Criteria of Discernment
in Interreligious Dialogue

Interreligious Dialogue Series

Catherine Cornille, Series Editor

Criteria of Discernment
in Interreligious Dialogue

edited by
CATHERINE CORNILLE

CASCADE *Books* · Eugene, Oregon

CRITERIA OF DISCERNMENT IN INTERRELIGIOUS DIALOGUE

Interreligious Dialogue Series 1

Cascade Books
A Division of Wipf and Stock Publishers
199 W. 8th Ave., Suite 3
Eugene, OR 97401

ISBN 13: 978-1-60608-784-8

Cataloging-in-Publication data:

Criteria of discernment in interreligious dialogue / edited by Catherine Cornille.

Interreligious Dialogue Series 1

xx + 284 p. ; 23 cm.

ISBN 13: 978-1-60608-784-8

1. Religion—Relations. 2. Dialogue—Religious aspects. 3. Religious pluralism. I. Cornille, Catherine. II. Title. III. Series.

BL410 C95 2009

Manufactured in the U.S.A.

For Brien O'Brien and Mary Hasten
in gratitude for their commitment to advancing
peace and dialogue between religions

Contents

Contents

Introduction: On Discernment in Dialogue

Catherine Cornille

Any dialogue between religions involves some degree of judgment of what is true or false, interesting or banal, valuable or futile, admirable or repulsive, appealing or strange in the other religion. Such judgments have been operative consciously or unconsciously, implicitly or explicitly throughout the history of encounter between religions. They have been manifest in the ways in which religions have borrowed symbols, teachings, and practices from other religions, often without acknowledging their source, as well as in the long history of religious apologetics. And they remain present today in the very choice of dialogue partners and in the choice of elements engaged at the center of the discussion.

Within the contemporary atmosphere of religious tolerance and acceptance of all religious expressions, the very idea of passing judgment on the teachings and practices of other religions is strongly resisted, indeed almost to the point of becoming taboo. All religious traditions are to be regarded as equal and the idea of subjecting a religion to any set of external norms is seen as simply unacceptable, if not untenable. Yet as well intentioned as this openness certainly is, it seems to miss the fact that normative judgments enter inevitably into the very encounter between individuals belonging to different religions already before any question of concepts and conclusions. Not only do religious individuals spontaneously perceive the world and others through a normative lens, usually shaped by their own particular beliefs and values, but insofar as dialogue aims at least in part at enriching one's understanding of the truth, such a work of discernment is in fact required. To be sure, every encounter with another religion presupposes at first a certain suspension of judgment in order to understand the other on its own terms. But eventually, the normative question of the validity and truth of the beliefs and practices of the other cannot but arise, at least for individuals who are seriously engaged with the truth and effectiveness of their own tradition.

While the necessity of norms in dialogue is generally recognized, there is disagreement among scholars about the understanding of the nature and the contents of such norms. Some scholars argue that the need for equality between the participants in dialogue calls for a complete abandonment of all religion-specific norms. Such criteria are said to entail a form of religious imperialism and arrogance, or to express a sense of the superiority of one's own religious framework over that of others. Rather than impose the criteria of one religion onto another, these scholars have proposed criteria that are thought to be neutral or common to all religious traditions. For example, the pluralist theologian John Hick has thus suggested that religions should be all equally judged according to the degree to which they make possible "the transformation of human experience from self-centeredness to Reality-centeredness."[1] Other criteria said to be neutral are commitments to socio-economic liberation, the equality between men and women, and genuine peace in the world. Such generic criteria certainly do have some validity insofar as they may sound a critical note with regard to the degree to which religions may neglect certain basic human rights or universal concerns. They may even provide a ranking of religions according to criteria that are undoubtedly shared by some individuals.

Yet it nonetheless seems clear that such criteria are in fact always in each case already colored by the worldview or the value system of each individual involved in the dialogue. And at any rate, in the dialogue between believers, such criteria are unlikely to have any special authority or to take precedence over those criteria derived from divine revelation or ultimate spiritual realization. Insofar as believers may embrace such criteria, it will thus not be because of their neutrality or because they represent the highest common denominator between religions, but because they happen to coincide with specific religious criteria.

Rather than in submission to some external or neutral criteria, it is in the very realization that every religion inevitably judges the other ac-

---

1. John Hick, "On Grading Religions," *Religious Studies* 17 (1981) 463.

cording to its own particular criteria that the equality between religions in dialogue is established. While each participant may remain convinced of the superiority of one's own religious criteria, the awareness of mutuality in this conviction tempers the arrogance and the aggression that is often thought to be associated with the use of confessional norms in dialogue. The use of confessional criteria in the dialogue between religions may thus be regarded as both an epistemological necessity and an expression of fidelity to the truth of one's own tradition. It also moves the dialogue beyond one's own individual judgment to an engagement between religious traditions.

One of the hesitations about applying confessional criteria to the judgment of other religions is their tendency to limit recognition of truth and validity in other religions to that which is identical to one's own religion, thus precluding the possibility of growth in dialogue. However, confessional norms may function in different ways. They may function as a maximal standard according to which only that which is mirrored in the other tradition may be considered valuable and true. But they may also function as a minimal standard, excluding only those beliefs and practices that are in direct contradiction with one's own. While the former approach may reduce the truth of the tradition to that which is already contained within one's own, the latter allows ample room for the recognition of truth in difference, and for the possibility of change and growth through dialogue.

Another perceived limitation of judging one religion according to the criteria of another is that it seems to fix religions into set hierarchical relationships. However, though it is certainly true that each religion will affirm the superiority of their own religious criteria, the content and interpretation of those criteria is by no means fixed and unchanging. On the contrary, not only may different believers and different schools identify different sets of essential criteria within a particular religion, but the understanding of these criteria may also change, at times as a result of the dialogue itself. It is indeed often in the course of the dialogue that believers become aware of their own essential criteria of truth through positive—and even more poignantly negative—responses to the religious other. But the dialogue may also shed new light on the meaning of these very criteria as the internal perspective becomes enriched through engagement with external perspectives. Therefore the use of confessional criteria in dialogue in no way implies the possibility of passing final judgment on the religious other.

◆ ◆ ◆

This volume brings together scholars from different religions and from different schools within different religions to reflect on the principles of discernment operative within their own religious traditions in the dialogue with other religions. As has been pointed out, these criteria generally operate implicitly or unconsciously and may thus be identified in a variety of different ways. Some focus on certain criteria that have emerged in the course of history, and in particular dialogues, while others propose sets of criteria based more on an internal reflection. Some start from Scripture while others derive their criteria from theological discussion and development. Some come to emphasize ethical principles while others use the doctrinal framework of their religion as the basis of discernment.

Some explain why, from the perspective of their religion, all the teachings and practices of other religions are essentially false and without any religious value or merit for their own religious reflection, while others reject the need or possibility of imposing one's own unique criteria of truth upon other religions.

Reflecting on the question of discernment from the perspective of the Jewish tradition, both Jonathan Magonet and David Elcott emphasize the prohibition against idolatry as the central criterion. This prohibition includes a rejection of tendencies to religious absolutism and to claiming complete and final knowledge of the truth. As a tradition of continuous interpretation of and commentary on the text, Judaism is particularly averse to scriptural literalism and to the rejection of diverging viewpoints and debate. For Elcott, this also extends to religious attitudes toward religious others: any religion that would claim exclusive truth would thereby automatically falsify itself, from a Jewish perspective. The validity of another religion is for him to be measured not so much according to the teachings of a particular tradition but according to the way of life of its practitioners. Elcott argues that the concrete contents of this ethical standard is itself not fixed and final but part of the continuous "messiness of moral deliberation." Magonet grounds this in the very reality of historical change and the development of social and religious consciousness.

Whereas gender equality may not have been a prominent norm in classical Judaism, it has become so, at least in non-Orthodox forms of Judaism. In addition to this, Magonet also points to religious attitudes that will inevitably play a role in the Jewish process of discernment: a focus on this world, on the meaning and purpose of time, and on the independence and responsibility of the human person in relation to God. Both Magonet and Elcott moreover point out that all of these criteria apply equally to the Jewish tradition itself.

The Christian theologians approach the questions from radically different perspectives, but wholly consistent with the traditions they represent. Speaking from a Roman Catholic perspective, Gavin D'Costa grounds his reflections in the official documents of the Church. He argues that, even though these documents do not recognize other religious traditions as valid means to salvation, they do acknowledge the presence of truth in the fact that the Holy Spirit may be at work in those religions. Countering Christian theologians who might argue for an independent activity of the Spirit in other religions, D'Costa insists that the working of the Spirit cannot be understood or discerned apart from Jesus Christ and the Church, and that any manifestation of truth and goodness in other religions is always accomplished through the grace of God. The figure of Jesus Christ thus remains the ultimate norm of discernment, and the Church the instrument of such discernment. In offering an example of discernment, D'Costa turns to the controversial example of *sati*, or widow burning, in India. Even though this practice raises many critical questions, D'Costa suggests that the element of voluntary self-sacrifice, not only to enhance one's own merit but also to transfer that merit to others, contains a distinctly Christic dimension. This goes to show that the practice of discernment often entails less a wholesale rejection or acceptance of particular teachings and practices of another religion than a careful discrimination of elements that may and elements that may not resonate with one's own religious worldview and beliefs.

Approaching the question of discernment from a Protestant Christian perspective, Reinhold Bernhardt derives his criteria solely from the Bible. He first distinguishes purely formal from material criteria, and within the latter, he distinguishes those that form the distinguishing characteristics of a religion, and those that are essential to a religion but possibly recurrent in other religions. Bernhardt suggests that the Bible points to four essential criteria of genuine religiosity that may be applicable, from a Christian perspective, to all religious traditions, including Christianity: transcendence, freedom, agape, and responsibility. These criteria may operate independently to judge particular religious phenomena, or in relation to one another to account for a truly integral view of the validity of religious expressions.

A particularly pertinent example of discernment in dialogue may be found in the document "A Common Word between Us and You," published in 2007 and signed by 138 Muslim scholars. Rather than on points of disagreement between Christians and Muslims, the document focuses on some of the essential beliefs that the two traditions share and that may become the basis of mutual understanding and cooperation: love of God and love of neighbor. Responding to this document from a Christian perspective, David Burrell emphasizes the importance of going beyond rigid truth claims to attend to their meaning. He points to various fault lines and conflicting doctrines that may be and have been the cause of tension between the two traditions, but that may in fact, when probed into their deeper meaning, open the possibility for fruitful dialogue. Burrell also reminds us that while the practice of discernment tends to be based on an attachment to the absolute nature of one's own claims to truth, authentic theology must start from an awareness of the analogical nature of its own beliefs.

The Islamic approaches to the question of discernment remain closely focused on the Qur'an as the ultimate source of truth. In her paper, Asma Afsaruddin discusses the very foundation and motivation for Muslims to enter into dialogue with other religions by focusing on particular Qur'anic verses and their commentaries by important Muslim thinkers. She demonstrates that certain verses may be and have been interpreted in very different ways, ranging from genuine openness to other religions to a direct condemnation of their distinctive teachings. Where negative judgments are made of the other, these seem to be directed mainly toward what is perceived as unethical behavior in these religions. But her discussion of the now-famous Qur'anic verse 3:64, which includes the words "a common word between us and you," also makes clear that belief in one God remains the ultimate religious criterion of truth from a Muslim perspective.

The contribution of Mustafa Abu Sway demonstrates that the Qur'an itself offers numerous examples of discernment, predominantly in relation to the religions of the book. He points out that the text allows for considerable openness toward teachings and laws that are not explicitly contradicted or abrogated in the Qur'an. Even though the Qur'an is regarded as a superior revelation, the teachings of Judaism and Christianity that are different from it are not to be automatically judged false or abandoned. On the other hand, Abu Sway also refers to teachings in both traditions that cannot be judged as revelatory from a Muslim perspective, and that he designates as "post-revelational human constructs."

The complexity of the process of discernment of particular teachings within another religion is made clear in the contribution of Joseph Lombard. Focusing on the Christian understanding of the incarnation, which has been traditionally rejected by Muslims, Lombard points out that the Islamic tradition in fact contains resources that may render this central Christian teaching intelligible, if not acceptable. He refers in particular to the concept of the uncreated Qur'an, which could open the way for a greater openness to the Christian teaching of the two natures of Jesus Christ. While this may not entail a full recognition of classical Christology, it does point to the fact that discernment does not merely involve a blanket acceptance or rejection of the teachings of the other religion on the basis of one's own set doctrines, but rather a careful negotiation of meanings embedded in one's own tradition as well as in that of the other.

While the challenge of the internal diversity of traditions and schools presents itself for every religion, this is particularly the case within Hinduism, which itself has generated religious worldviews and belief systems ranging from nondualism to radical dualism. In this volume, we have contributions from scholars discussing each of these extreme approaches to the subject. Anantanand Rambachan reflects on the question of discernment from the perspective of the nondualist tradition of Advaita Vedanta. While Advaita Vedanta has often come to be associated with the belief that all religions are true or at least lead to the same ultimate goal, Rambachan points out that the founder of the tradition, Shankara, had a decidedly more normative and critical understanding of the truth of other religions. In reconstructing Shankara's arguments against his adversaries, Rambachan offers a set of criteria that may still serve as the basis for Advaita discernment in dialogue today.

Deepak Sarma approaches the question of discernment in dialogue from the perspective of the dualistic Madhva tradition, which represents a radical negation of the presence of any valid truth outside of the tradition, and outside of the select group of virtuoso readers who are entitled to read and interpret Scripture. Rather than discussing criteria of truth, he thus focuses on the dynamics of exclusion operative in the tradition. These dynamics, though in many specifics unique to the Madhva tradition, also have analogues in certain traditions or schools within other religions. It is thus important to keep in mind that the very notion of discernment of truth in other religions requires a particular conception of truth that is not always in the self-understanding of religions.

The Buddhist approach to the question of discernment in interreligious dialogue features two Tibetan Buddhist scholars, Judith Simmer-Brown and John Makransky, and a scholar belonging to the Pure Land tradition of Buddhism, Mark Unno. Characteristic of Buddhism, at least in its Mahayana forms, is its emphasis on the ultimate emptiness or insubstantiality of all reality. John Makransky points out that this has led to the development of both negative and positive criteria of judgment of other religions. On the negative side, it has led to a rejection of all religious tendency to absolutize one's own truth claims, conceptions of the absolute, and conceptions of the self. But on the positive side, Makransky states that Buddhism affirms the need for teachings and practices as "skillful means," judging their truth and validity on the basis of whether they lead to "freedom from the subtlest habits of confusion, clinging and aversion" and whether they engender the qualities of enlightenment: compassion, love, humor, joy, equanimity, and humility. With examples from the life of the Buddha and from contemporary Buddhist scholars, Makransky demonstrates that these criteria have led to a vigorous scholastic critique of theism but also to the recognition of non-Buddhist teachers as embodying enlightenment.

Judith Simmer-Brown focuses mainly on the Dalai Lama, extracting from his example certain Buddhist principles for discernment in dialogue. She points to the nineteenth-century Ri-me tradition of Buddhism as one of the important sources of inspiration for the Dalai Lama's approach. Characteristic of this tradition is its open approach to the different Buddhist schools of teaching and practice in Tibet, based on the belief that there might be something for everyone in the variety of teachings. In the course of time, the Dalai Lama has come to adopt a similar approach toward other religions. Simmer-Brown points out that in judging another religion, the Dalai Lama focuses less on the teachings or the philosophy of a particular religion than on its fruits, in particular "its ability to produce warmhearted human beings."

Offering a very clear exposition of the basic teachings of Shin Buddhism, Mark Unno rejects the very notion of judgment of other religions, based on the relativity and the temporality of all religious "forms." Rather than applying the essential teachings of Shin Buddhism to judge the truth and validity of other religions, he offers examples of ways in which the encounter between different experiences and religious worldviews may at times break open a sphere of genuine insight and realization that transcends religious judgment.

◆ ◆ ◆

In surveying the criteria of discernment in dialogue operative in various religious traditions, it is clear that many of the contributors focus less on the truth or falsehood of particular teachings in the other religion than on the fruits of a particular religious tradition—on the lifestyle, values, and ethical attitudes manifest among members of a particular religion. This emphasis on the fruits rather than the contents of religious teachings need not be regarded as a way to avoid the difficulty of judging one religion according to the highly particular belief system of another. It is also more than a turn to a highest common ethical denominator. The ethical criteria used are themselves firmly grounded in the worldview and teachings of particular religions. And in some cases, the call to judge other religions according to their fruits is itself a scriptural injunction or an admonishment of the founder. The fruits according to which a Muslim judges a Buddhist will be different from those according to which a Buddhist judges a Muslim. However, the focus on the fruits of one's faith does open the possibility for a greater openness toward the other religion and a first step to affirming the possible validity and truth of the teachings related to certain ways of being and acting. It is indeed the encounter with exemplary moral and spiritual individuals in other religions that tends to shatter assumptions that all other religions are false or futile and that nourishes interest in the specific teachings and tenets of the other religion.

In reflecting on the more doctrinal or conceptual criteria of truth, the different contributions attempt to isolate some of the essential or irreducible characteristics of their own tradition. These may range from general but essential religious principles (love, freedom, etc.) to very concrete religious teachings (belief in a creator God, the insubstantiality of the self), and from more common beliefs to teachings that distinguish one's own religion from all others. While probably yielding little recognition of other religions, it is not altogether surprising that the search for essences leads to a focus on the distinctive teachings of one's tradition. But the criteria of a religion need not coincide with what is unique or distinctive about a religion. Every religion contains a complex whole of beliefs and practices, some distinctive and some common to more than one religion, which may become the basis for discernment. But insofar as all religious beliefs and practices are always embedded in a particular religious framework, the process of discernment will always be a matter of selective hermeneutical negotiation.

It is striking that none of the papers in this volume focuses on ritual practice as a criterion of discernment. This is not surprising. Even though ritual forms an integral part of all religious traditions, it also forms the most specific part of religions. While believers may tend to judge the practices of other religions as either effective or not, this will usually be based on one's general worldview rather than on the specifics of one's own ritual life.

While most of the papers discuss the principles of discernment, few focus on the processes of discernment operative within their respective traditions. This involves the question of *how* a religion comes to discern what is valuable in the other tradition, and *who* is considered the final authority in these matters. Most often, the process of discernment is a slow one, left to the discretion of individuals directly involved in the dialogue. However, if dialogue is to have a broader religious impact, the fruits of discernment are to be somehow brought to bear upon religious traditions as a whole. And this may require in time a more concerted and communal endeavor.

It is thus clear that the process of discernment of truth in interreligious dialogue involves a complex procedure combining faithfulness to one's own tradition and openness to the other, critical self-awareness and serious engagement with the teachings and practices of others, daring judgment and continuous openness to correction. Since the process of dialogue itself sheds light on the essential criteria of a particular religion, each new dialogue may enhance awareness of the criteria of truth operative within one's own religion. And these criteria may themselves also change and grow as the dialogue may at times lead to a deeper understanding of one's own religious principles. But insofar as criteria of truth are always operative in dialogue, this volume will hopefully spark further systematic reflection on the topic within religious traditions and thus lead to a greater self-awareness in dialogue. And this greater self-awareness and transparency about motives and principles of discernment may in turn enhance the sense of mutual trust and sincerity among dialogue partners, as well as openness to the possibility of discovering genuine truth in other religions.

Part I
Jewish Perspectives

1

Jews in Dialogue: Towards Some Criteria of Discernment

Jonathan Magonet

When I was starting to prepare this paper, a particular memory came to mind of an early experience of interfaith dialogue. It relates well to the theme of "Dialogue and Discernment," insofar as we are considering the presuppositions, not to mention prejudices, about the 'other' that we bring to the dialogue situation. Some of these are conscious, being based on previous knowledge of the particular 'other' before us—either from history or from contemporary cultural or political information, or disinformation. At another level we are also looking at the deeper structures within our own faith that determine our values and assumptions about how religion in general is to be experienced, expressed, and conducted. We often take it for granted that such understandings that may be ours alone are actually universal. It is then a small step to the belief that they are the essential components of any "authentic" religion, precisely because they are our own, and indeed so much a part of our way of seeing things that we hardly need to express them. Because we know that they are fundamental, we might even assume that these are objective measuring instruments against which any faith community is to be evaluated. However, having once been confronted with such a set of criteria from the perspective of another religion, I can see the value of attempting to uncover and express these assumptions, and then to subject them to critical appraisal. But first the event itself.

I can no longer locate the actual place where the encounter took place. It would have been in the early seventies at one of the first of what would become an annual international Jewish-Christian-Muslim student conference. In my mind's eye the session took place outdoors on a lawn at a conference center, probably in Arnhem in Holland. The speaker was an earnest young Muslim who, I presume, wanted to lay before us a set of objective measurements of the values and authenticity of our three monotheistic faiths. (I suspect that like certain Jewish fundamentalist groups, he wanted to show how his fundamentalism was capable of using the language and "objective" methodology of science as proof of its time-less truth!) To do so he drew up a grid, listing across the top of four col-umns the criteria to be evaluated, and vertically the three faiths (Judaism, Christianity, and Islam) to be subjected to analysis.

The criterion given at the top of the first column was "pure mono-theism." In the appropriate box, both Judaism and Islam got a tick. But clearly Christianity, as viewed from his perspective, was highly prob-lematic. Given the Christian deification of a human being, Jesus, (who is respected but only as a human prophet in Islam), not to mention concepts like the Trinity, clearly the Christian box did not get a tick, but, perhaps appropriately, a "cross."

The second column addressed the question of fidelity to revealed Scripture. Once again the Islamic column received its automatic tick. I think that Christianity got the benefit of the doubt on this occasion and received a tick. But Judaism was clearly at fault in this category. It seems that there is a strand of Islamic thinking that asserts that Jews had falsi-fied their Scriptures for their own purposes. It was the Jewish turn for a cross.

The third criterion was "universalism." Here again both Islam and Christianity got a tick as faiths that embraced the entire world. But Judaism, with its obvious exclusiveness, its emphasis on peoplehood, sim-ply could not compete—we got another objectively determined cross.

As far as I recall, the fourth criterion was about commitment to righ-teousness and justice. By now it goes without saying that Islam, presum-ably because of its legal tradition and not least, in the popular imagination, its historical record of tolerance in the Golden Age of Spain, got a tick. I don't recall the fate of Christianity. Probably the wrongs perpetrated in the Crusades gave it another cross. But regarding Judaism there were no such doubts. The injustices done to the Palestinian people were enough to give us a final cross.

I do not recall anything of the subsequent discussion. Perhaps we were so shell-shocked by the naivety of the presentation that we dismissed it with a few polite remarks, not wishing to hurt his feelings. Or else we jumped in to defend one or other of the negative judgments.

However, when I tell this story, I immediately add that there are Christians and Jews who could equally easily set up such a self-serving chart. I presume that high on the Christian list would be the word *love* and the degree to which the other's theology and practice exemplified it. A Jewish list might seem rather self-serving, with questions about the level of anti-Semitism the other faith expressed being high on the list. But if this represents a kind of parody, however unintentional, of the exercise before us, it is a warning about how easy it is to rig the scorecard. It evokes the comment by the late Krister Stendahl: "I would apply the same rules for good leadership that I often do for effective interfaith dialogue: let the other define herself (don't think you know the other without listening); compare equal to equal (not my positive qualities to the negative ones of the other); and find beauty in the other so as to develop 'holy envy.'"[1]

The Noachide Laws

When it comes to listing things that Judaism would use to evaluate the religious credentials of another faith, a particular rabbinic concept comes immediately to mind: the *sheva mitzvoth livnei noach*: "the seven commandments given to the sons of Noah," that is, to the ancestors of the reestablished postflood humanity.

The seven commandments are a rabbinic development, partly direct, partly by interpretation, of laws to be found in the opening chapters of Genesis and in the Ten Commandments. Different versions of the seven commandments have minor variations, and they are amplified to thirty in some mediaeval formulations. Of the basic seven, six are prohibitions: against murder, adultery/incest, theft (including kidnapping),

---

1. Yehezkel Landau, "An Interview with Krister Stendhahl," *Harvard Divinity Bulletin* 35 (2007). Online: http://www.hds.harvard.edu/news/bulletin_mag/articles/35-1_stendahl_interview.html/.

idolatry, blasphemy, and eating a limb from a living animal (presumably related to the prohibition on consuming blood—Gen 9:4). The seventh is positive, to establish courts of law, thus emphasising the task of teaching "righteousness and justice" as "God's way," as explicitly stated regarding God's choice of Abraham (Gen 18:19). These laws are seen as common to all humanity and capable of being reached by human reasoning alone. Maimonides even goes as far as to differentiate between those who fulfil them with the intention of fulfilling the divine will, whose reward is in the "world to come," and those who do them as a result of intellectual reasoning, and who receive their reward in this world.[2] Yet precisely because of the universal application of these laws, with possibly one exception, they do not quite address the specifics of discernment we are considering.

Idolatry

The exception, which is also the most ambiguous and in some ways most pertinent to our discussion, is the prohibition on idolatry. Given the power of the biblical prohibitions and the constant struggle to annihilate idolatry in ancient Israel, one might expect it to feature prominently in the Jewish approach to other religious traditions. Instead Judaism follows the direction indicated by, among other passages, Deuteronomy 4:19, which argues that God apportioned the "sun, moon, stars and the hosts of heaven" as legitimate sources of worship "to all the peoples under heaven." Such worship is accepted, perhaps in a somewhat patronising way, as permitted to others provided they do not insinuate it or impose it on Jews.

The most obvious physical representations of deities arise today when Jews come into contact with Eastern philosophies and religions. However, their geographical and spiritual distance evoke on the part of Jews a tolerance, a respect, and indeed a curiosity. Precisely their difference from any familiar Jewish or Jewishly derived agenda within Christianity or Islam makes them particularly attractive to Jews seeking an alternative spirituality, as the phenomenon of "Jubus," "Jewish Buddhists," would attest. Again, anecdotally, I recall an event in London when a number of religious representatives were invited to a Hindu religious festival. We

2. *Mishneh Torah*, Book of Judges, Laws of Kings 8:11.

stood on the stage dominated by a huge representation of a deity—clergy of various Christian denominations, assorted members of other faiths— watching politely as various acolytes laid bowls of food at the feet of the "idol." It was an interesting and indeed moving occasion, but none of us felt the need to denounce it as an idolatrous practice or as requiring us to walk out for fear of compromising our immortal souls. Of course this was several steps below proper dialogue, and should perhaps be considered under the rubric of British politeness. But in the absence of any mission-izing purpose, physical threat, or supercessionist ideology, the prevailing mode was that of good neighborliness within a multicultural setting.

A Talmudic story tells how the rabbis captured the "evil inclination to idolatry" and slew it, since which time "idolatry" ceased to be a real is-sue for Jewish people.[3] Indeed the Talmud records a discussion about the presence of a statue to Aphrodite in a bathhouse. Surely a Jew could not enter such a place, as it might imply worshipping the goddess. The answer suggests a degree of pragmatism. "We do not say that the bathhouse was built as an ornament of Aphrodite, but we say that Aphrodite is an orna-mental attachment to the bathhouse!" But the same Mishnah continues: "What is treated as a god is forbidden, but what is not treated as a god is not forbidden."[4] This leads in part to the unease of Jews in being invited to attend religious services in a church.

The Hebrew Bible clearly considers idolatry to be a real threat to faith in the One God, experienced in the struggle against the nature deities of Canaan and the more sophisticated theological challenges of Babylon.[5] Nevertheless, even the more overt and seemingly simplistic parodying of idol worship in the Hebrew Bible may have had its own internal didactic purposes. For example, Psalm 115 points to the absurdity of worshipping idols:

> They have a mouth, but do not speak.
>
> They have eyes but do not see.
>
> They have ears, but do not hear.
>
> They have a nose, but do not smell.
>
> With their hands they do not feel.

3. Babylonian Talmud, *Yoma* 69b.

4. Mishnah, *Avodah Zarah* 3:4.

5. See Isaiah 45:7.

With their feet they do not walk.

They make no sound in their throat.

They have human forms but lack even human powers, let alone divine ones, and thus whoever worships them is effectively dead like them. This seems on one level to be a rather crude dismissal, ignoring whatever ideas and belief system may lie behind worshiping the physical form. However the lesson seems to be that the God of Israel, who is invisible and has no physical attributes, nevertheless can see, hear, smell, and speak, and that those who worship Israel's God receive the blessing of "life."[6]

The opening of the psalm suggests precisely why "idolatry" is so pervasive and subversive: *lo lanu, adonai, lo lanu, ki l'shimcha, ten kavod.* ("Not to us, O Eternal, not to us, but to Your name give honour.") In what circumstances might we be tempted to place greater honor on human beings than on God? When we worship the artifacts that we ourselves have created. As Chanan Brichto suggests, it is possible that this psalm itself is consciously self-referential, with the psalmist's questioning his own hubris at his literary creativity: "Not to us . . . but to Your name!"[7]

This temptation of self-worship is well analysed by Erich Fromm:

> The approach to the understanding of what an idol is begins with the understanding of *what God is not.* God, as the supreme value and goal is *not* man, the state, an institution, nature, power, possession, sexual powers, or any artifact made by man . . .
>
> An idol represents the object of man's central passion: the desire to return to the soil mother, the craving for possession, power, fame, and so forth. The passion represented by the idol, is at the same time, the supreme value within man's system of values. Only a history of idolatry could enumerate the hundreds of idols and analyze which human passions and desires they represent. May it suffice to say that the history of mankind up to the present time is primarily a history of idol worship, from the primitive idols of clay and wood to the modern idols of the state, the leader, production and consumption—sanctified by the blessing of an idolized God . . .

6. For an analysis of the psalm, see Magonet, *A Rabbi Reads the Psalms*, 2nd ed. (London: SCM, 2004) 147–56.

7. Chanan Brichto, "The Beauty of Japhet and the Tents of Shem—An Exegesis of Psalm 115," *Journal of Reform Judaism* 29 (1982) 26–32.

> The idol is the alienated form of man's experience of himself. In worshiping the idol, man worships himself. But this self is a partial, limited aspect of man: his intelligence, his physical strength, power, fame and so on. By identifying himself with a partial aspect of himself, man limits himself to this aspect; he loses his totality as a human being and ceases to grow. He is dependent on the idol, since only in submission to the idol does he find the shadow, although not the substance, of himself.[8]

A similar idea is expressed by Arthur Miller: "An idol tells people exactly what to believe, God presents them with choices they have to make for themselves. The difference is far from insignificant; before the idol men remain dependent children, before God they are burdened and at the same time liberated to participate in the decisions of endless creation."[9]

This level of evaluating idolatry leads us to the problem of ideologies, political structures, and religious systems themselves that need constant monitoring if they are not to become agents for dehumanisation. In this broader sense of idolatry, Jews are no more immune than anyone else. The record of the biblical prophets offers a constant reminder of the need for a self-critical awareness, and a willingness to recognise and acknowledge the traps we fall into. Jews are proud of the dissident tradition of the prophets, though we share a common human tendency to resist criticism when it challenges our personal or communal comfort. To some extent the legitimating and practice of self-criticism, individually and as a people, find liturgical expression in the actions and rituals of the High Holy Days. Nevertheless it tends to be amongst secularised Jews that the strongest critical voices are to be heard today, regarding actions committed by Jews, notably with regard the political policies of the State of Israel and, more commonly, regarding wider social issues.

The willingness to call into question the values of our own religious tradition with a degree of detachment is a notable feature of post-Enlightenment Judaism. That kind of openness is another criterion that Jews would expect to find in other religious communities. We are genuinely puzzled by the seemingly uncritical expressions of faith and the unchallenged authority of religious leaders to be found elsewhere. The interpre-

---

8. Erich Fromm, *You Shall Be as Gods: A Radical Interpretation of the Old Testament and Its Tradition* (Greenwich, CT: Fawcett, 1966) 36–37.

9. Arthur Miller, *Timebends: A Life* (London: Methuen, 1987) 259.

tation of the name 'Israel' as one who struggles *with* God as well as *for* God gives popular expression to this self-understanding. This, in turn, leads us to examine the nature of the Jewish relationship with God.

The Covenant

The central defining concept of the relationship between Israel and God is the *berit*, the 'covenant,' a contractual and binding association of mutual responsibility. However, what makes it more than simply a legal contract is that it is underpinned by *chesed*, an untranslatable term that expresses a mutual loyalty and faithful love that transcend time. Being a contract, the Jewish obligations and responsibilities to one another, to others, and to God are defined under the concept of *mitzvot*, 'commandments'; hence law, *halakhah*, is a central religious mode for Judaism. However, such a relationship with God raises the expectation that God too can be called into account for the fate of the Jewish people. However much such an expectation is bounded by other considerations of the relative insignificance of humanity in the face of the power and 'otherness' of God, nevertheless Judaism does expect that due respect be given to human beings and hence asserts our right to argue with God. The models for this are clearly present in the Hebrew Bible: Abraham's regarding Sodom; Moses's defending Israel; Jeremiah's challenging God's justice in the face of manifest social corruption; Job's asserting his innocence, which is ultimately vindicated by God. Such a robust relationship, which becomes one of the 'norms' from a Jewish perspective, has little patience with or understanding of the submissiveness to the will of God that seems to be assumed within Islam, and indeed Muslims find the more combative Jewish attitudes to God shocking. Nor do Jews appreciate what appears to be the difficulty apparently experienced by Christians in expressing their own legitimate anger and outrage against God in the face of tragedy. From outside, it seems to be related to the sense of helplessness when confronted with the suffering of Jesus. With a father-figure God, one can have a good fight; with a suffering 'son,' a very different set of psychological expectations are evoked.

The difference of approach is illustrated by a rabbinic distinction between the nature of the relationship with God experienced by Noah and Abraham. In Genesis 6:9 we learn that *et ha-elohim hithallekh noach*

('Noah walked with God') whereas in Genesis 17:1, God says to Abram, *hithallekh l'fanai* ('walk before Me.'). What is the difference? It is like a king who had two sons: to the younger he said, 'take my hand and walk with me,' but to the older he said, 'walk before me.'[10] There is an assumption here about the maturity of an Abraham, and thus the Jewish people, who can retain a degree of independence and indeed be pathfinders for God, compared to the more dependent situation of the 'Noachides.' Naturally such an idea, from the rabbinic aspect, should immediately be qualified by a 'so to speak,' but it does indicate a degree of independence and self-respect that is an important part of Jewish understanding of the relationship to God, something that Jews bring to the dialogue table.

This degree of responsibility and independence is dramatically illustrated by the rabbinic reworking of the story of that first act of disobedience in the Garden of Eden. The 'knowledge of good and evil' that is acquired through eating the fruit of the forbidden tree (Gen 2:17; 3:6) becomes viewed in a positive way in Jewish liturgy. In the first of the petitions in the Amidah, the 'Standing Prayer' or 'Eighteen Benedictions,' recited daily by Jews, the text reads literally 'You grace (*honen*) Adam with knowledge.' The word 'Adam' implies both the first man and humanity in general; the word for 'knowledge' is precisely that used in the Genesis narrative, but here understood as something not acquired through disobedience but as given to us by an act of grace by God:

> You favour human beings with knowledge and teach mortals understanding, favour us with the knowledge, understanding and discernment that come from You. Blessed are You God, who favours us with knowledge.

Here it is not simply the Jew who gains from this gift, but all human beings. However, the very placement of this blessing at the beginning of the Amidah reflects another dimension of Jewish religiosity that must colour our approach to other faiths. Study and the acquisition of knowledge are key Jewish spiritual values. The Bible contains many examples of 'wisdom literature': knowledge derived from empirical observation and received tradition (Proverbs) but also challenging debates about its values and views and limitations (Ecclesiastes, Job). The term *hokmah*, 'wisdom,' refers originally to craftsmanship but like the Greek, *sophia*, moves on

10. *Tanchuma*, Noah 5.

from practical skills to address the more abstract processes of reasoning. When the Torah scroll is taken out from the ark and paraded around the synagogue, a verse is sung taken from the book of Proverbs: 'it is a tree of life to all who grasp it.'[11] Clearly in the immediate context this must refer to the Torah itself, though if one checks the source of the phrase, the actual referent is not Torah but *hokmah*, 'wisdom,' (Prov 3:13). This opens the door to a Jewish insistence that all knowledge, whatever its source, is to be valued and respected, which would allow, for example, no dichotomy between science and religion. Thus, intellectual rigour and a commitment to lifelong study are religious values that Jews might expect to find in other faiths.

Human Nature

Three biblical passages set the tone for the Jewish understanding of human nature. The first is obviously Genesis 1:27 'God created the man in His image, in the image of God He created him, male and female He created them.' What precisely this 'image' implies is open to endless speculation. Nevertheless human beings must ultimately be seen as sharing some aspect of the divine, which demands respect for all human beings and a positive assessment of human nature. Within humanity as a whole, Israel is called upon to share something of the 'otherness,' 'holiness,' of God, to be *kadosh* just as God is *kadosh* (Lev 19:1). This will find its expression in later rabbinic teachings in terms of imitating those divine attributes that reflect God's compassion and generosity.

A second pair of biblical verses points to the reality of human wrongdoing and destructiveness. Genesis 6:5 asserts that 'the Eternal saw that great was the evil of human beings in the earth, and all the imagination of the thoughts in their heart were only evil all the day.' After the flood God decides no longer to curse the ground because of 'Adam,' 'because the imagination of the heart of the human being is evil from his youth' (Gen 8:21). The term translated as 'imagination,' *yetzer*, derives from a verb meaning 'to form,' to manipulate existing materials, and is indeed the verb used of God's creation of 'Adam' in the 'second' creation story in Genesis 2:7: 'the Eternal God formed the man, dust from the ground . . .'

11. Proverbs 3:18

Thus this 'imagination' within human beings, however it might express itself, owes something to their creation by God, 'in the image of God.'

It is the rabbinic tradition that filled out this term by conceiving of two contrasting 'inclinations' or 'impulses' in constant struggle within the heart of human beings, the *yetzer ha-tov* and the *yetzer ha-ra*, respectively the good and the evil inclinations.[12] The latter is present from childhood as a kind of undifferentiated energy, often identified with the sexual drive; the former emerges at puberty as a self-disciplining element.[13] In a well-known comment on God's act of 'formation' in Genesis 2:7, the rabbis derived the idea that the 'evil inclination' was actually 'good': 'but for the evil inclination, no man would build a house, take a wife and beget children.'[14] The task of human beings therefore is to control the evil inclination, with the Torah as the God-given aid.[15]

If the concept of the two inclinations expresses the physical and psychological parts of human beings, there remains the mysterious factor, the life force, that distinguishes the living creature from an inanimate body. The biblical terms *nefesh*, *n'shamah* and *ruach*, partly overlapping, partly differentiated, represent different perceptions of this force. As Rachel Elior explains:

> In the Bible, body and soul are viewed as one, and existence and meaning are attributed to the soul on the physical, human and historical plane. With the passing of time, however, the soul came to be viewed as a metaphysical entity that belonged to, affected, and was affected by the realm of the divine, transcending the confines of history and nature . . .
>
> The talmudic conception of man has its roots in the biblical worldview, but it was also influenced by developments in religious

12. There are variations in the combination of the two words. Jastrow lists *yetzer tov* and *yetzer ha-tov*, but only *yetzer ha-ra*. The form *yetzer tov*, a noun and adjective, suggests that 'the good inclination' is intrinsically good, whereas the construct form *yetzer ha-tov; yetzer ha-ra*' suggests 'an inclination towards goodness' or 'towards evil,' which might imply that the 'good inclination' was a more dominant aspect. Marcus Jastrow, *A Dictionary of the Targumim, the Talmud Babli and Yerushalmi, and the Midrashic Literature*, 2 vols. (1903; reprint, Peabody, MA: Hendrickson, 2005).

13. Inevitably one thinks of Freud's 'Id' and 'Superego.'

14. *Genesis Rabbah* 9:7.

15. For a discussion on various rabbinic understandings of the 'Evil inclination,' see Daniel Boyarin, *Carnal Israel: Reading Sex in Talmudic Culture* (Berkeley: University of California, 1993) 61–70.

thought and by ideas current in the postbiblical world, especially within Hellenism, which embraces the possibility of the soul's simultaneous existence on both a physical and spiritual level.[16]

The rabbis regarded sleep as 'one sixtieth part of death.' Thus the soul departs temporarily from out body, only to return to us again in the morning when we awake, each awakening being in some sense a rebirth. One understanding of the relationship between the body and the soul is expressed in one of the opening passages of the daily Jewish liturgy: 'My God, the soul You have given me is pure, for You created it, You formed it and You made it live within me. You watch over it within me, but one day You will take it from me to everlasting life.'

The task demanded by this prayer is to preserve the soul in that purity until we die. The annual elaborate programme of actions, prayers, and confessions of the High Holy Days provides the mechanism for ensuring that this cleansing takes place. But the fact that the soul, even in our life, belongs in part in the heavenly domain means that Judaism assumes that there is some kind of life beyond death. This belief is formulated in the second paragraph of the Amidah, which states five times that God *m'chayei metim*, 'brings the dead to life.' It is possible that one of them refers to the daily awakening, but the others suggest bodily resurrection, though the precise nature of that has been heavily debated. In general, there is relatively little emphasis on the subject either in Jewish liturgy or in Jewish teachings. Non-Jews (and indeed Jews!) who ask are even surprised to discover that Judaism does indeed contain a belief in the afterlife.

The promise and the paradox are nicely expressed in a saying attributed to Rabbi Jacob: 'This world is like a vestibule before the world to come; prepare yourself in the vestibule that you may enter the hall. He used to say, Better is one hour of good deeds and repentance in this world than the whole life of the world to come; and better is one hour of blissfulness of spirit in the world to come than the whole life of this world.'[17]

---

16. Rachel Elior, "Soul," in *Contemporary Jewish Religious Thought: Original Essays on Critical Concepts, Movements and Beliefs*, eds. Arthur A. Cohen and Paul Mendes-Flohr (New York: Macmillan, 1987) 889–90 [887–96]. For a broader discussion on the relationship between body and soul in rabbinic literature see Boyarin, *Carnal Israel*, 31–60.

17. Mishnah, *Pirqe Avot* 4:21–22.

After our individual death there is a time of judgment, but the tradition is forceful in limiting this to a year at most as reflected in the length of time when we should daily recite memorial prayers for the dead. Any longer might imply the deceased was so wicked as to require the extra intervention! In this final judgment, at least anecdotally, before God's all-knowing wisdom, wrongs will be righted, suffering compensated and righteousness rewarded. But undoubtedly the Jewish emphasis is 'this-worldly' rather than an 'otherworldly' religion, with our focus firmly on responsibilities in the here and now. This too becomes a basis for evaluating the related teachings of other faiths.

Such teachings and perceptions must inevitably colour a Jewish approach to other religious and philosophical understandings of human nature. If the soul is pure, and if the propensity for human beings to do evil deeds is a feature of our biological makeup but is nevertheless capable of being controlled, this leaves little room for concepts like 'the fall' and 'original sin,' at least as popularly understood. (Nor is there a place for intermediaries between the individual Jew and God, though the folk tradition knows angels, lost souls, and '*wunder Rebbes*.') It is significant that in the biblical narrative about the disobedience by Eve and Adam in the Garden of Eden, no word for 'sin' is used. (It first appears in the story of Cain's jealousy of Abel, and then only as a temptation that he should be able to resist [Gen 4:7].) On this reading, 'sin' is an individual action and not a permanent human state that requires some external divine intervention to remove it. Rather, the theology of the High Holydays puts the responsibility for what we do wrong firmly on our shoulders, to acknowledge it consciously, and practically to attempt to repair the damage we have done and restore relationships that have been harmed. The term for all this activity is *teshuvah*, often translated as 'repentance,' but its Hebrew meaning is to 'turn' in all its many dimensions, away from wrongdoing and returning to God. Only then may we seek forgiveness from God expressed in the term 'atonement,' *kapparah*, literally to 'cover over' the consequences of our misdeeds that human actions alone can no longer achieve.

Memory and Time

Central to the covenant and all the actions of the High Holydays is the view that what the Jewish individual does has consequences for the people as a whole, for good and for bad. One expression of this interdependence is our collective memory, which plays a significant role in Jewish self-understanding, as expressed particularly in the oft-repeated biblical command to remember you were slaves in Egypt. This is used in some cases to ensure the proper treatment of those who are 'strangers in your midst,' the frequency of the repetition within the Hebrew Bible suggesting that this is one of the hardest lessons for liberated slaves to learn! As Rabbi David Lillienthal once expressed it in a sermon, remembering we were slaves is to prevent our turning into a Pharaoh.

But the word for remember, *zakor*, carries its own particular weight. To remember is literally to 're-member,' to bring back into existence something from the past so that it is again existentially present. This re-living the past in the present moment is well illustrated by the Passover Haggadah. 'In every generation it is the duty of all to regard themselves as if they had personally gone forth from Egypt.'

The punishment of the Passover drama's 'wicked son,' who does not accept the significance of the ritual, is that had he been there in Egypt, he would not have been redeemed! It is precisely the act of remembering that dictates the Jewish understanding of the calendar and ultimately of time itself. Each year at *Pesach*, Passover, we leave Egypt; at *Shavuot*, 'the Feast of Weeks,' we stand and receive the revelation at Sinai and enter the covenant, and at *Sukkot*, 'the Feast of Tabernacles,' we wander again in the wilderness on the way to the 'promised land.' In the summer we remember and mourn the events leading up to the catastrophe of the destruction of the Jerusalem Temple, taking comfort from the prophetic passages of consolation that are read in the following months leading up to the New Year. Alongside the secular calendar where 'real' history takes place, we live out another cyclical history, itself more 'real' because it re-enacts the sacred drama of our eternal life lived with God.

The cycle of six days work and the Shabbat of rest impose another pattern of time, time that is filled with meaning precisely because the days are counted from one Shabbat to the next. Shabbat rest, as well as commemorating God's rest after the six days of creation, is also deemed to be in memory of the liberation from slavery that came with the exodus from Egypt, when servants too are to experience and share that rest. The Shabbat, that 'cathedral in time,' also points towards a messianic future, and is itself a foretaste of that future. If 'memory' pulls Jews back to a past that is somehow ever present, the messianic hope pushes Jews forward towards a better future, even though the language to describe that future is imprecise: 'the end of days,' 'the world to come,' 'the days of the Messiah.' Again the emphasis is upon the nature of the world that we create moment by moment by our own behaviour in that same eternal present. As the Baal Shem Tov expressed this tension within Jewish existence, 'Remembering is the first step to redemption.'

But even secular time is filled with potential meaning for each individual life. Ecclesiastes reminds us that 'for everything there is a time and a season for every purpose under heaven' (3:1). But that generality becomes an urgent personal task for the psalmist contemplating the transience of life: 'teach us how to count our days so that we acquire a heart of wisdom' (Ps 90:12).

It must be pointed out immediately that the power of these patterns of ritual and celebration are much diminished in the postemancipation Jewish world. As 'Jews by choice,' free to choose to remain within a Jewish spiritual world or depart from it, we are selective in our approach to all aspects of Jewish tradition. In the past the festivals of the year helped determine our understanding of contemporary events, sometimes even blinding us to their own reality. (For example, the simplistic identification of any enemy with the villainous, genocidal Haman of the book of Esther may limit stratagems for identifying, evaluating, and appropriately addressing a particular threat.) Today, in a significant reversal, Jews may need to draw on their experience in life and the world to bring a depth of meaning to the festivals. Nevertheless, however this dynamic is played out, time as spiritually full of meaning and purpose is another criterion for 'authentic religion' that Jews would expect to find amongst other faiths.

Exile

While the Jewish perception of human nature is generally positive, Jews are more sanguine about the challenges and sorrows of life itself. Job's 'man is born to trouble as the sparks fly upwards' (Job 5:7) reflects a bitter sense of inevitability. Ecclesiastes, ever the materialist, asks quizzically or despairingly 'what profit has a man for all his labour under the sun?' (Eccl 1:3).

The limitations of life are bluntly described in Psalm 90, which at first glance seems merely to provide a catalogue of human sinfulness lived out under the threat of divine anger and punishment. But the psalm is constructed to give two perspectives on human life, contrasting human time 'from generation to generation' (v. 1) with divine time 'from age to age' (v. 2) before even the world was created. It offers a dark, imagined divine perspective that sees only the transience of our lives (a thousand years in your sight are like a yesterday that is past [Ps 90:4]), lives lived out under the threat of divine anger. But in protest at this judgmental theology it offers our human perspective that recognises that our life is a mere 'seventy years, eighty years with strength' and that they are 'full of trouble and sorrow' (Ps 90:10). It is only when God and human beings work together that we can find joy, and that God can come to bless the 'works of our hands' (Ps 90:17).[18]

The paradigm for the inevitability of human suffering is established with the banishment from the Garden of Eden. On one level it is banishment from the security of childhood, a life where all is provided and little expected. Yet, as the thrust of the book of Genesis suggests, it is only through our experience outside Eden that we can live a life in the freedom to make mistakes and to grow into our full humanity.

The individual situation becomes a collective one in Judaism through the experience of exile. Literally *galut*, 'being uncovered', hence 'exile', refers to the expulsion from the 'promised land', first under the Babylonians, and subsequently and for most of two thousand years, by the Romans. This dimension of exile includes the loss of national autonomy and self-rule, with all the necessary institutions in place to guarantee the correct ongoing relationship with God. In exile there is no Temple, only the synagogue, an improvised short-term solution that itself became an institution and centre for Jewish life. Exile means also to be subject to the whims of the prevailing political powers, and Jewish history is a catalogue of settlements and expulsions, of relative freedoms and dire persecutions.

18. For a fuller analysis of the structure of this psalm, see Magonet, *A Rabbi Reads the Psalms*, 165–76.

But exile is also a theological category. The physical expulsion from the land was interpreted as a divine punishment, ultimately deriving its justification from the 'small print' in the contract with God, the blessings for fulfilling it, the curses for failing to live up to it, spelled out in Leviticus 26 and Deuteronomy 28 with nightmarish precision and accuracy. The memory of what was lost, and the understanding of life as a state of exile, are symbolically embedded in Jewish life—from the unplastered patch of ceiling in a Jewish home to the glass that is broken at a Jewish wedding to the fast days recalling the destruction of Jerusalem and the Temple.

But it goes deeper. It is surely no coincidence that the cycle of Pilgrim Festivals is celebrated for their historical associations and hardly at all for the harvests that they originally expressed. Moreover, this historical remembering and re-enactment concludes at *Sukkot*, still in the wilderness on the way to the land, before beginning the cycle once again at *Pesach* back in Egyptian slavery. Similarly the Torah itself, the Five Books of Moses, is read cyclically, reaching its climax in the festival of *Simchat Torah*, the Rejoicing in the Torah. But on that occasion no sooner do we conclude by reading of the death of Moses on the border of the Promised Land than we return immediately to the narrative about creation. In our spiritual year we hover on the border of the 'Promised Land' but never enter it. Exile is a state of soul.

Yet the memory of the land itself, the promise of return, are the necessary complement to the experience of exile, and without them despair might have long since undermined all desire to survive as a people and a faith. The adjustments made in the Jewish calendar by the periodic insertion of an extra month ensure that the festivals coincide with the times of harvest in the land of Israel. The expectation of return, in God's own good time, is an every recurrent topic in Jewish liturgy and the theme of poets, dreamers, and travellers throughout two millennia of exile. 'My heart is in the East and I am at the edge of the West. How then can I taste what I eat, how can I enjoy it?' wrote Judah Halevi in the twelfth century. That yearning is summed up in a song, suffused equally with that tradition and the spirit of nineteenth-century nationalism, that became the national anthem of the State of Israel:

> As long as a Jewish soul
> still yearns in the innermost heart,
> and eyes turn eastward

gazing towards Zion,
then our hope is not lost,
the hope of two thousand years
to be a free people in our land,
the land of Zion and Jerusalem.
—Naftali Herz Imber

To have a home, physical roots, a connection to the earth, and a fully restored relationship with God, are all to be found in this Jewish yearning. But the emotional longing and the pride of ownership are challenged by the religious tradition itself, lest the land too becomes another idolatrous trap. Again it is the Torah that provides the context for understanding the nature of the relationship with the particular territory: 'The land shall not be sold in perpetuity for the land is Mine, for you are visitors and tenants with me' (Lev 25:23). The behaviour of the Israelites is seen as affecting the land itself, whether or not it yields its harvest (Deut 11:13–21), and in disgust the land might vomit out its inhabitants (Lev 18:28).

It is at this point that theology bumps up against brutal political realities. The State of Israel is established, not in some spiritualised realm but in a tangible geographic location, with real territorial and ideological enemies, and a highly complex, in many ways post-Holocaust emotionally damaged, Jewish population. Two thousand years of a religious system, based on survival, a limited degree of autonomy, and accommodation to external powers, must now adapt itself to the responsibility of governing a modern nation-state and having power over others. On another level we are acting out that deepest of Jewish inner conflicts, the acknowledgment of the call to be 'holy,' 'other,' in some ways special before God, and the wish simply to be 'normal,' 'like everyone else,' without the burden that the covenant imposes. In terms of our topic, Jews bring a newfound ambivalence to the encounter with Christianity and Islam. In the past we might have approached them with a kind of triumphalism of the victim, by pointing to their abuse of power. Now we find ourselves defending, or being unable to defend, in public arenas and privately, the effects of the actions of the State of Israel, perceived as some ultimate expression of Judaism. Time alone will tell how this radically changed political and spiritual situation will be acted out, and indeed what role dialogue itself might have in changing perceptions, attitudes, and political actions.

Revisiting the Four Categories

Perhaps it is appropriate at the end to revisit the four categories proposed by the young Muslim. They do represent four valuable criteria, so what would happen were we to appropriate them ourselves?

Clearly with the concept of monotheism we are in full accord, particularly as it allows us to view positively both Christianity, albeit with some reservations, and Islam. Nevertheless one qualification exists insofar as there is a risk that 'monotheism' slips very easily into 'monolatry', in the sense that it is only our perception of the One God that is 'real' and authentic and ultimately the 'true' understanding to which all should come. This tendency exists in Judaism, for example, in the *Alenu* prayer that comes towards the end of most services. It consists of two paragraphs. The first is highly 'particularistic' in that it asserts our uniqueness as a people and our special task as Israel to witness to God in this world. In some versions it dismisses all forms of worship by other peoples as serving things of emptiness and vanity, and the text was frequently subjected to internal and external censorship. Yet having asserted the uniqueness of Israel, the second paragraph expresses the hope that the establishment of God's rule over the world will come soon, when idolatry will be abolished, when the wicked will turn to God and all will come to worship God and accept God's rule over them. It is universal in its sentiment, but still particularistic in its expression, as it is to Israel's perception of God that they are invited to turn. Fortunately Jews have never had the political power to impose such a view on other peoples, but instead have repeatedly throughout history been subject to such attempts by both Christians and Muslims. When is 'universalism' merely 'particularism' writ large? Monolatry, like other forms of idolatry, is a seductive trap, a false spiritual arrogance and assertiveness that may often only be recognized and acknowledged in historical retrospect. A contemporary version of the *Alenu* prayer speaks instead of a partnership of different faiths to bring about '*tikkun olam*', the repair of the world.[19]

With regards to universalism itself, another of the four criteria, all three faith communities face the same problem of affirming their unique-

19. The text can be found in Magonet, ed., *Seder Ha-t'fillot, Forms of Prayer: Daily, Sabbath and Occasional Prayers*, 8th ed. (London: The Movement for Reform Judaism, 2008) 313; based on a prayerbook of the Israeli Progressive Movement.

ness, and at the same time acknowledging that they are part of humanity as a whole; asserting the truth of their understanding of their relationship to God while at the same time having to come to terms with at least the 'partial truths' of other faiths. The question today is how far that acknowledgement changes the inner self-understanding of each without undermining some essential element of their identity. It is precisely where that identity is perceived to be under threat that ranks are closed and dialogue is seen as adding to the danger. The recognition that God is greater than any limited understanding we may have offers the possibility of accommodation within a broader monotheistic awareness, but that is a major step for any institutionalised religion.

The criterion 'commitment to righteousness and justice' becomes all too often a weapon in slanging matches between different religious faiths, and internally amongst different movements within each faith. Though this violates Krister Stendahl's 'compare equal to equal,' it does allow a degree of righteous indignation at the perceived abuses committed by others, until the counterattacks arise. While the squabbling continues, so does the suffering. We have probably never been so aware of injustices perpetrated throughout the world as today, through the impact of globalisation and the knowledge of so many trouble spots brought into our homes through the selective eye of the media. No group is guiltless, and no group without its dedicated people who fight for justice for themselves and others. Jews can point with pride to a figure like Rene Cassin and his role in helping establish the Universal Declaration of Human Rights, and to any number of other Jewish individuals who have contributed to justice within society. But we can also identify Jews who fail to live up to the kind of 'righteousness and justice' that Abraham was to pass on to his descendents. As indicated above, the very nature of Israel as a sovereign state raises questions on a dimension not experienced by Jews since biblical times. Nevertheless our responsibilities and actions in this area remain central questions that all must ask ourselves, internally as religious faiths and communities, as well as challenging one another.

The criterion, 'fidelity to revealed Scripture' is actually a two-edged sword. Setting aside questions about the accurate transmission of the received text, if 'fidelity' means an uncritical acceptance of the text at its face value, then Jews are indeed sinners. Judaism is highly critical of what is often termed a 'fundamentalist' approach to Scripture, though the attitude is better defined, as by the late Father Gordian Marshal, as 'selective literalism.' For Jews it is precisely because Scripture/Torah is the word of God that it must be open to infinite levels of interpretation, just as God is infinite. Numbers of rabbinic statements attest to this view: 'There are seventy faces to Torah,'[20] 'Turn it and turn it again, for everything is in it.'[21] Indeed the entire postbiblical development of Judaism is a record of debate about the actual and potential meaning of every sentence, word, even letter of the Hebrew Bible, the subsequent texts being themselves subject to precisely the same scrutiny and interpretive activity.

Moreover, precisely because the Torah comes from God, it can only represent the highest moral and ethical values. So when the overt meaning of a Torah passage fails to live up to the best of contemporary values, the rabbis have had no qualms about reinterpreting it to meet those values, while at the same time assuming they were working within a legitimate, divinely sanctioned methodology.[22] In our postemancipation world the 'chain of tradition' has become broken, or rather, a variety of movements claim to be the authentic inheritors of that tradition. But the principle of interpretation as the way of finding God's will in contemporary life remains dominant.

Many of the views of 'what Judaism believes' expressed until now reflect the reality of a preemancipation Judaism. As indicated from time to time, in the modern world the rigid halakhic and social structures that characterised Jewish life have been radically transformed. Alongside those who attempt to remain true to all aspects of past beliefs and practices are those who reject them out of hand, and those who seek to edit, amend, reinterpret, or completely innovate within the classical framework. Nowhere is this tendency so obvious as in the slow emergence from patriarchy. It characterised biblical religion: the partner with God in the covenant is the adult Israelite male to whom belong wife, children, land, slaves, animals. The concept of the Oral Torah, which formed the basis of rabbinic tradition and authority, expressed itself in the phenomenal intellectual constructs of the two Talmuds (Palestinian and Babylonian) and the many volumes of Midrash, and their subsequent legal codifications and responsa. Yet this entire activity was the work of men who defined

---

20. *Oti'ot d'rabi Akiva.*

21. Mishnah, *Pirqe Avot* 5:25.

22. 'If one translates a verse literally he is a liar!' Babylonian Talmud, *Kiddushin* 49a.

also the nature, role, and status of women. While they did their best to remove inequalities and injustices to be found in the biblical record, particularly in matters of marriage and property laws, the 'secondary' status of women, for example being unable to initiate divorce proceedings, remained. In addition restrictions were placed upon their opportunities to study Torah, perceived as a strictly male preserve. It has taken the inroads of modernity to undermine the authority structures that sustained this culture, and the women's movement to expose its assumptions and challenge its gender prejudices. Half a century is a short period in a history measured in millennia, but undoubtedly, with the exception of a relatively small but significant ultraorthodoxy, Judaism is undergoing a revolution, spearheaded by the non-Orthodox religious movements with, for example, the ordination of women as rabbis, alongside the day-to-day political and cultural reality of Jewish communities. Thus expectations of religious equality for the two genders are today significant factors in Jewish approaches to dialogue, precisely from those within the 'liberal' wings of Judaism who are also most prominent in dialogue itself.

All Having Been Said

This paper has of necessity sought to be detached and analytical in exploring the nature of the Jewish relationship with God and the expectations of other faiths that flow from this. But there are other dimensions of passion and commitment that defy such immediate evaluation. In particular it is the poets of Israel who explore the inner experience of a life lived with a God who is at one and the same time far and near, unknowable and intimately present, almost an abstraction yet as demanding as any lover. The psalmist can write:

> My soul is thirsty for You,
> my flesh is pining for You
> in a dry and weary land
> where there is no water.
> So I looked for You
> in the holy place,
> to see Your power and glory.

Because Your love is better than life,

my lips shall praise You. (Psalm 63:2–4)

The kabbalistic tradition explored this dimension further as attested by the poem 'Yedid Nefesh' of the sixteenth-century Rabbi Eliezer Azikri:

Beloved of the soul,

source of mercy,

draw your servant

to do Your will,

to run to You swift as a hart,

to bow down low

before Your majesty,

finding Your love

sweeter than the honeycomb

and every tempting savour.

On Yom Kippur, the Day of Atonement, we chant repeatedly a set of verses, "Ki Anu Amecha," that draw on the many metaphors for the relationship between God and Israel, each of which could generate further areas for comparison with other faiths; so let them provide the last word.

For we are Your people and You are our God.

We are Your children and You are our father.

We are Your servants and You are our master.

We are Your community and You are our portion.

We are Your inheritance and You are our destiny.

We are Your flock and You are our shepherd.

We are Your vineyard and You are our keeper.

We are Your work and You are our creator.

We are Your beloved and You are our friend.

We are Your own and You are our nearest.

We are Your people and You are our sovereign.

We are the people known to You and You are the God
    made known by us.

2

Meeting the Other: Judaism, Pluralism, and Truth

David M. Elcott*

Posing the Questions

Judaism does not speak with one voice on any issue, lacking as it does a singular decider or an authoritative catechism, so any claims made about Judaism when it looks beyond itself to see other religious beliefs and faith communities will be highly personal. I know that my tradition is multivoiced, reflecting radically varied contexts, ages, and geographic communities. A disinterested broker of Jewish thought provides contradictory traditions, creating anachronistic but potentially rich dialogues that would span millennia. This study will provide cursory recognition of the variety of historic Jewish responses yet will follow a path directed by my teacher, Yitz Greenberg, whose work on a principled pluralist Judaism, emerging both from within the tradition and from modern Jewish experience, speaks most clearly to me. It is from this vantage point that I will address the essential principles and processes of discernment that a Jew committed to dialogue and relationship with other religious communities brings in to conversation. I will highlight and encourage a tradition that will build on three claims grounded in Jewish texts and traditions.

The first claim affirms that access to the experience of God is available to all human beings as expressed in the *midrashic* claim that *eyn*

* Dedicated to my teacher, Rabbi Irving Yitz Greenberg.

26

makom panu'I miney ("Entrances to holiness are everywhere"). The possibility of ascent is all the time, even at unlikely times and through unlikely places."[1] Any engagement with the non-Jewish world is grounded in an understanding that God's presence is far reaching and well beyond the boundaries of Judaism. This naturally leads to a principle of Jewish pluralism not as concession but as part of the divine plan, the most effective mechanism to upgrade the presence of God in the world. It is best expressed within Judaism in the words of Rav Abraham Kook, chief rabbi of Palestine and one of the most powerful and respected voices of twentieth-century Judaism:

> For the building is constructed from various parts, and the truth of the light of the world will be built from various dimensions, from various approaches, for "these and those are the living words of God . . ." It is precisely the multiplicity of opinions, which derive from variegated souls and backgrounds, that enriches wisdom and brings about its enlargement. In the end, all matters will be properly understood and it will be recognized as impossible for the structures of peace to be built without all those views which appear (to us) to be in conflict.[2]

This in turn will lead us to a second Jewish understanding that informs the ways a Jew meets a non-Jew. At the Jewish core is a deep challenge to absolutist religious claims, a challenge that derives from a Jewish understanding of God's revelation in which Sinai is a multifaceted approximation of God's word, but certainly not the same as God. As the founding rabbis of the first centuries of the common era understood the Oral tradition, revelation continues to unfold as humans better apprehend God's will, but no one can ever claim absolute knowledge of God. No one, therefore, and no religious tradition can own all of God's truth. To make that claim would be to submit to idolatry. Jews will resist those who claim they alone know God or what God demands.

I am then led to examine Judaism in terms of its perception of other religious and ethnic communities and its treatment, in theory if not in practice, of those who are not part of the Jewish community. As I am

1. *Bamidbar Rabbah* 12:4, with added commentary by Lawrence Kushner, *Honey from the Rock* (Woodstock, VT: Jewish Lights, 1995) 48

2. Abraham Isaak Kook, *Olat Raya*, vol. 1 (Jerusalem: Mosad Harav Kook, 1962) 330–31.

less bound by the chain of tradition and the traditional community that seeks to uphold it, I will be more prepared to call for embedding a clear critique within, or even for eliminating those elements of, the tradition that undermine the fundamental pluralism and openness that, for me, are at the core of the Judaism I live and seek to promote. The logic for excising the "othering" texts and traditions of Judaism results from an exploration that will challenge the monotheist and Enlightenment positions that the veracity and authenticity of any religion is based on whether that religion is true or false. I will propose that the Jewish test of a religion's power and value is whether it creates partnerships with other religious communities to seek God's truths, provides meaning to those who follow it, and advances God's goodness and healing in the world. This derives from the Jewish understanding that human beings, created in God's image, are *shutafim haKadosh Baruch Hu*, partners with God in repairing the brokenness of the world. This is perhaps the most obvious principle of discernment operative when a Jew engages with other faiths: what are the fruits of belief? The degree to which a religion is capable of succeeding in providing meaning, motivation and behaviors that upgrade all life reflects the truths it has to offer.

Entrances to Holiness Are Everywhere

Judaism struggles over how the Other is seen, whether there is a place in God's plan for those of other faiths and truths to be found in the multiplicity of beliefs. Biblical Israel seemed to fear the religious Other (if not all "others") as a seductive force that would tear the faithful from obedience to God.[3] So we are not surprised that a section of Psalm 115 is recited on Jewish festivals, as a reminder of the falseness of other faiths:

> They have mouths, but cannot speak;
> Eyes, but cannot see;
> They have ears, but cannot hear,
> Noses, but cannot smell . . .
> Those who fashion them,
> All who trust in them,
> Shall become like them.

3. See for example Deuteronomy 12.

Aleynu, the liturgical culmination of each service recited three times a day, is meant to attest to the unique and singular truth of Judaism:

> It is incumbent upon us to praise the God of all . . .
>
> Who did not make us as all other nations and peoples
>
> Who did not give us their portion or destiny . . .
>
> We therefore hope in You, God, and may we soon behold the glory of your might: sweeping away the false gods of the earth, utterly destroying idolatry . . .
>
> So that all humanity will invoke Your name.[4]

While written in the early centuries of the common era, the latter prayer, *Aleynu,* was placed in the *Siddur* in the thirteenth century, long after classical idolatry had ended. Verses excised under Christian pressure ("for they bow down to nothingness and emptiness, and pray to a god that will not save") have in recent years been reintroduced in certain circles in Israel and abroad. This mindset, as old as biblical Israel in the psalm cited above, through rabbinic Judaism[5] and into medieval times,[6] reflects the view that other religions are dangerous and impure. Jacob Katz notes of Christianity, but this clearly would apply to other faith communities: "avoidance of contact with the visible expressions of the Christian faith became almost an instinct with the Jew, who felt himself endangered spiritually, and perhaps even physically, whenever he encountered a Christian gathering performing its religious rites."[7] It is fair to say that since Jewish theology is inextricably rooted in the Jewish historical experience, any encounter with other Abrahamic faiths will occur on a platform of memory—Crusades, Inquisition, anti-Jewish riots and pogroms, anti-Israel behaviors and, of course, the Holocaust.[8] For

---

4. See Boston College, *Jewish Understandings of the Other: An Annotated Sourcebook, Liturgy: Daily Prayers,* http://www.bc.edu/research/cjl/meta-elements/texts/cjrelations/resources/sourcebook/Aleynu.htm.

5. See, for example, Mishnah, *Avodah Zarah* 4:7; or Babylonian Talmud, *Megillah* 25b.

6. Jacob Katz, *Tradition and Crisis* (New York: New York University Press, 1993) chap. 4, inter alia.

7. Ibid., 43.

8. Note that in a "first" ever event, an address given by a rabbi—in this case, the chief rabbi of Haifa, Shear-Yashuv Cohen—to a Synod of Bishops, could not avoid the history of Roman Catholic-Jewish relations: the church's efforts on behalf of Jews during World

Jews, recalling carnal memory and not philosophy or classical theological discourse is an essential aspect of discernment that informs interfaith encounter. Better said, history is the language of Jewish theology. What "you" did to "us" begins (and often ends) dialogue with Jews.

So the instinctual tendency of "othering" does reflect Katz's sensitive read of the Jewish way of processing information. Just as the biblical redactors and the rabbis of the early centuries sought to divide the world between "us "and "them," medieval Jews—often segregated and unable to imagine social intercourse with their Christian or Muslim counterparts—felt endangered by contact. The cathedral, with its icons and dark chambers and the faithful crossing themselves, was naturally threatening. The Muslim rulers, however noble, enforced policies that not only separated Jew from Muslim but confirmed the domination of Islam by forbidding Jewish equal standing with Muslims and enacting humiliating laws. One need not list the rules and regulations or even the pogroms and riots that occurred in Europe and North Africa to recognize that Jews formed their personal and communal identity not only from within but also in the ways their lives reflected against the Other. Upon awakening, Jews were expected to recite the words, "Blessed are you God, who has not made me a Gentile."[9]

Whatever role such separation and discrimination against other faith communities may have served in earlier ages, its damage to Judaism has become more apparent now. The Jewish experience of the Other confirms in so many ways that "[t]he relationship of culture and power is clearly evident in the practices of exclusion and othering that characterizes ethnographic practices"[10] And such othering is never benign exactly because, as Derrida notes, the Other compels a community to question itself, being shadowed and haunted by those it claims are Other.[11]

Insofar as identity presupposes alterity, any effort by a group to establish the parameters of its own identity entails the exclusion and/or

---

War II. See *HaAretz*, "Haifa Chief Rabbi at Vatican: Wartime Pope Let Jews Down," July 10, 2008. online: http://www.haaretz.com/hasen/spages/1026980.html/.

9. For all but the Orthodox Jewish community, this blessing has either been reframed—"Blessed are you God who has made me Israel"—or removed entirely.

10. Laurence J. Silberstein and Robert L. Cohen, *The Other in Jewish Thought and History: Constructions of Jewish Culture and Identity* (New York: New York University Press, 1994) 5.

11. Ibid., 7.

silencing of the voices of Others. Consequently, the process of identity formation entails acts of violence against the other.[12]

For many, a Judaism based on praising a God "who did not make us as all other nations and peoples" whose gods and, therefore, their lives are nothingness and emptiness, says little constructive about who and what Jews are. In fact, from biblical research that links Scripture with other ancient cultures to Chassidic garb and Zionist nationalism, Judaism has gained a great deal from the ways it learned from or even mimicked the Other, even if the source of such appropriation was denied. There are periodic glimmers that non-Jews could be good people, could earn their place in the world to come, and even that Gentile religions and civilizations could do good. Although experiencing themselves as under attack by a hostile world, the rabbis who founded rabbinic Judaism in the early centuries of the common era could not deny the obvious, that there were righteous Gentiles and that other cultures produced just and constructive societies.[13] Within most Jewish circles, there is now little debate on the matter. The great majority of twenty-first-century Jews engage in a wide range of relationships with members of other faiths, including serious and deep dialogue. This should and often does lead to encounters that transcend acceptance and, instead, seek a partnership with other faith communities in which, as Greenberg notes, "Each partner affirms that its truth/faith/system alone cannot fulfill God's dreams. The world needs the contribution that the other religion can make for the sake of achieving wholeness and perfection for all. A partner affirms (today, I would say: celebrates) that God assigns different roles and different contributions to different groups."[14] While certainly understandable, fear and anger and the "othering" of religious and ethnic groups cannot frame the way Jews encounter others in the world. So how can a community grounded in ancient texts and generations of exegetical commentaries and legal codes find truths in the faiths of others with whom they now share a more intimate existence?

One way is to selectively read inherited texts, a few examples of which I will provide. While the common culture in Jewish communities

12. Ibid.

13. Mishnah, *Avodah Zara* 4a; Bereshit Rabbah, *Bereshit* IX, 13.

14. Irving Greenberg, *For the Sake of Heaven and Earth* (Philadelphia: JPS, 2004) 43.

often claimed to have limited encounters with non-Jews, we can find medieval responses to the religious Other that allow us to construct a chain of relationship from the written word authored by rabbinic authorities whose purview and strengths lay in making halakhic legal decisions. They seldom spoke of values or ethics, cultural observations or attitudes. The answer to questions concerning other religions would play out within a legal framework. If Islam was seen as idolatrous, we would know it based on (for example) a responsum over wine. Yet here we read that Rabbi Nissim ben Gerondi, who lived in Barcelona from about 1340 to 1380, says that "perhaps it is permissible" to drink Muslim wine in a setting not conducive to socializing (socializing with non-Jews is forbidden in a separate ruling). A later reading by Rabbi Joseph Messas, a halakhic authority of the twentieth century in North Africa, clarifies why certain authorities disregard the Gaonic view that permits one only to obtain benefit from this wine but does not allow one to drink it. Rabbi Messas explains: "There is no unity [of God] like the unity found in Islam; therefore, one who forbids [drinking] wine which they have handled turns holy into profane by regarding worshippers of God as worshippers of idols, God forbid."[15] The legal rendering reads as follows: Jews cannot drink the wine of idolaters. We learn that Muslims are viewed as monotheists because we can drink their wine. While they may be in error in their rejection of Judaism, they are true monotheists who believe in the one God.

Christianity is more complex for the rabbis. The Trinity that was initially understood as affirming multiple gods, Jesus as both human and divinity, providing a physical form to God, God's impregnation of Mary, along with the iconography and general sense of Christianity as heresy, made it easy to claim that "they bow down to nothingness and emptiness." However, perhaps from more direct encounters with Christianity during the Enlightenment, a shift takes place that constructs from medieval traditions a view of Christianity as a fellow monotheist tradition. Citing one example, when twentieth-century German rabbi Marcus Horowitz was asked by a colleague for a halakhic ruling on whether it is permissible for Jews to help fund a church, he reminds the petitioner that Christians are not idolaters:

15. Marc B. Shapiro, "Islam and the Halakhah," *Judaism* (1993). See online: http://findarticles.com/p/articles/mi_m0411/is_/ai_14234286?tag=artBody;col1.

"They, dear Jews, worship the Maker of Heaven and Earth." *Shituf* (joining in concert) was permitted for non-Jews. No less an authority than R. Moshe Isserles, whose glosses on the *Shulhan Arukh* were incorporated into its text, here so ruled. Since normative Jewish law held that Christianity was a form of monotheism, Horowitz stated that it was a commandment for a Jew to donate charity money to a church. He concluded his responsum by thanking God for allowing Christians, through their teachings, "to be among the pious and great men of the world.[16]

Again, the halakhic rendering marks a shift, joining Christianity to Islam and Judaism as monotheist faiths that provide access to God—even in the unlikely place of mosque or church.

The issue of Buddhism, Hinduism, and other Eastern religions is even more complicated for the obvious reasons that the main body of world Jewry had little engagement with them, knew little about their faiths, and, prima fascia, statues of gods, goddesses, demons, and Buddha forms were easily seen as idolatrous. The key response to Hindus—and perhaps we may include Buddhists—is found in the often cited Maimonides's *Guide to the Perplexed* from the twelfth century: "No one is antagonistic to Him or ignorant of His greatness except the remnants of this religious community that has perished, the remnants that survived in the extremities of the earth, as for instance the infidels among the Turks in the extreme north and the Hindus in the extreme south. These are the remnants of the religious community of the Sabians. This was a religious community that extended over the whole earth."[17] Certainly Maimonides reigns authoritatively as the medieval halakhic decisor. Yet we also must acknowledge that he knew little of Buddhism and Hinduism, viewing them as relics of an ancient idolatrous culture that once knew the one God and then rejected that God. We now know that these cultures developed independently of Western influence. What if he, like the German-Jewish philosopher Martin Buber, chose to explore Eastern religions? Not surprisingly, Buber, in "The Spirit of the Orient and Judaism," comes to a radically different conclusion. Seeing through the physical artifacts and plastic manifestations of divine beings in Hinduism and Buddhism, Buber writes:

16. As cited by Peter Ochs, "The Jewish View of a Christian God," in *Christianity in Jewish Terms*, edited by Tikvah Frymer-Kensky et al. (Boulder: Westview, 2000) 75.

17. Maimonides, *Guide to the Perplexed*, III 29 (translated by Shlomo Pines) 515.

But whatever its guide, there is always the same inspirited demand for the good life, the fulfilling life, for the "way." Knowledge of the nature of the world, on which the Occidental who wants to master it depends, is forever subservient to the knowledge of the *way*. What is said of Buddha may be said of all Eastern teachings: he did not lecture on whether the world is eternal or temporal; he taught only the way . . . The East perceives that the full manifestation and disclosure of the world's inner substance is thwarted; that the primally intended unity is split and distorted; that the world needs human spirit in order to become redeemed and unified; and that this alone constitutes the meaning and the power of human existence in the world . . . [t]he East's timeless greatness and its timeless import for humanity reside in the fact that this perception is wholly turned toward life.[18]

Buber provides a pathway to reach out and welcome adherents of Eastern practice and religious life as partners in the search for the divine and as actors whose works can help construct the structures of peace.

Yitz Greenberg amplifies Buber's analysis from his own perspective by reframing the Noahide covenant, which too often is used by Jewish leaders as a grudging minimalist acceptance of other religions. The Noahide covenant, which the rabbis derived from God's renewed covenant found in Genesis 9, provides both a biblical and rabbinic acceptance of the potential righteousness of all humanity and its inclusion in God's covenantal promise. Maimonides makes this point, even given his limitation that Gentiles must acknowledge the authority of Torah, affirming that those who observe these core humanist commandments are counted among the righteous and have a place in the world to come.[19] Greenberg writes: "The universality of the Noahide covenant does mean, however, that henceforth every religion that works to repair the world—and thus advance the triumph of life—is a valid expression of this divine pact with humanity . . . Abraham's covenant—a pioneering, world-transforming revelation that teaches God's presence, concern, and obligation—is but one of a series of divine initiatives to redeem suffering humanity."[20] While it would be naïve to claim that Jews meet non-Jews only on these terms—

18. Martin Buber, *On Judaism*, ed. Nahum N. Glazer (New York: Schoken, 1967) 61–62.

19. Maimonides, *Yad, Hilkhot Melakhim* 9.1.

20. Greenberg, *For the Sake of Heaven and Earth*, 57.

the memory of anti-Jewish attacks and the fear of further attack remain a vital pulse in the Jewish community—the experience of Jewish encounter with non-Jews allows for levels of engagement today that would have been unimaginable in the past. If we are to explore essential principles and processes of discernment that are operative as Jews encounter others, then an expansive read of the covenant with Noah and his descendants provides a constructive framework of openness. Again, the midrash is so helpful in its recognition that access to the sacred and awareness of God is not limited to any one space, language or set of behaviors or beliefs. Otherwise, it seems to me, there would be no need to claim that "There is no place on earth without the Presence (of God)."

The Battle against Idolatry

Judaism stakes its historical legitimacy on the revealed awareness that God is beyond human consciousness, infinitely impossible to comprehend. Idolatry, then, must imply much more than bowing to graven images onto which the worshiper has projected supernatural powers. The pagan world knew that their gods did not actually reside in the sculpted form. The Torah's attack on idolatry had less to do with the pagan forms than with the underlying beliefs of a pagan world, that gods are themselves subservient to a natural order. For Judaism, nothing can impede Judaism's contention that the world can be improved exactly because God and we enter history as partners to challenge the accepted absolutist claims of those who accept the world as it is.

The pagan world to which the Bible responds revels in predetermination; change is never possible, the natural world and the universe itself are complete, and we are forced to acknowledge our particular condition as unchanging. The gods themselves are regulated by natural cycles and forces of fate over which they have no control. Human life mimics with recurring cycles and patterns. It was possible for the pagan world to contain many gods, because no matter how many there were, they still were not free. Ultimately, the gods had to bow to the absolute control of the natural world. If the gods themselves were controlled, how much more so were the people who served those gods. The hierarchies of the gods were mirrored in the human societies that worshipped them—where birth determined a person's status and fate. Pharaoh and Caesar, Judaism declares, like nature itself, ultimately must be subservient to a force beyond human apprehension—the only absolute. Contemporary theologian Gordon Tucker amplifies this point:

> [I]t is ultimately futile to try to capture all that can (or perhaps must) be known in the systems we devise, no matter how cleverly and piously. There are inevitably truths greater than those that are humanly conceived and designed formalizations can capture for us—be they number theory, or physics, or ethics, or religion. As given in a quote of unknown attribution brought by (the dean of Modern Orthodoxy Rabbi) Soloveichik, there is "music that is better than it can be played."[21]

As monotheist religions, Christianity and Islam will be met with hostility to the degree that they tend toward absolutist claims. Buddhism and Hinduism (ironically, given Jewish concern about pagan worship) may offer a more comfortable encounter with Jews exactly because they are seen as more open to multiple understandings of God. But any community that claims it has achieved temporal, this-world perfection is seen as engaging in a form of dangerous alien worship. And a religious tradition that claims full knowledge of God, that it has access to the divine truth, is also idolatrous, because in spite of claims to the contrary, the world is not yet perfect, and we are not yet one with God. Greenberg explains that "humans, by definition, cannot enclose the infinity of God, either in its expression or by their comprehension. There is a real danger that the human version/understanding, which is by definition finite, will be extended by believers into an infinite claim that allows no room for the other. This human extension ends up with a pseudo-infinite; *this is the definition of idolatry*. Idolatry is the partial, created or shaped by finite humans, that claims to be infinite."[22]

Here we have located the sacred core of God's revelation that promotes a principled Jewish pluralism that eschews absolute truths, even a Torah that was given to Moses on Mount Sinai. The Zohar refers to the idolatrous nature of those who seek a literal reading of the Torah: "So this story of Torah (the Five Books of Moses) is but the garment of Torah. The

---

21. Gordon Tucker, "Can a People of the Book also Be a People of God?" *Conservative Judaism* 60 (Fall/Winter 2007–2008) 17.

22. Greenberg, *For the Sake of Heaven and Earth*, 210 (italics original).

body is clothed in garments, the stories of this world. Fools of the world look only at the garment, the story of Torah; they know nothing more. Those who know more do not look at the garment but rather at the body under that garment . . . In the time to come they are destined to look at the soul of the soul of Torah."[23]

Although the thirteenth-century Spanish kabbalist authors of the Zohar were most certainly elitist mystics, their claim resonates with an earlier, populist midrashic text that touches a primal understanding of revelation itself: "All the people saw the voices"—How many voices were there? . . . The Torah was meant to be heard in voices according to the strength of each human listener as it says in Psalms 'The voice of God is in the power'—the power of each human being." In the same way God appeared to each generation in a different way and the manna tasted differently to each age bracket."[24]

That, I believe, is why the rabbis insisted as a cardinal axiom of faith that the Oral Law is as divinely given as the Written Law, that it is ongoing and belongs to mortal and fallible human beings who cannot deign God's truth, but can modestly grasp only an approximate version that is, at the moment, accessible to them. Stepping back from the issues of power and authority that certainly contributed to the rejection of a hereditary priesthood for a merit-based rabbinic leadership, the rabbis make a striking claim: "Moses received the Torah from Sinai and transmitted it to Joshua; Joshua to the elders; the elders to the prophets; and the prophets handed it down to the men of the Great Assembly,"[25] not to prophets who know God's word, but human beings whose debates, disagreements, and arguments end up being the word of God. They go so far as to forbid God to intervene when the Great Assembly of Rabbis is trying to make a decision. In this story, Rabbi Eliezer's legal viewpoint is validated by God's intervention with divine miracles—and then God is overruled by the majority of rabbis. "Rabbi Yehoshua stood up and protested: 'The Torah is not in heaven!' (Deut. 30:12). We pay no attention to a divine voice because long

---

23. *Zohar* III:152a: translated in Daniel Matt, *Zohar: The Book of Enlightenment* (New York: Paulist, 1983) 44–45.

24. *Mekhilta d'Rabbi Yishmael*; see also *Shemot Rabbah* 29,1; and *Pesikta Drabbati* on Exodus 19.

25. Mishnah, *Avot* 1:1.

ago at Mount Sinai You wrote in your Torah at Mount Sinai, 'After the majority must one incline' (Ex. 23:2)."[26] Noam Zion elaborates:

> Rabbi Yehoshua rejects the interpretative move of Eliezer who "consults the author" regarding the authoritative reading of the Torah. Yehoshua claims *authorial intention is irrelevant to interpretation* even if the words of God are called *mitzvot*, that is, expressions of God's will . . . Thus Rabbi Yehoshua's viewpoint is a radical one. He uses it to challenge a God who in the story is unsure that giving up control of the interpretation of Torah is good. "It is not in Heaven" is then a *radical* defense of human interpretation by rejecting the prophetic voice from heaven that would have stopped controversy by authenticating one view.[27]

Yitz Greenberg translates this remarkable rabbinic tradition into a Jewish principled pluralism that does not merely accept the existence of the Other and validate its right to be in the world, but sees encounter with the Other as the best way to understand God's will and to avoid the idolatry of human absolutism:

> When culture and values are no longer embedded in structures that are fixed, "genetic," or absolute, and when the spirit of choice and freedom is strong, then the sense of absolute claims, which typically undergirded classic religions, is lost. For many, if not most people, the result that emerges is relativism, which is the loss of capacity to affirm any standards. But the deepest religious response is pluralism—the recognition that there are plural absolute standards that can live and function together even when they conflict. The deepest insight of pluralism is that dignity, truth, and power function best when they are pluralized, e.g., divided and distributed, rather than centralized and absolutized.[28]

This is the authentic Jewish response to the absolute truth claims of other religious and political cultures as well as an internal critique against those who have fetishized Torah and Halakhah into idolatrous forms. Principled pluralism, at least in the Jewish context, is the most effective way to come closer to God, to humbly seek justice and practice mercy as

---

26. Babylonian Talmud, *Baba Metzia* 59b.

27. Noam Zion, "Elu v'Elu: Two Schools of Halakha Face Off On Issues of Human Autonomy, Majority Rule And Divine Voice of Authority," in Shalom Hartman Institute, online: http://www.hartmaninstitute.com/uploads/Holidays/Elu-02062008_0957_45.pdf/.

28. Greenberg, *For the Sake of Heaven and Earth*, 201.

partners with all human beings who seek to approach God by doing good, a foundational point to which I will shortly return. Greenberg concludes: "The essential difference between pluralism and relativism is that pluralism is based on the principle that there still is an absolute truth. There still are valid values; we still can and must say no to certain systems and ideas . . . The pluralist affirms absolute values but has come to know their limits. The absolute values do not cover all the possibilities. Pluralism is an absolutism that has come to recognize its own limitations."[29]

Judaism, with all its traditions and historical experience and rich texts, cannot achieve its messianic dream alone. We each can only claim part of the story and a fraction of the truth. As Mark Johnson notes, "It takes no great insights to recognize that our moral understanding is complex, multidimensional, messy, anything but transparent and utterly resistant to absolutes and reductive strategies . . . We negotiate our way through this tangled maze of moral deliberation, one step at a time, never sure where we will end, guided only by our ideals of what we, and others, and our shared world might become."[30]

Judaism revels in the messiness of moral deliberation. This messiness, and not God's truth, is both principle and process. In Jewish–non-Jewish encounter, there should be no surprise when Jews challenge hoary faith assumptions and bridle when truth claims are too coherent, too compelling, too absolute, leaving no space for textual, historical, and behavioral alternatives. Expect in any dialogue that Jews will be particularly prickly if a conversation includes, "There is only one path to salvation." We choose to live with the messiness that "All these and those [other contradictory viewpoints] are the living words of God." Recognizing and respecting the paths we all have taken to reach this moment, at this juncture at least, I believe that this is the humble way that most Jews enter into dialogue as we approach, hear and try to be obedient to God.

29. Ibid., 203.

30. Mark Johnson, *Moral Imagination: Implications of Cognitive Science for Ethics* (Chicago: University of Chicago Press, 1993) 260.

Excising "Othering" from Contemporary Judaism

Judaism or, better yet, Jews are still struggling with how to encounter other faiths. Grounded in a pluralism that sees potential entrances to holiness everywhere and hears in contradictory voices the living word of God, what do I do with those elements of the Jewish past that have, for the very understandable reasons of oppression, anger, and fear, deviated from the core Jewish pluralist message? What can a Jew committed to interfaith encounter do with those aspects of Judaism that are not hospitable to dialogue? Understanding this internal struggle is essential for non-Jews who enter into dialogue with the Jewish community.

Years ago, in trying to locate within the contemporary Orthodox community an authentic way to promote equality for women, my study partner cited the benevolence of Deuteronomy 21:10–14. In that text, a captured woman is allowed one month to lament her father and mother after which the man who captured her in battle is allowed to go to her and make her his own. Then, if he no longer wants her, he must release her outright and can neither sell nor enslave her. I stopped our study session in pain, for what I read was that a man goes to war and comes home with booty that (not whom) he rapes until he decides to discard her. This text is in our Torah, handed to Jews as an inheritance from millennia past. But now faithful Jews must reject this particular inheritance.

I include in the categories of traditions that must be rejected as a desecration of God all biblical genocidal claims, even if never actualized, against the inhabitants of the land of Israel as well as the acceptance of slavery, capital punishment, homophobia, and, of course, the overall inequality of women in the Bible. One can certainly explain the sociological context of key texts, find the literary and legal elements taken from other traditions, or make a positive comparison to more brutal cultures. But that is no longer adequate. Because we are to be faithful to the Torah's vision that each human being is created as an image of God imbued with infinite value, cherished uniqueness, and the right to divine equality, Jews are therefore commanded to reject degrading and "othering" texts and traditions because they diminish God in the universe.[31]

And Judaism must not limit its rejection to the Bible, but is obligated to examine those elements of rabbinic Judaism that further exacerbate

31. Elcott, *A Sacred Journey* (Northvale, NJ: Aronson, 1995) 10–12.

many of these issues even as it attempted to ameliorate others. Among the sacred texts received but now to be rejected, I cite Shimon Bar Yohai, one of the great rabbis of the Mishnah that was compiled during the early centuries of the common era. He gives us the phrase: "The best of the Gentiles should be killed,"[32] which helps explain such statements as the following: "Cattle may not be left in inns of idolaters because they are suspected of bestial sodomy; a Jewish woman may not remain alone with them since they are suspected of lewd lechery; and a Jewish man may not remain alone with them for they are suspected of murder."[33]

Beyond such "othering" projections in the legal midrashic tradition, there is a general training that permeates popular liturgical texts, that the *goyim*—what became a pejorative term from the Hebrew word "nations"—try to destroy us and we call on God to destroy them first. So, after reciting the verse that in every generation, "they" arise to destroy us, the Passover Haggadah adds: "Pour out Your wrath on the nations that know You not . . . Pour out Your rage upon them and let Your fury overtake them. Pursue them in anger and destroy them from under the heavens of the Eternal." Such words desecrate God's name even if we understand the pained context in which they were authored and included in the tradition. They may be studied only to show that Judaism has recognized these statements as a misunderstanding of God's will. They cannot be taught without the critique and rejection built in, for Jewish tradition eschews reading Bible without commentary. Contemporary commentary infused with a principled Jewish pluralism would need to place caution symbols next to the unacceptable words just as Jews demand that Christians excise or reframe anti-Jewish liturgical and Gospel texts and that Muslims rid themselves of anti-Jewish diatribes.

I am grateful that there are other texts for me to cite instead that contradict or lighten the intensity of those that disturb me. I am commanded to care for the stranger, to feed him, to clothe her, to offer work, to try to heal and to bury Gentiles who have no one else to care for them.[34] And the Mishnah tells us to seek out the welfare of the Gentiles—even idolaters—because we value the ways of peace.[35]

32. Palestinian Talmud, *Kiddushin* 4:11.
33. Mishnah, *Avodah Zarah* 2:1.
34. Babylonian Talmud, *Gittin* 61a
35. Mishnah, *Gittin* 5:9.

I am not alone in my concern that uncompromising absolutist texts of the Bible are a misread of God's truths. Those genocidal biblical texts against the Canaanites and the Amalekites made the rabbis terribly uncomfortable as well. In the Talmud, the rabbis declare that the seven condemned pagan nations have been scattered by repeated conquest and can no longer be identified.[36] By the time we reach the *Mishnah Torah*, the famous twelfth-century legal work of Maimonides, we are taught that any commanded war against the seven Canaanite tribes cannot be applied to any other nation or people, even if they inhabit the sacred land of Israel.[37] The second category of mandatory wars, that of the war to the death against the Amalekites, was rendered harmless by claiming they no longer exist as a nation, or that God will fight them directly in messianic times.[38]

In other words, while Jewish tradition chose not to deny the authenticity of the original command to destroy the seven Canaanite tribes that occupied the land of Israel as well as the Amalekites, it at least made two claims: first, that these nations cannot be found, and, therefore, there is no *mitzvah* to fulfill; and, second, that the rabbis denied the right of Jews to use those commands to ever attack any other people. In this age, Jews must be more affirmative that God is not found in genocide and ethnic cleansing. In this case, it is Jewish idolatry that must be uncovered and discredited.

Sensitized to the capacity of religion today to wreak damage in the name of God, we are pushed to explore more effective ways to teach the faithful to engage with those of other faiths. This includes engaging as a community in a deep and thorough investigation of all Jewish sacred texts. It means making informed and conscious decisions about which texts will continue to be taught, and how Jews are to teach them. Religions must take responsibility for the potential violence and divisiveness in their sacred narratives. As religious human beings, we are commanded to eradicate idolatry from the world. Jews, before asking this of other faiths that have offended us, properly must begin this work with the focus on Judaism.[39]

36. Babylonian Talmud, *Yoma* 54a.
37. *Hilkhot Melakhim* 5:4.
38. Babylonian Talmud, *Yoma* 54a.
39. J. Shawn Landres and Michael Berenbaum, eds., *After The Passion Is Gone:*

Here the essential principle and process of discernment that is operative challenges the authority of any religion's "othering" texts and narratives. Jews will be suspicious of any interfaith encounter at which participants fall back on the position that God's word, that sacred Scriptures, cannot be read differently, since at the heart of Jewish tradition is ongoing human interpretation and a resistance to literal readings. A common Jewish expression used to prod change is, "Where there is a rabbinic will, there is a rabbinic way." Jews will expect other faith communities to be open to change as well.

Seeking Truths

In excising or overriding dangerous "othering" scriptural and traditional voices from the past, I understand the contradiction in my own argument, for I firmly believe that all these (contradictory) words are the living word of God. Greenberg weaves for us a means of listening that derives from the Jewish belief that each human being is created in God's image yet leaves space for disagreement and critique.

When we deny other views or other value systems the right to be heard on the grounds that our system holds the absolute truth, we are denying the image of God of the speakers/believers of the other truth. By implication, it takes a dignified, value-laden system to nurture an image of God. Therefore, if an image of God is advocating this system, this creates the presumption of validity for the ideas or values in question. Admittedly, this presumption may prove to be wrong upon analysis, but, until then, the other faith system is entitled to be heard. If one treats another religion or value system as being so illegitimate as to have no right to be heard or taught, then by implication one is denying the image of God of the people who believe or advocate those ideas.

It may well be that particular ideas are so evil that people who advocate them may be degraded monsters rather than equal, dignified images of God, but this must be proved. Once proved, that system may legitimately be delegitimated. Thus, we may conclude that a group of Nazi mass murderers preaching their evil have no right to be heard. Still the normal presumption is that every system held or lived by images of God

American Religious Consequences (Walnut Creek, CA: Alta Mira, 2005) xiii, 348.

is true or, at least, valued enough to be heard. It has the intrinsic right to be considered, to be made available—even if it conflicts with another system known or believed to be true, even if that other system is perceived as divinely sanctioned.[40]

To see the image of God in the Other opens pathways to a shared language of discourse that allows us to participate in conversation, create partnership, and disagree with fervor and conviction. To do so, we reject true-false dichotomies or reframe them to instead respect each other's narratives. Narratives rather than truth statements bridge even conflicting theological claims. As Alasdair MacIntyre reminds us: "Narratives have remarkable power. Man is in his actions and practice . . . a story telling animal. He is not essentially, but becomes through his history, a teller of stories that aspire to truth. But the key question for men is not about their own authorship; I can only answer the question 'What am I to do?' if I can answer the prior question 'Of what story or stories do I find myself a part?'"[41]

As I have noted, the rabbinic method is a narrative strategy, not a scientific one—it seeks understandings, not the Truth. Emmanuel Levinas, the twentieth-century French thinker, claims that this is adult faith, accepting the loss of a consolatory heaven, that God has withdrawn from the world and that we are left to do the work of healing "through the intermediary teaching, the Torah. It is precisely a discourse, not embodied in God that assures us a living God among us."[42] And when the Torah is wrenched from its dialogic character, its multivoiced potential, and seeks objective and scientific truths, it can become a destructive agent. Levinas elaborates his thesis in his analysis of a talmudic discussion concerning impure hands:

> Due to the fact that the hand touches the uncovered Torah scroll,
> the hands are declared impure. But why? Is it certain that the bare-
> ness of the scroll only means the absence of a covering over the

40. Irving Greenberg, "Seeking the Religious Roots of Pluralism: In the Image of God and Covenant," *Journal of Ecumenical Studies* 34 (1997) 389.

41. Alasdair MacIntyre, *After Virtue*, 2nd ed. (Notre Dame: University of Notre Dame Press, 1984) 216.

42. Levinas, *To Love the Torah More Than God, Difficile liberte*, trans. Helen A. Stephenson and Richard Sugarman (Paris: Michel, 1963) 219, as quoted in Susan A. Handelman, *The Slayers of Moses* (Albany: State University of New York Press, 1982) 172.

parchment? I am not sure that that absence of covering does not already and especially symbolize a different bareness ... And is the hand just a hand and not a certain impudence of spirit as well, that seizes a text savagely, without preparation or teacher, approaching the verse as a thing or an allusion to history in the instrumental bareness of its vocables, without precautions, without mediation, without all that has been acquired through a long tradition strewn with contingencies, but which is the opening of horizons through which alone the ancient wisdom of the Scriptures reveals the secrets of a renewed inspiration. Touched by the impatient, busy hand that is supposedly objective and scientific, the Scripures, cut off from their inner breath, become mere onctuous, false or mediocre words, matter for doxographers, linguists and philologists. Therein lies the impurity of these inspired texts, their latent impurity.[43]

God, then, is present not in the law, not in the personal existential encounter, but in the cross-generational, human experiential dialogue that takes place in reading the text. Otherwise, God is absent from the conversation. Susan Handelman adds: "This point is crucial to understand the schism between Jews and Greeks ... *absence does not equal* nonexistence ... [it comprises] a vocabulary that seeks to evade the either/or trap of being-or-nonbeing of Greek philosophy."[44] Judaism is dialogic hearing/voicing, not scientific seeing/proving.

Jean-Francois Lyotard, a postmodern theorist, referring to the twentieth-century version of this split over truth and narrative, seeing and hearing, further challenges the true-false rules by which some religious leaders make their absolutist truth claims. Scientists, he explains, do not accept narrative truths, certainly religious narrative, because they are not subject to argumentation or proof. They would claim that narratives belong to a different mentality, far more primitive and underdeveloped. Modern religion desperately tries and, I would claim, appropriately fails to transcend the scientific critique. Lyotard's twist in the argument is that even scientific knowledge cannot know and make known that it is the true knowledge without resorting to narrative knowledge itself.[45] At the

43. Levinas, *In the Time of Nations*, trans. Michael B. Smith (Bloomington: Indiana University Press, 1994) 32–33.

44. Handelman, *The Slayers of Moses*, 172.

45. Madan Sarup, *Post-Structuralism and Postmodernism* (Athens: University of Georgia Press, 1993) 136–37.

same time, Lyotard challenges the abuse of the narrative when it weds itself to power, to an absolutist metanarrative that demands fealty:

> Simplifying to the extreme, I define postmodern as incredulity toward meta-narratives. This incredulity is undoubtedly a product of progress in the sciences, but that progress in turn presupposes it . . . The narrative function is losing its functors, its great hero, its great dangers, its great voyages, its great goal. It is being dispersed in clouds of narrative language elements—narrative, but also denotative, prescriptive, descriptive, and so on . . . The decision makers, however, attempt to manage these clouds of sociality according to input/output matrices, following a logic which implies that their elements are commensurable and that the whole is determinable. They allocate our lives for the growth of power . . . Where, after the meta-narratives, can legitimacy reside?[46]

Because metanarratives are relied upon to assure power, to assert power, they are even more dangerous in our age than in the past, because their followers possess a modern capacity to wreak havoc in the name of their particular metanarrative. The melding of scientific proofs and over-arching metanarratives should cause us to pause, to reevaluate the narrative process. Yes, we all are dependent on the stories we tell, and, therefore, the framework or ground rules of our lives and our faith depend on the story. What must be asserted is that our sacred narratives and the truth statements and meaning we derive from our sacred narratives are significant only when they are contextual and helpful in the human enterprise of repairing the world. And they are always limited and must never be absolutized. The sadness is that rather than accept that there are multiple narratives, each with the potential to illumine an aspect of the infinite God, too many believers have attempted for the past few hundred years to prove that there is but one single true metanarrative. Under the pressure of the modern age, truth claims seem to have become a necessary criterion for the believer, yet these truth claims often are a masquerade of piety and faithfulness, for they lead us to a false faith and to destructive behavior. Claiming truth in God's name does not necessarily lead us to a meaningful religious life.

46. Jean-Francoise Lyotard, *The Postmodern Condition: A Report on Knowledge* (Minneapolis: University of Minnesota Press, 1993) xxiv–xxv.

On the "true-false" scale, the destruction of a "false" religion by murdering its adherents, bombing its holy sites, denigrating its symbols, denying the veracity of its story and its history makes perfect sense. In so doing, religion becomes both trivial and dangerous. The antidote: If your understanding of God's truth commands you to destroy in God's name, don't give up on God. Give up on that truth.

So there is great potential danger when an interfaith event or religious debate asks my religious tradition to evaluate the truth of others when we meet in interfaith encounters. Political philosopher Iris Marion Young correctly notes that "[a] group exists and is defined as a specific group only in social and interactive relation to others. Group identity is not a set of objective facts, but the product of experienced meanings."[47] And meaning, hopefully, leads not to exclusionary truth claims but to action. Jews are more at home recalibrating the focus so that ours becomes a theological discussion that pragmatically evaluates the products of a religious life. In understanding a carnal Judaism, as has been discussed above, it comes as no surprise that Jews would not only be asking what one believes, but also what meaning one derives from such beliefs, and then what religious believers actually do. Here, perhaps, in a simple question one finds the essential principle by which Jews will seek to discern other faith communities: What have you done because you are a believer?

This does not diminish interfaith dialogue but expands its obligation to be more than conversation among erudite thinkers. As Abraham Joshua Heschel, a twentieth-century theologian writes, "Philosophy, to be relevant, must offer us a wisdom to live by—relevant not only in the isolation of our study rooms, but also in moments of facing staggering cruelty and the threat of disaster."[48] We certainly should encourage theological discourse, plumbing our beliefs and exploring our religious concepts. As my colleague Volker Haarman, a Christian theologian, reminds me by referencing Leora Batinzky's analysis of Rosensweig:[49] "We must not give up on this kind of controversial theological discourse, in which coming to

---

47. Iris Marion Young, "Together in Difference," in *The Rights of Minority Cultures*, ed. Will Kymlicka (Oxford: Oxford University Press, 1999) 161.

48. Abraham J. Heschel, *What Is Man?* (Stanford: Stanford University Press, 1965) 13.

49. Leora Batnitzky, "Dialogue as Judgment, Not Mutual Affirmation: A New Look at Franz Rosenzweig's Dialogical Philosophy," *Journal of Religion* 79 (1999) 523–44.

an agreement is not the aim, but to deepen our judgment of one over and against the other for the sake of deepening our self-judgment. Otherwise, don't we lose the appreciation of the richness and the diversity of theological insights that the religious traditions provide?"[50]

Dialogue can open each participant to another voice, to be challenged on the most profound level, to provoke radical reassessments, enriching the narratives and allowing all who partake a generative exploration of alternative ways to see the world. Where such dialogue feels most valuable is when participants are impelled to return to their own religious settings ever more capable and motivated to pursue goodness, more generous toward those we once would have called Other, more willing to roll up our sleeves and reengage in acts of healing.

David Saperstein, who oversees the Jewish Religious Action Center, amplifies the value of this type of interfaith theological conversation:

> I side with those theologians who suggest that when creating the universe God left one small part of creation undone. That part was social justice. Then God gave to us that which was given to nothing else in creation: the ability to understand and choose between wrong and right. In allowing us to be partners with God in completing creation, God ennobled humanity, raised us above mere biological existence . . . and gave to our lives destiny, meaning, and purpose. The work of repairing the world is holy work. And that is the work to which we are called.[51]

We see here a rejection of what is perceived as an arrogant search for religious truth while replacing that process with a more modest search for religious meaning and action out of which, quite possibly, God's goodness/sacredness will emerge. There are truths, divine truths, but we should whisper them with angst and trepidation, for we are claiming a knowing that is terribly presumptuous. Modest religious narratives, on the other hand, can be sensitively shared, validating the many truths that such stories and storytellers can offer each other. As pedagogue Robert Cole says so simply, "This story, yours, mine—it's what we all carry with

---

50. Volker Haarmann, relayed in personal conversation.

51. David Saperstein, "The Use and Abuse of Jewish Tradition in Political Debate," *CCAR Journal* (Spring 2008) 33.

us on this trip we take, and we owe it to each other to respect our stories and learn from them."[52]

The Jewish story is that God needs us as partners to complete the vision of creation. In meeting colleagues of other faiths, as in meeting fellow Jews, one would not ask if this understanding of partnership with God is true or false, but rather, what type of life does a believer live. Yitz Greenberg concludes: "Creation teaches us that the universe is infused with values and shaped in accordance with a divine plan to maximize life in the world. One should live—and judge—life by standards that advance this plan. A neutral or wasted life is one that does nothing to advance the cause of Creation; an evil life is one spent in diminishing life or in opposition to the perfecting of the world."[53]

Today the Jew who enters interfaith dialogue hopefully will make no claim to truth or seek or deny the truths of others. Rather he or she will transmit a Judaism that teaches us how to live a life of meaning and will embrace all those whose traditions help illumine our path as we work with God together to perfect the world.

---

52. Robert Coles, *The Call of Stories* (Boston: Houghton Mifflin, 1989) 30.

53. Greenberg, *For the Sake of Heaven and Earth*, 53.

Part II

Christian Perspectives

3

Coordinates for Interreligious Discernment from a Protestant View: Transcendence—Freedom—Agape—Responsibility

Reinhold Bernhardt

I would like to present four "material" principles of interreligious discernment. They are derived from the Christian tradition—more precisely from a modern Western interpretation of that tradition. Before I develop them, let me make some methodological remarks as to how the criteria I employ have been determined.

Three Categories of Criteria

It seems useful to distinguish between three categories of criteria for the discernment and evaluation of religious phenomena.

Formal Criteria

First there are the formal criteria applicable to every value-system (whether religious or secular), moral order, or worldview. Here we find such criteria as the inner consistency of the system, or its faithfulness to the normative origins of its tradition, or the correspondence between ideal and reality, theory and practice. These are important but purely formal criteria.

Klaus von Stosch[1] develops another set of four formal criteria that do not arise out of the material content of the religious traditions, but refer instead to fundamental intellectual attitudes. Imagine two crossing coordinates: The first line is drawn between relativism and fundamentalism, the second between rationalism and fideism. These four intellectual attitudes spring from misconceptions of the given belief system and arise without regard to its specific content. *Relativism* waters down the validity of the given beliefs to purely contingent and subjective preferences; *fundamentalism* on the contrary denies the historical contingency of religious beliefs and congeals them into assertions regarded as immediate divine truths, and as such, they need not and indeed must not be subjected to analysis, discursive reflection, or discussion. *Rationalism* neglects the expressive, regulative, and orienting functions of religious beliefs, reducing them to a cognitive-propositional *fides quae*; *fideism*, on the other hand, focuses only (or mainly) on the expressive and regulative aspects of religion, downplaying the cognitive-propositional dimension. According to Stosch, such lopsided conceptual frames of religious beliefs are to be avoided.

Formal criteria are not dependent on the material essentials of the religions but belong to a general hermeneutical critique of traditions. Of course even the hermeneutics of a tradition is part of the tradition; nevertheless, the basic rational standards of that hermeneutics are not immediately derived from its specific material content and can therefore be applied to other traditions as well. In any event they do not touch on the character traits of the *particular* religion or on its nerve centre, which directs the whole system and requires commitment from the religion's adherents and gives them orientation. Even though an intellectual critique of the manifestations of a religious tradition's formal criteria may be important, they are irrelevant for its functioning in the life of the particular religious community.

---

1. Klaus von Stosch, "Das Problem der Kriterien als Gretchenfrage jeder Theologie der Religionen: Untersuchungen zu ihrer philosophischen Begründbarkeit," in *Kriterien interreligiöser Urteilsbildung*, ed. Reinhold Bernhardt and Perry Schmidt-Leukel, Beiträge zu einer Theologie der Religionen 1 (Zürich: TVZ, 2005) 37–57.

Material Criteria

At the other end of the spectrum we find highly specific *material* crite-ria—so specific that they are not applicable (or only in a negative way) to other religions. They do not permit an interreligious comparison, because they both presuppose and propose the incomparable validity of the rev-elation that constitutes their own tradition. Such criteria simply set forth the *propria* of one's own religion over and against the other religions that lack them.

The most striking example of such a position was held by Karl Barth. For him the all-decisive criterion was the name of Jesus Christ. This name is "the essence and source of all reality."[2] Even if some of the phenomena of other religious traditions may seem very similar to comparable phe-nomena in the Christian religion, the name of Jesus Christ draws a clear-cut line of demarcation. It constitutes a qualitative difference between Christianity—which, through God's undeserved grace, has the honor to bear this name—and any other so-called religions of grace, such as the Amida Buddhism of the Japanese Jodo Shinshu school.

Barth knew that according to Shinran, the founder of Jodo Shinshu, enlightenment is achieved not by one's own efforts but by trust in the compassion of the Amida-Buddha. The similarity to the Protestant doc-trine of justification by faith alone was so striking that the Jesuit Francis Xavier, who came to Japan as the first missionary in the middle of the six-teenth century, believed that he had encountered the "Lutheran heresy" there.[3] But Barth refused to admit that a so-called religion of grace that was not gifted with the name of Christ could be seen as a manifestation of God's universal und unconditional grace. Here Barth followed Acts 4:12: "There is none other name under heaven given among men, whereby we must be saved."

Propria Criteria

As distinct from purely formal and general criteria, which are readily ap-plicable to other traditions but are not helpful for discerning and evaluat-

---

2. Barth, "Der Inbegriff und die Quelle aller Realität," in *Kirchliche Dogmatik* I/2 (Zurich: TVZ, 1938) 381.

3. Ibid., 374.

ing their material content, the self-referential "*propria* criteria" that are identical with the core convictions of a given tradition are not applicable to other traditions.

Now in contrast to these two types of criteria, I suggest a third approach: I suggest we look for material criteria that are deeply rooted in the sources of their own respective religious traditions and yet at the same time applicable to other traditions as well.

The normative principles I suggest are not simply identical with the name of Jesus Christ; on the other hand they are not simply reducible to the ethical "lowest common denominator" of the world religions, as Hans Küng's "Project World Ethos" elaborates it. Instead they are utterly central features and applications of the God-relation that the gospels proclaim and to which they call. Therefore, my attempt to present those principles can be understood as—and indeed is—an attempt to present the essence of Christianity as I see it.

I find these material principles for interreligious evaluation not in the *fact* but in the *content* of the revelation of God in Jesus Christ—which is to say, in the God-relation that Christ embodied in his preaching, acting, suffering, and dying; in the God-relation that is confirmed in God's final word on him (as expressed in the symbol of the resurrection) and into which he called his followers. I find these principles not in the first instance in propositional beliefs *about* Jesus Christ but in the foundational attitudes Jesus Christ proclaimed to be essential for the God-relationship and that thus have become essential for Christian faith at the existential level. They describe existential patterns of Christian life-orientation that are not to be understood as static states of being but as dynamic motivations and driving forces in the process of developing personal and communal identities. They function as attractors, calling upon the believer to actualize the Christ-mediated God-relation ever anew, thus reforming the attitudes and the self-actualization of individual persons or communities in the image of Christ. If we think of *being Christian* as the ongoing, teleologically impelled movement towards *becoming Christian*, then these existential patterns serve as markers along the path upon which Christ precedes us.

But the values I would like to elaborate upon for the evaluation of religious phenomena are not confined to that path. Even though they are characteristic essentials of the Christian tradition, they are not absent from other traditions and can thus be applied to non-Christian forms of religious life-orientation as well. Essentials need not necessarily be discriminators. The center does not necessarily double as a fence.

According to Schleiermacher, each of the religions has its own focal principle that structures the implicit and explicit axioms of the whole system in its intellectual, cultic, and ethical dimensions. Though the focal principles are unique, the worldviews and value systems they generate can indeed be considered and weighed in relation to each other, for they all address their adherents' basic human needs in coping with life and death.

This is the point where the evaluation process can and must come into play. All religious traditions offer the prospect of ultimate well-being. In each case, that prospect emerges out of a particular determination of the four fundamental relations in which human beings live: the relation to themselves, the relation to other humans, the relation to the world, and the relation to the divine ground of being. These four basic relationships constitute a "grid," so to speak, with respect to which the various religions develop and exhibit their varying frameworks for life-orientation. With respect to this grid their varying answers can be closely examined, related to each other and evaluated by adherents of other traditions. A judgment on a given religion is arrived at on the basis of these answers.

This approach is not intended, however, to be applied on the macro-level to a religion as a whole or to "religions in general," but rather at the micro-level—applied, that is, to very specific, concrete religious forms; to particular communities and groups, to interpretations of particular traditions in a particular context by a particular community, as the approach of comparative theology suggests. Religious teachings, practices, psychological and social structures can be investigated with regard to how they value and foster these impulses—or how, on the contrary, they suppress them.

There is no "Christian imperialism" or even inclusivism intended in this approach; what is at work here is rather the attempt to view Christian and non-Christian religious formations from the perspective of Christian theology. Other religious traditions will—and indeed should—apply their own identity markers to the phenomena of the Christian religion.

The conceptual framework for the interreligious hermeneutics I propose is thus a *mutual inclusivism*.[4]

Moreover, this interreligious assessment is applicable not only to other religious traditions (whether classical religious groupings or new religious movements); it should also be applied to phenomena within one's own tradition, thereby providing the opportunity for an intrareligious self-critique.

The material principles of interreligious discernment themselves belong to the topics with which interreligious dialogues have to deal. The aim of interreligious dialogue is not only to promote mutual understanding but also to open the field for critical discourse, as recommended in the Qur'an 29:46, where a fair dispute between Muslims, Christians, and Jews is proposed.

Principles of Interreligious Discernment

Following these remarks on methodological questions we can now set forth from a Christian perspective the four material principles for interreligious perception and evaluation. I label them "transcendence," "agape," "freedom," and "responsibility." Religious teachings, practices, psychospiritual and social structures, can be closely questioned as to how they encourage their adherents, both as individuals and as groups, to develop religious identity formations that are committed to self-transcendence, agape, freedom, and responsibility—or whether, on the other hand, they suppress such endeavours.

Transcendence

Not only in Christianity but in all religions constituted in a revelation, there is a deeply rooted consciousness of the difference between the reality of God, the revelation of God, and the religion that refers to the revelation but cannot claim to be identical with it. The revelation transcends the religion and God transcends the revelation. The presence of this distinction functions as an indicator of authenticity in a religion, a

---

4. See Bernhardt, *Ende des Dialogs? Die Begegnung der Religionen und ihre theologische Reflexion*, Beiträge zu einer Theologie der Religionen 2 (Zürich:TVZ 2006) 206ff.

clear sign that a religion is not centred on itself—i.e., on its own historical constructions and analyses—but centered rather on the divine self-manifestation and indeed on the reality of the divine that ultimately is beyond its grasp. With respect to God, this awareness presumes a polarity between the self-communication of God on the one hand and the enduring, impenetrable mystery of God on the other—a mystery that is neither disclosed nor deciphered by its "revelation." Rather, the revelation reveals it *as* a mystery. The mystery remains. The revelation is held to be totally authentic, yet it does not exhaust the whole reality of the revealing God. God is greater than his revelation, as a person is 'greater' than all of his/her self-revelations. The 'word' of God is the representation of God, but it is not God. It is a mediation of God, which establishes the relation to God. But the transcendent God transcends even these revelations. The infinite and unfathomable mystery remains sovereign over all forms of God's revelation, transcends them and relativizes them.

Jesus obviously had a clear consciousness of the distinction between himself and God. He pointed beyond himself to God and the kingdom of God: "Why do you call me good? No one is good but God" (Mark 10:18). Indeed, even the theologians of the Johannine community, with their high Christology, did not simply identify Christ as the logos of God *with* God. According to John 5:43, Christ came in the name of God. He is the mediator between God and humankind, who does not seek honor for himself but seeks to promote the honor of the One who sent him (John 8:50) and on whom he is dependent (John 5:19ff; 10:29; 14:24b, 28; 17:1ff.). In stressing the difference between Christ and God, the authors of the Gospel of John repudiate the accusations of those Jewish leaders who had accused Jesus of identifying himself with God (John 5:18; 10:33; 19:7). According to 1 John 3:20, God is the *Deus semper major*, who "dwells in unapproachable light, whom no man has ever seen or can see" (1 Tim 6:16).

With this consideration we arrive at the first of the four criteria for assessing religious phenomena. I summarize it as follows: Has the religious form in question developed a consciousness of the difference between God, revelation, and religion? Is it centered on itself as the only representation of God, claiming to be in full accord with his will, and therefore the normative interpreter of God's revelation as well as the supreme power regulating its applications in the life of the faith community? Or is it centered on God's self-communication, on the revelatory movement of his mediation, open to being affected by it and striving to respond and correspond to it? Does it claim to be in possession of God's truth or strive rather to live within that truth that is always beyond its grasp? That is the understanding of the Gospel of John: The truth is not something that can be claimed, but only something that might be lived in and lived up to.

Does a religious form place itself under an 'eschatological proviso,' longing for an ultimate fulfilment that would transcend all religions and revelations—the final breakthrough of the light of God, as promised in 1 Corinthians 13:12 and 2 Corinthians 3:18, where the believers are told that *now* they see as through a dark glass, but *then* they will see face to face? Then even the Son of God will be subject unto God, so that God may be all in all (1 Cor 15:28).

If Christians take that proviso seriously, then they cannot claim absolute or ultimate validity for their own religion. And the same applies to other religions that refer to a transcendent God and his revelation. Revelation is not only the foundation of the religious tradition but also its critical principle: Paul Tillich referred to this as the prophetic principle. It calls all religious forms into the unceasing activity of self-transcending.

From this perspective it follows that religious forms that diminish or deny the difference between their own reality and the reality of their divine point of reference need careful scrutiny. A religious phenomenon that is not seen as a way but instead as the ultimate goal, not as a historical and therefore relative mediation of divine truth but as the eschatological realization of that truth here and now—such self-divinization needs to be criticised as idolatry. Idolatry means the deification of historical entities and the confinement of the reality of God within certain strands of history. It all begins with the claim that it is absolutely necessary to participate in one specific historical realization of the presence of God in order to achieve grace or salvation.

Against such a confinement of the truth found among particularistic interpretations of the theistic religions, it must be insisted that God is not a tribal God belonging to a particular community, but the ultimate reality that encompasses the whole cosmos. Even if there are singular relationships between God and certain peoples who are ordained to let his light shine in the world, there is no people that has been left without a relationship to the Creator (Acts 14:15–17). Divine election is not a privilege but an obligation to give testimony to the universal grace of God toward all humankind. Particularism can be a form of idolatry needing to be criticized because it refuses to take up that continuously self-transcending movement—i.e., the self-transcending movement of the given religion towards that religion's constitutive revelation, and then the transcending of that revelation towards the God who has revealed it. Where this movement is taken up, an intrareligious self-critique will follow, a theological critique of the religion that points to the fact that a religion is not self-centered but God-centered and thus authentic.

Freedom

According to Mark 2:27, Jesus proclaimed that "the Sabbath was made for humans, and not humans for the Sabbath." He "turned the order between acceptability and acceptance . . . into its opposite. Acceptance comes first, acceptability follows . . . Paul cast this inversion of the covenant-law paradigm, from the conditional, scrutinizing acceptance of the acceptable to the unconditional, suffering, redeeming acceptance of the unacceptable, into abstract theological terms."[5] According to his critique of the legalism of the Jewish authorities, especially as expressed in his letter to the Galatians, he stressed that in Christ a relationship to God is established in which all people can be called to participate without having to fulfil religious preconditions beforehand. Not even believing in God's unconditional grace can be a precondition of justification, if the gift of grace is given without any condition to be fulfilled by the one who is thus gifted.

The freedom I speak of here refers not only to religious rules but also to interpersonal relationships, to the social sphere. It grants the otherness of the other, respecting his or her independence and self-determination; it obliges one to maintain a certain distance in the relationship to the other and allows a person even to detach and free him- or herself from that relation—a freeing that may well be experienced as a kind of redemption. (Freedom can thus take a turn *away* from agape, for agape tends to intensify interpersonal relations.)

---

5. Klaus Nürnberger, "A Biblical Critique of Jewish-Christian Exclusiveness," in *Theology and the Religions: A Dialogue*, ed. Viggo Mortensen (Grand Rapids: Eerdmans, 2003) 347.

Accordingly, freedom affects all the manifold concerns of life in the world. In the first letter to the Corinthians (7:29–31) Paul advised the addressees to "have" the things of the world as though they did not have them. The relation to God mediated in Christ leads to a detachment from the world—comparable to the Buddhist notion of detachment.

Though freedom may be employed with reference to religious laws, to relations with other human beings, and also to worldly matters, it refers in the first instance to one's relationship with oneself. First and foremost it consists in the opening of the *cor incurvatum in se ipsum* (the heart turned in upon itself), the liberation from self-centeredness, from the *amor sui* (to use Augustine's term). It is what Luther called the freedom of a Christian ("Freiheit eines Christenmenschen") who is subject to no one and nothing. The one, ultimate dependence upon God sets the human being free from all pre-ultimate dependencies.

This consideration brings me to the second of the four criteria for assessing religious phenomena. I summarize it as follows: Does a form of faith break through and open up the self-centeredness of its adherents? Does it contribute to their liberation—a liberation from bondages: the bondage to the ego, to legalistic religious regulations, to other human beings, and to worldly concerns? Does it liberate them from a religious selfishness concerned primarily with one's own salvation? Does it recall its followers to the insight expressed in Matthew 10:39 and 16:26 as well as Mark 8:35 and 9:24—that a person who tries to found his/her life upon his/her own existential capacities will lose that life, whereas the one who trusts in the constitution of his/her own life as already given by the ground of being will find it?

Freedom emerges as the result of a continuously self-transcending movement taking place within the individual in relation to God. This dynamic is set in motion through what the Christian tradition calls the Holy Spirit, the power of God's transforming presence. Does the religious phenomenon in question work towards establishing the conditions that would make it possible for this power to unfold its dynamically inspiring potential, or does it aim instead to subordinate the religion's adherents to the religion's authorities?

This material principle of discernment applies not only to the individual person (in his or her relation to him- or herself and to worldly concerns) but also to the religious community. I thus ask: What about the psychological and social structures within a religious community? Do they tend to be coercive? Or liberating? Do they resort to manipulation as a means of winning new members? Do they entangle their adherents in psychological, social, or economic dependencies? Do they tolerate and perhaps even respect differences, or is there an authoritarian leadership that pressures community members to conform? Do they support an education that allows critical thinking, open discussions, and the option of holding a variant position? Are the members forced to obey heteronomous moral rules, or are they allowed to follow their own consciences? Do the members enjoy equal rights with respect to a participation in the leadership, or are there restrictions in terms of gender, race, or caste? How does a community deal with those who have decided to leave it in order to convert to another community or even to another religion? Do they grant religious liberty? Do they allow and in fact foster the freedom of criticism and self-criticism, even towards the religious authorities?

Just as important as freedom in the negative sense of "freedom from" is freedom in the positive sense of "freedom to," whereby a person is empowered to develop his or her potential ("charisms," 1 Cor 12) for the sake of the community and of neighbors in need. Does it give a person orientation and inner strength to cope with the contingencies of life? Does it permit its members to discover and develop their own needs, or does it sustain them in delusion? Does it support stable relationships and social networks? Does it encourage engagement for the well-being of others and ultimately for the comprehensive well-being of creation?

Obviously these considerations are linked to a normative framework that has been shaped not only by the Christian tradition but also by the Enlightenment and by the modern movements in the eighteenth and nineteenth centuries. The crucial question becomes whether or not this framework can be applied to other cultures having other values and moral standards. What from my perspective appears to be oppression may not be felt and regarded as oppression by the "oppressed" him- or herself; it is simply part of his/her cultural environment. In such a case, an intercultural critique of ideologies cannot be avoided. Anthropological values held to be of universal validity need to be distinguished from cultural values that reflect the particular. The former outweigh the latter: If values claimed to be universal in scope clash with one another, then we must endeavour to arrive at a hierarchy of values. Though we find only tradition-bound value systems and have no access to a neutral position from which the conflict can be decided, it does not follow that all values are merely grist for the mill of cultural relativism. Of course in terms of their genesis, their interpretation, and their application, values are always de facto dependent on a specific cultural context, but at least in terms of their validity ('in principle'), the basic human rights can be and must be held to be independent of the situations in which they emerged and developed.

Agape

According to the first letter of John, God's very essence is love (1 John 4:8, 16). This essence—"love"—is realized in the inner trinitarian *perichoresis* and is itself the primal and defining term in God's extratrinitarian relation to creation. Creation itself is an act of love, an act of self-differentiation, self-communication, and self-alienation. God creates a reality beside and yet within the reality of God—as an 'other' reality to which he is in relation. The realization of the relation is not only a manifestation of love but indeed in its very constitution: already the calling of the created reality into existence bears within itself the relation of love. The creature is called to respond to as well as correspond to that love—in the relationship with God, with him- or herself, with other creatures, and indeed with created reality as a whole. *Being in agape* is the foundational characteristic of Christian existence. It must then impact upon the Christian's most fundamental ways of seeing, finding expression in behavior. The one side of agape is empathy and compassion; the other side practical caring: hospitality; social action; commitment on behalf of the suffering, the guilty, the enslaved, the oppressed, and the poor. The mandate for self-giving service is set forth in Mark 10:42–45.

Agape is lived out not only as solidarity in the personal sphere but also as justice in the public sphere. From the perspective of Christian social ethics, the structures and functions of social institutions, political organizations, and economic systems can be critically questioned as to whether or not they encourage justice, fairness, and a balance of interests. This is "structural agape."

Love strives for justice, but on the other hand it can also provide the corrective for a static, legalistic application of norms of justice, in terms of equal treatment. It calls for empathy, for a recognition of individual distinctiveness, for a consideration of the demands of special situations. Agape requires creative intuition, creative participation in the existential needs of other humans. It thus surpasses tolerance and nurtures genuine respect and the accepting of differences. It creates openness and—not least—interreligious openness.

Paul describes redemptive agape not only as an interpersonal reality but as a transpersonal and transrelational power. It can be envisioned as a field of noncoercive force encompassing the whole of creation and affecting the humans who live in it. Paul calls the realizations of that force as reflected in the attitudes and behavior of human beings "fruits of the Spirit" of God, as manifested in the way Jesus preached and practiced unconditional agape towards those who were regarded as nonpersons.

This reflection leads me to the third of the four criteria for assessing religious phenomena from my Christian point of view. The questions: Does a religious belief lead to agape in the forms described just above? Does it make clear the close link between the relation to God and the relation with other human beings, or does it instead proclaim selfish ways to salvation? Does it stress the importance of neighbourly love and oblige the believer to struggle for the welfare of other creatures? Does the faith-form include the spiritual, mental, and bodily 'healing' of other lives?

Yet agape refers not only to interpersonal relations but also to the other basic relations of the human person: towards God, towards nonhuman creation, towards him- or herself. Authentic self-acceptance includes all of one's *bodily* dimensions as well and constitutes an important aspect of agape. Thus agape is not to be set up in opposition to eros but indeed embraces it. In other words, agape is not a purely spiritual form of love but encompasses all facets of the divine, the human, and the nonhuman reality.

Jürgen Werbick, a Catholic theologian from the University of Münster, once stated that those religious phenomena that correspond to and cultivate agape cannot be dismissed as lacking authentically divine truth—regardless of the religious form in which they appear—and thus have to be acknowledged. Those that, on the other hand, controvert agape require controversion.[6] That statement may be read as a commentary on

---

6. Jürgen Werbick, "Toleranz und Pluralismus," in *Christentum und Toleranz*, ed. Ingo Broer and Richard Schülter (Darmstadt: Wissenschaftliche Buchgesellschaft, 1996) 117.

the famous phrase: *Ubi caritas, ibi deus est* ("Where charity prevails, there is God").

Agape, when considered in terms of the four foundational relations (the relation of the human person to him- or herself; to other human beings; to the nonhuman creation, and to the ultimate ground of being) calls for balance; which is to say, a form of agape that tries to favor one dimension at the expense of the other three should be regarded as problematic. If for example agape is directed only towards God but not towards other human beings, or if it is restricted only to the members of one's own community, or if an altruistic charity is paired with self-neglect and self-negation, or if there is no overarching cosmic solidarity with both animate and inanimate creation, then it needs to be re-examined.

Freedom and agape form two poles within a polarity. When agape is overemphasized, it can lead to the dissolution of the self, to questionable relationships, and dependency. If, on the other hand, freedom is overemphasized, the dissolution of relationships, self-isolation, and apathy may well result. What is called for is that balance—balance between agape and freedom, between self-centeredness and other-centeredness, between world-centeredness and God-centeredness.

Responsibility

The fourth principle I would like to suggest as a norm in assessing religious phenomena is responsibility. It stands as the opposite pole of transcendence. If the call to transcend one's dependence upon finite realities (including religious systems) becomes overemphasized, a retreat from active commitment to social, political, and economic affairs may be the result; in its extreme form it can lead even to loathing and contempt for the world. Against such an attitude that evades entanglement in worldly concerns, the Jewish, Christian, and Islamic traditions call for responsible action in the world in order to support "eco-human well-being" (as Paul Knitter expresses it) for the sake of present and future generations.

No exclusive salvation *apart* from the rest of the world is promised in the Christian gospels—neither for the individual nor for a specific religious group. Instead we encounter in the gospels the hope of salvation for the whole world, including all creatures. The dominant vision of Christian eschatology is not an apocalyptic destruction of the world but rather the forming and reforming of the world towards the kingdom God—not freedom from the world but freedom in the world and for the world. This requires us to respond to the needs of the suffering creation as set forth in the basic ethical demands of the biblical testimonies and the Christian tradition. It requires striving for peace and justice at the micro-level of the community, at the meso-level of society and at the macro-level of humanity. It requires striving for the protection of the ecosystems and the active enforcement of human rights.

Religious faith-forms that commit their adherents to responsible action aimed at promoting freedom and agape in the world comply with this fourth principle. Thus the necessary questions follow: Does the given religion call for charity towards the underprivileged, the poor, and the oppressed? Does it call moreover for political engagement in order to generate social structures that improve the living conditions of those groups? Thus in its expression, the principle of responsibility comes close to that of agape, while transcendence corresponds to freedom.

How to Apply the Principles?

Of course each of these four material principles can be interpreted and applied in quite different ways. They do, however, offer a rough normative orientation in the wilderness of religious phenomena. Applying them in a negative way—i.e. asking which phenomena do not accord or comply with the principles—is more useful than looking for positive correspondences; the former leaves space for phenomena that do not require our judgment. That is, there are a lot of religious manifestations that are simply different and that can be tolerated, respected, acknowledged as simply different, without evaluation or assessment. Only those that may conflict with essential and fundamental values in one's own belief system will call for closer scrutiny. Thus the four principles function as "minimum standards" that can help to identify problematic instances.

Paul's injunction to "prove all things; hold fast to that which is good" (1 Thess 5:21), opens out into the broader horizon of a positive assessment; yet it can also foster an inclusivist attitude, unable perhaps to respect the different phenomenon in *its own* value and dignity, and willing to recognize it only insofar it meets the standards of one's own belief system. This problem can be avoided if we understand "holding fast" not in terms of integration but in terms of acknowledgement. Paul's instruction can be interpreted in the light of 1 John 4:1: "Believe not every spirit, but try the spirits whether they are of God." According to the Christian tradition, the normative revelation of God is Jesus Christ, and so from a Christian perspective the norm for assessing religions phenomena will be whether they seem to be inspired by that Spirit that suffused the person of Jesus Christ and shone through in his words and deeds. Fruits of that divine Spirit are to be found throughout the multiplex landscapes of religion. That makes interreligious expeditions so fascinating.

4

Roman Catholic Reflections on Discerning God in Interreligious Dialogue: Challenges and Promising Avenues

Gavin D'Costa

I want to develop an argument that has two stages with a methodological interval acting as a bridge. In the first stage I want to ask: What are the theological principles and parameters within the Roman Catholic tradition (which I will call Catholic from now) that exist from which we might base an answer to two questions? First, are there elements of the good and true within another religion? And second, does God work within other religions? These are two distinct and also overlapping questions. To answer this I will attend to recent Catholic teachings. Catholic theologians cannot be involved in interreligious dialogue without reference to the teachings of the Catholic Church, even if they do not like or agree with these teachings. The Catholic theologian has to sail from charted waters into unchartered territories. Some rudder is required for the expedition, as well as flexibility and imagination to tack the sails to negotiate the unexpected. In the second stage, I want to ask, if Catholic teaching acknowledges a set of interesting answers to the question of truth and God's presence in other religions, how then does the Catholic go about discerning these realities? I shall be arguing that this act of discernment is far from a purely intellectual exercise, for discernment is a performative event requiring the Church to rethink its practices (traditionally called inculturation), to learn how to proclaim the truth of Jesus Christ (traditionally called mission), and to be challenged (its being open to God).

In what follows I shall not speak about the response of the religious other to this act of discernment, for that of course is not my provenance. I certainly disagree with those who posit rules for dialogue that must be obeyed by both dialogue partners (found in some American and German theologians), for this is usually the imposition of modernity upon all religions. [1] As Alastair MacIntyre has argued, no one comes from nowhere; traditioned rules and presuppositions underlie every approach in social and religious practice. [2]

Stage One: The Teachings of the Catholic Church on Truth and Goodness and the Holy Spirit's Presence within Other Religions

I cannot carry out a close exegesis of recent magisterial documents on this topic, and the following interpretation I offer is contested. [3] I will briefly outline my reading of the documents of the Second Vatican Council and the post-Conciliar magisterium on this issue. These document set out six important markers in answer to the question. I should also counter an objection to this methodology that might be forthcoming: why start at a priori teachings on the religions rather than inspect the actual situation of dialogue with the religions? I suggest that this is a false dichotomy, for the teachings of the Council present reflection on practices through the history of the Church. In two thousand years from now, Mumbai II or Lima IV or Vatican X, ecumenical Councils of the future, might develop these

1. For example, in the work of Len Swidler et al., *Death or Dialogue?* (London: SCM, 1990); and Hans Küng and Helmut Schmidt, eds., *A Global Ethic and Global Responsibility: Two Declarations* (London: SCM, 1998).

2. See Alasdair MacIntyre, *Three Rival Versions of Moral Enquiry* (London: Duckworth, 1990). MacIntyre's argument undercuts the universalist, read modernist, assumption in writers mentioned in note 1 above. See D'Costa, "Postmodernity and Religious Pluralism: Is a Common Global Ethic Possible or Desirable?" in *The Blackwell Companion to Postmodern Theology*, ed. Graham Ward (Oxford: Blackwell, 2001) 131–43.

3. See D'Costa *The Meeting of Religions and the Trinity* (Edinburgh: T. & T. Clark, 2000) 101–17; and Jacques Dupuis, *Towards a Christian Theology of Religious Pluralism* (New York: Orbis, 1997) 158–79.

teachings in the light of reflection on the praxis of Church communities. There will be a continuity of teaching but also renewal, development, and surprise.

First, *The Dogmatic Constitution on the Church* (*Lumen gentium*, 1964, 13–16 [abbreviated *LG*]) reiterates the ancient teaching: *extra ecclesiam nulla salus* ("there is no salvation outside the church").[4] This indicates the continuity of dogmatic teaching contrary to those who argue for a change in Catholic doctrine. Second, it is also taught that that no unevangelized person is without the means of salvation, for the "Saviour wills all men [and women] to be saved (cf. 1 Tim. 2:4)" (*LG*, 16), and God is just and merciful. This is not universalism, which has been formally condemned. Third, both *Lumen gentium* and the *Declaration of the Church to Non-Christian Religions* (*Nostra Aetate*, 1965 [abbreviated *NA*]) set out a series of concentric circles expressing the closeness of relation to non-Catholics. First, there are other Christians (differentiations are made within this class), followed by the Jewish people, then Muslims, then Hindus and Buddhists, and nonreligious people who seek truth sincerely. Fourth, when we ask how it is that these folk (the unevangelized among them) might be saved, the initial answer tends to express the inner response to grace, not the external elements that form a religion: "Those who, through no fault of their own, do not know the Gospel of Christ or his Church, but who nevertheless *seek God with a sincere heart*, and, moved by grace, *try in their actions to do his will* as they know it through the *dictates of their conscience*—those too may achieve eternal salvation" (*LG*, 16, my emphasis). Thus the heart and conscience are primary in generating good actions, and it is the former that is central in relating a person salvifically to God. To emphasize good works alone would amount to Pelagianism (the doctrine that good works alone can attain salvation).

Fifth, we can fill out this initial answer further, for the earlier part of this paragraph describing Judaism and Islam indicates detailed external elements that are prized by the Church. *NA* fills this out further

4. *LG*, 14: *Docet autem, sacra scriptura et traditione innixa, Ecclesiam hanc peregrinantem necessariam esse ad salute* ("Basing itself on scripture and tradition, it teaches that the Church, a pilgrim now on earth, is necessary for salvation": Austin Flannery, ed., *Vatican Council II: The Conciliar and Post Conciliar Documents* (Dublin: Dominican Publications, 1975); all English translations are from Flannery. For the history of this ancient teaching, see Francis Sullivan, *Salvation Outside the Church? Tracing the History of the Catholic Response* (New York: Paulist, 1992).

and gives more attention to Hinduism and Buddhism. Reading these two documents together, and focusing on Islam and Buddhism (to choose a theistic and nontheistic tradition), we find that the elements singled out in the documents are aspects of beliefs and cultic practices that are not in contradiction with beliefs and practices found in the Church. For example, in Islam, belief in a God who is creator, judge, and merciful is extolled, as are the practices of "prayer, alms-deeds and fasting" (*NA*, 3). In Buddhism, which provides a tough test case for agreement of central beliefs, the documents praise the deep insight of "essential inadequacy of this changing world." Obviously, the specialists within these traditions can fill out these details with complexity and nuance, but what is important is that beliefs and practices, not just the inner heart and conscience is given positive treatment.

Sixth, what is the theological significance of these elements? Here we step into a heated debate. The documents say five clear things about these elements. First, that none of these positive beliefs and practices is rejected: "the Catholic Church rejects nothing of what is true and holy (*vera et sancta*) in the religions" (*NA*, 2). This is important, as the first term, *vera*, can indicate natural truths known through reason that relate to God (such as God's existence, goodness, and so on); and the second term *sancta* is a formal term which can either relate to a holiness that comes from God or indicate the designation of something that becomes holy and sacred because of its relation to God. Second, it is said that these elements "often reflect a ray of that truth which enlightens all men" (*NA*, 2). That is, they can reflect truths that relate to Christ, the fullness of truth, "the way, the truth and the life" (John 14:6) cited in (*NA*, 2). Third, these reflections are conceptualized as *preparatio evangelica* in *LG*, 16, citing Eusebius of Caesarea's teachings, where all truth in cultures is seen as preparing peoples for the truth of Christ. This is classic fulfillment theory: grace does not destroy nature but fulfills it; and at the cultural level, all that is good and true and holy is transformed into the fullness of truth and goodness. Fourth, since these elements exist within a larger whole, they cannot without further transformation and purification be affirmed as truth per se. Indeed *LG* is blunt in saying these elements can be mixed with untruths and even be under the influence of the 'Evil One' (and this is echoed in the document on Missionary Activity) although *NA*, focusing on the positive relation alone, does not mention it. Fifth, in both documents, *NA* and *LG*, immediately after these positive statements, mission is emphasized: *NA*, 2; and *LG*, 16.

After Vatican II there was and still is animated debate about whether these positive elements might be considered as salvific means. I want to say a little about this issue, as this helps to focus our question further. We can see from above that the documents are happy to affirm elements of truth and goodness in other religions and to affirm the holiness to be found there and to affirm elements of beliefs and practices that are positive. And the obvious question follows: do these all amount to affirming possible means of salvation, given the clear affirmation that God does not leave anyone without the means to salvation? Two very astute commentators, Karl Rahner and Jacques Dupuis, both argue that the Council was silent on this question.[5] Others, such as Mikka Ruokanen and Paul Hacker, argue that the Council would not countenance such a teaching, and both read the achievements in other religions as basically anthropological achievements: the best the human spirit can achieve in moving towards the living God.[6] Others like Paul Knitter, at the opposite end of the spectrum, have argued that the Council documents clearly imply that other religions are salvific means to their adherents.[7] Elsewhere, I have argued that the Council is silent on this particular point. But since the Council (and during his pontificate), significant comments by Pope John Paul II count as a clear development of doctrine on this question. Two particular points need comment.

First, John Paul II formally taught that the Holy Spirit might not only be present in the hearts and consciences of the unevangelized but also in their traditions. The most explicit of a number of texts (see also *Redemptor Hominis* [1979] 6, 11, 12; *Dominum et Vivificantem* [1986] 53) is *Redemptor Hominis* 28: "The Spirit manifests himself in a special way in the Church and her members. Nevertheless, his presence and activity are universal, limited neither by space nor time . . . The Spirit's

---

5. Dupuis, *Towards a Christian Theology of Religious Pluarlism*, 168–70; and Karl Rahner, "On the Importance of the Non-Christian Religions for Salvation," in *Theological Investigations*, vol. 18 (London: Darton, Longman & Todd, 1984) 288–95.

6. See Paul Hacker, *Theological Foundations of Evangelisation* (St. Augustin: Steyler, 1980) 61–77; and Mikka Ruokanen, *The Catholic Doctrine on non-Christians according to the Second Vatican Council* (Leiden: Brill, 1992).

7. Paul Knitter, "Roman Catholic Approaches to Other Religions: Developments and Tensions," *International Bulletin of Missionary Research* 8 (April 1984) 50.

presence and activity affect not only individuals but also society and history, peoples, cultures and religions." This statement certainly questions those who argued that the Council only affirmed that which was naturally possible within other religions. It acutely raised again the question of whether other religions could be called salvific structures, especially in the light of the acknowledgment that the Holy Spirit worked through those structures. Second, during John Paul II's reign, a document from the Pontifical Council for Interreligious Dialogue and the Congregation for the Evangelization of Peoples titled *Dialogue and Proclamation* (1991) was issued that seemed to consolidate the salvific means, for it said: "The mystery of salvation reaches out to them [the nonevangelized], in a way known to God through the invisible action of the Spirit of Christ. Concretely, it will be in the sincere practice of what is good in their own religious tradition and by following the dictates of their conscience that the members of other religions respond positively to God's invitation and receive salvation in Jesus Christ, even while they do not recognize or acknowledge him as their Saviour" (29). Both these documents seemed to push in a particular direction, but both require to be read in the context of all previous documents as well.

The later Jacques Dupuis builds his case on these passages, especially the latter, to argue that other religions might be counted as 'participated mediations' in the mystery of God's salvation, in effect, means of salvation certainly not independent of Christ, but independent of his Church. I cannot enter into this complex debate here, but the teaching magisterium issued two documents that both questioned this development in Dupuis' position, refusing that salvation could be independent of the Church or that other religions could be regarded as salvific means in an *ex opere operato* manner.[8] That is, they could not have any objective salvific efficacy such as is attributed to the sacraments of the Church, which Trent

---

8. *Dominus Iesus*, 21: "Certainly, the various religious traditions contain and offer religious elements which come from God, and which are part of what 'the Spirit brings about in human hearts and in the history of peoples, in cultures, and religions.' Indeed, some prayers and rituals of the other religions may assume a role of preparation for the Gospel, in that they are occasions or pedagogical helps in which the human heart is prompted to be open to the action of God. One cannot attribute to these, however, a divine origin or an ex opere operato salvific efficacy, which is proper to the Christian sacraments. Furthermore, it cannot be overlooked that other rituals, insofar as they depend on superstitions or other errors (cf. 1 Cor 10:20–21), constitute an obstacle to salvation."

conceptualized formally in terms of *ex opere operato* to stress the objective and unambiguous action of God's saving act.

We are now in a position to answer the first question set. Yes, Catholics can look for signs of truth and goodness as well as signs of the Holy Spirit within the cultures and religions of others. They can also look for the workings of the Holy Spirit in the hearts and conscience of persons within those religions. Second, all this does not mean that other religions can be salvific means in the way that the Church is, nor does it mean that these positive elements are the only reality to be found: untruth must also be engaged and challenged. Third, all these positive Spirit-moved elements form a preparation for the gospel, without which these elements have not reached their fullness and completion. Fourth, all this can be said while also saying there is no salvation apart from the Church and Christ, and that God never leaves the unevangelized without the means of salvation. Only by holding together these four statements in tension, rather than resolving them in a liberal or conservative direction, can we be faithful to the Church's teachings. I hope this gives enough rudder to see the possible direction that we might move in and also enough leeway to negotiate each particular tradition as we engage it.

Methodological Interlude

Before moving to the second stage, there is a raft of objection that must be met regarding the intended second stage move: asking how we discern goodness and truth and the action of the Holy Spirit in other religions.

First, there is an intra-Catholic question regarding those who follow the Hacker line outlined above (that no supernatural grace can be attributed as acting within the religions). While I shall give grounds for my disagreeing with the reading of Hacker et al., Hacker's approach still allows for mutual cooperation and activity by religions on a whole range of ethical matters: the environment, human sexuality, family life, economic wealth and poverty, and so on. It does not require wholesale agreement about any doctrinal issue or mutual affirmation viz. viewing each other as differing means to salvation or anything of the sort. It allows for ad hoc points of common concern to bring religions together. It also allows for a critique of other religions for failing to observe the natural law so that the engagement is not an anodyne process but one that draws folks into tough discussion. Insomuch as the natural law in this model is entirely dependent on reason, it even allows the possibility of rational argument between religions in the attempt to convince folk on matters of truth. Here then is one possible answer from within the Christian tradition to the question being asked on dialogue and discernment. I need to indicate briefly why I do not want to answer the question in this way before moving on.

First, reason seems to operate within the context of revelation in the majority of religious traditions, and the almost-rationalist model outlined above is rare to find prior to the seventeenth century. I do not know enough about other religions to see how this applies to them. This is not to say that reason should not be used to expose poor arguments, contradictions, and falsehoods, or that reason is dispensable in any way as explicating revelation and its implications, at least to my sort of Catholic Christian. It is simply to say that pure reason alone as the means to getting to God is a dream more dreamt in the European Enlightenment than in the Catholic psyche. Second, the location of the transcendentals of truth, goodness, and oneness has more recently been recovered within their life in the divine life, rather than being viewed as autonomous elements within creation. This is in part due to the recovery of a fourth transcendental, beauty, in Romantic philosophy and then within Catholicism through Jacques Maritain's groundbreaking work, which sought to reread Aquinas and reestablish this transcendental. Hans Urs von Balthasar sought to show how this fourth transcendental, beauty, actually defines and further unites the three traditional ones. I am aware that this excessively telegraphic account of a rather important development in recent Catholic thought requires much unpacking.[9] The significance of this development is a warning against naturalizing the presence of the supernatural: because all real truth, beauty, and goodness are anchored in the living God, not in human reason—just as finally reason too is anchored in the divine *logos*. Equally, this development, especially in the hands of Balthasar, means that the particular revelation of the divine Trinity in the narrative of Israel and

---

9. For a good explication of the issues, see Jacques Maritain, *Art and Scholasticism and Other Essays*, rev. ed. (London: Sheed & Ward, 1943); and on Hans Urs von Balthasar, drawing together various writings into a synthetic whole, Aidan Nichols, *Redeeming Beauty: Sounding in Sacral Aesthetics* (Aldershot, UK: Ashgate, 2007) 53–70.

of Jesus and his Church mean that every instance of beauty, truth, and goodness is related to this generative narrative. There is both a centrifugal and centripetal force that must be held in tension. Third, the poverty of reason-alone natural theology is in its exclusion of supernatural grace to the hearts and cultures of non-Christians when post–Vatican II magisterium has said otherwise. This perhaps is the most compelling reason to adopt a different hermeneutical approach to the question at hand.

Another methodological problem relates to what might be termed an existential individual and structural problem. What follows in stage two is an inexact science, for two precise reasons. First, when we are trying to discern the causes involved in the shaping of the hearts and souls of men and women, we are dealing with the depths of the mystery of the human person. Their inner subjectivity is not available to us in a forensic fashion, and even if we are that person's confessor or very close associate, it is still difficult to be sure of a person's deepest motivations and inner life. This cannot stop us asking the question of how we might discern the possible activity of the Holy Spirit in a person's life, but we should be warned of the genuine limitations in answering this fully in the complexity of human life. Further, if the human heart is finally impenetrable to an outsider, the semiotics of a culture analogically has a certain inexhaustible depth (if it is not totally 'closed' and not totally evil). Both persons and cultures cannot be interpreted exhaustively, although for differing reasons. By *semiotics*, I mean the prayers, rites, customs, the social and political practices, and so on, that form a person within, let us say, a Hindu or Muslim culture. Here we face two difficulties. First, when we engage with the complex semiotics of a religious culture, we are faced with the question of what I call insider interpretation, that is, interpreting the signs 'as if' from the inside of that semiotic system. This means 'going native,' learning the languages and practices that are part of that world and learning to see the world from that person's view. There are challenging theoretical debates here regarding the incommensurability and/or translatability of sign systems, as well as their alleged homogeneity.[10] I think commensurability and translatability are defensible, both on a philosophical and anthropological level, and most importantly, from a theological level as well. So a premise, to be defended some other time,

10. See D'Costa, *Disputed Questions in the Theology of Religions* (Oxford: Blackwell, 2009) chaps. 2–3.

is that every human is made in the image of God (outside interpretation is here unavoidable), a metaphysical belief which allows the possibility of translatability, without denying various difficulties. Homogeneity is a red herring here, as each tradition might defend its internal coherence in differing ways and with different rules and stipulations. In principle, it might not be concerned with this question (although in my limited knowledge, I do not know of any such religion). Hence, the first difficulty is establishing genuine and rigorous insider interpretation—but it is possible.

A further methodological difficulty is now mapping outsider interpretative criteria upon this material. I am asking a Christian theological question (is the Holy Spirit at work here?) to materials that are not Christian and do not contain the narrative actor of the Holy Spirit, although there may be analogues within that tradition. I face three obvious objections. First, this is an imperialist exercise, as it involves the imposition of alien categories upon materials not part of those categories. Second, this fails to be open to the otherness and novelty of another tradition, for it tries to translate everything into familiar terms. Third, this judges another by what I already know, so it is like looking at another and asking 'how much do you look like me?' *Narcissism* is the usual word for this process.

I need to give brief answers before proceeding. First, all interpretation is an imperialist exercise if we take this stricture maximally, even the interpretation that all interpretations are imperialist. Minimally taken, and far more interestingly, it is possible to argue that when outside interpretation coincides with inside interpretation, we have the basis for some engaging conversation (say when two traditions agree that they should together resist a social practice, be it abortion, usury, or capital punishment). When outsider and insider interpretations do not coincide, it requires the interpreter to find a way of engaging with the interpreted so that this interpretation might challenge the interpreted tradition (as in arguing that voluntarism leads to a type of ethics that is not subject to reasonable defense—as was the case with Pope Benedict's not entirely successful venture into this area at Regensburg). Alternatively, it might simply act for the interpreter's community as a sign of affirmation or criticism (such as the Vatican II documents) and do not require per se any interpretative agreement from the interpreted community.

The second objection (that interpreting from an alien community fails to engage with novelty) cannot, I would argue, be made into a hermeneutical principle. It must be checked in each instance, as some interpretative frameworks are more open and some less to engaging with difference. For example, ideological historical Marxism interpreted religion in a way in which novelty or questioning-back is not often possible; this is quite different from psychoanalytic Marxism, in the hands of Lacan, where rich possibilities are uncovered even if one does not accept the entire reading strategy. Likewise, there are closed Christian interpretative grids and more open ones; and I would argue that Vatican II provides us with the most open grid possible, which allows the possibility of the human spirit, Satanic forces, angelic powers, and divine action to have extensive operation. Is all this narcissism? No, because the exercise is only conducted for one reason: to trace the workings of the living God, not to extol the human community of the Church or any individual Catholic. And is there a structural egotism, insomuch as God is already known in Christ? Here the answer must be both yes and no, if one accepts the terms of the question which I would not, as God cannot contradict what God has disclosed in Jesus Christ but can only deepen and enrich our appreciation of that revelation.

Another question, the last, regards recent teachings and their harmonizing with earlier traditions. If we ask, how is the presence of the Holy Spirit traditionally discerned? As a way of addressing our own question about discerning the Holy Spirit within other religions, we come to a very curious tension. In the New Testament witness, there are of course many rich trajectories regarding the nature and purpose of the Holy Spirit, but a dominant overarching one is that the Holy Spirit, this self-gift from God, this enabling grace, is given for the sole purpose of glorifying Jesus, for forming those who so respond to the Spirit into Christ-like bodies, the 'body of Christ,' which in the New Testament is the Church. The Holy Spirit is discerned as making present the Church. Further, the traditional seven *gifts* of the Spirit: wisdom, understanding, counsel, fortitude, knowledge, piety, and fear of the Lord are seen as completing and perfecting the human and theological virtues and cultivating a community of character who are ready to obey the divine demands. These are preparatory for becoming Christ, who is the fullness of these gifts. On the other side, there are the *fruits* of the Spirit, extolled by Paul (Gal 5:22–23), and the Church traditionally lists twelve: charity, joy, peace, patience, kindness, goodness, generosity, gentleness, faithfulness, modesty, self-control, and chastity.

The point about both these *gifts* and *fruits* is that they take their definition from the Christic narrative, not as abstractions or values that can be removed from this Christ-centered story of redemption. Therefore, at one level, to apply tests for the presence of the Holy Spirit, given the context within which these tests are traditionally understood, seems like a classic category mistake. The Holy Spirit's primary role is christological and ecclesiological, which seems to be precisely *not* what we are looking for when engaging other religions. Or is it precisely what we should be looking for? That is the question.

I'd like to suggest that it is this motif that must be kept central to the act of discernment, for the engagement with other religions, as intimated earlier, cannot be kept independent from inculturation (coming to know the fullness of Christ), mission (proclaiming that which we cannot own, the risen Christ), and thus is a profound learning and transformative process. It is also of course a hope that there may be mutual benefits and challenges, but none of this should be stipulated for the other. How might the christological motif be explicated? What is Christ-likeness? It starts and finishes with the particular historical man Jesus, made universal in the resurrection and ascension—a theme central to the Johannine tradition.[11] This means that whenever we discern the Holy Spirit in persons or religions, we are saying that there is implicitly or inchoately the face of Christ breaking through. The terms 'implicitly' or 'inchoately' are not terms of meanness or restriction, but terms that respect that another religion is not explicitly or choately concerned with following Christ as a Person. This is important; Christ is a Person first and foremost and cannot be reduced to an idea, a program, a blueprint for social action or ritual action. He is quite simply the Second Person of the divine Trinity, consubstantially united with human nature in the Person of Jesus Christ, through whose life we come into communion with the divine life. So in a moment when I do start abstracting, please remember that Christ-like characteristics are slightly analogous to describing Violetta-like characteristics (if I can be permitted to draw from Verdi's *La Traviata* for a moment). We just cannot speak of Violetta-like characteristics without the music and words and action of the opera, be it in an instantiation of the opera in reading the score, listening to a CD, or in a live performance, whether in English,

11. See D'Costa, *The Meeting*, 109–32, where I have dealt in detail with these Johannine themes.

Dutch or Italian, either in modern dress and based in New York or in traditional costume based in Paris and the surrounding countryside. The analogy breaks down, as Violetta, unlike Jesus, is not the metaphysical ground for God-talk. Nevertheless, from a christological perspective, one might start speaking of Violetta as Christ-like, looking at the theme (there's the abstraction) of selfless love, self-sacrifice for another, and forgiveness of wrongdoing against innocence. Verdi did not like the Church but was bought up in a Christian culture, so some of this reading might not be fanciful eisegesis. Indeed his heroines do have a penchant for taking on the suffering of the world and in this action being destroyed. There are all sorts of complexities here: Catherine Clement has criticized Verdi for his misogyny in destroying woman after woman in his operas, apparently all for the sake of love;[12] although Clement's reading can be questioned, because in *La Traviata* Violetta's death is both an unmasking of Germont's patriarchal control over his son (in the name of his daughter's future!) and of Alfredo in his violent jealousy and quick condemnation of Violetta. She unmasks the dark forces of this world but pays for it with her life, although the analogy begins to break down, as Violetta's consumption that destroys her is present before the tragedy is generated.

Stage Two: Discerning God's Spirit in the World Religions

I have chosen an opera to start this strategy of looking for Christ-likeness, as it makes immediately present the plethora of difficulties involved in actually dealing with a semiotic, Western product generated from within the Christian culture that is not ecclesial or christological in its explicit structure. I've pointed to the question of its christological motifs, but what about its ecclesiological motifs? This is not actually any more difficult because the opera is a story of a community of persons learning the costly meaning of forgiveness, and how self-deception (Alfredo) and status and power (Germont) fail to acknowledge the value of self-sacrificial love found in the sector of society where it is least expected: Violetta is a courtesan. To put this rather bluntly and overpersonally, every time I watch this opera, I am called into question, called to plumb the depths

12. Catherine Clément, *Opera, or, The Undoing of Women* (London: Virago, 1989) 60–65.

of what being a Christian is, looking at the costly shape of forgiveness and the tragic shape of love. Verdi's opera bears within it the resurrection every time it is performed, because the beauty and truth of what takes place does not overwrite the tragedy in a facile way, but neither does it leave tragedy as the only enduring sensibility; rather it sings the triumph of love over death itself.

When we turn from nineteenth-century Italian opera to non-Western religious cultures, we have some new and deeply interesting challenges. I want to take the most uncomfortable and difficult example I can muster, precisely as it will bring out the complexity of the discerning hermeneutical task. Vatican II is understandably cozy in drawing on obvious points in common, but what about less obvious points? For instance, does the Holy Spirit act in the heart of a free and dutiful *sati,* and through its institutional role, within the Hindu tradition? I think most Christians and Hindus would say no, not only because the Holy Spirit as Third Person of the Trinity is an alien term to the Hindu tradition. In Hinduism, quite terrifyingly, I want to suggest that one finds a flash of the Christ-like in the horrific practice of *sati*, the self-immolation by a widow. I realize that choosing this example raises all sorts of problems, not least because most educated Hindus, especially in the West, do not defend this practice as part of authentic Hindu tradition and actively campaign against its periodic reappearances. In all its horror, it still holds an important Christ-likeness that I want to explore without in any way endorsing or valorizing the practice.

In terms of the eighteenth-century text, *Stradharmapaddhati* (*Guide to the Religious Status and Duties of Women*), written by the Hindu orthodox pandit Tryambakayajvan, we get one explanation of a righteous freely undertaken act of *sati*. We have a very important instance of how the good wife, through her own meritorious action, might freely undertake to destroy and pay off the bad karmic merit due to her husband and to others. Here the cosmology of Hinduism, based as it is on the truth and righteous of *dharma*, and the karma generated by each action, is central to the framing of this sacrificial act; and while there is literally a world of difference between this cosmology and the Abrahamic teleological, noncyclical concept of time, there are still enough analogical relations to make some point of contact within a greater difference.

The merit due to the *sati* is threefold. First, her ritualized act of righteous devotion releases her from all bad merit that she has accrued during her life. Second, a bad wife has every reason to perform *sati*, for this will be a definitive chance to purify herself. Tryambakayajvan puts it clearly, indicating that intentionality and consequence are not unilaterally identified: "Women who, due to their wicked minds, have always despised their husbands (while they were alive) and behaved disagreeably towards them, and who none the less perform the ritual act of dying with their husbands when the time comes—whether they do this of their own free will, or out of anger, or even out of fear—all of them are purified of sin."[13] The latter two causes (anger and fear) can certainly conspire towards forced *sati*, but it is clear that Tryambakayajvan is not intending to support these forms of *sati*, for his argument is precisely to extol the free choice of *sati* because it is *dharmically* coherent and attractive in securing righteousness in the world. For Tryambakayajvan, *sati* has the quality of 'sufficient atonement' (*prayascitta*) for the deeds of the bad wife. The third and most significant meritorious aspect is the transferential merit gained for the husband and his family as well as for the *sati's* own ancestral family. Merit is usually accrued by the one who undertakes a ritual act, although there is a long tradition going back to the Vedas whereby merit can be attained for another. The sati atones for the sins of her husband and has the power, in her action, to release him from the fires of hell (a provisional, not eternal hell). In some texts, it is clear that this atoning power also applies to the wider families in the marriage and to those who visit the shrines of the *satimata* (lit.: "truth/virtuous mother"). Tryambakayajvan cites many texts. Here is one showing the extent of the *sati's* atoning power. Her self-sacrificial love of duty breaks the bounds of hell, as through her free act she liberates her husband, even if he committed the most heinous crime, such as murder of a Brahmin. Tryambakayajvan put it like this: "Even

13. I. Julia Leslie, *The Perfect Wife: The Orthodox Hindu Woman according to the Stradharmapaddhati of Tryambakayajivan* (Delhi: Oxford University Press, 1989) 43r.7–9. In this, Tryambakayajvan crosses a line that is contested by other jurists, some of whom argue that *only* the *sativrata*, the good wife, can follow this course as her decision to do so (*samkalpa*) must be immediate and without deliberation, an expression of her virtuous character that has been practiced throughout her married life. A bad wife would not come to such a decision spontaneously and immediately. Admittedly, the weight of the tradition paradoxically imputes the death of a husband prior to his wife's as the fault of the wife, who should have looked after him better—obviously not applicable to a warrior.

in the case of a husband who has entered into hell itself and who, seized by the servants of Death and bound with terrible bonds, has arrived at the very place of torment; even if he is already standing there, helpless and wretched, quivering with fear because of his evil deeds; even if he is a brahmin-killer or the murderer of a friend, or if he is ungrateful for some service done for him—even then a woman who refuses to become a widow can purify him: in dying, she takes him with her."[14] Or with more dramatic and succinct force, Tryambakayajvan cites another verse: "Just as the snake-catcher drags the snake from its hole by force, even so the virtuous wife (sati) snatches her husband from the demons of hell and takes him up to heaven."[15]

What do I want to say about this ritual action in terms of its Christ-likeness and churchly shape? Two things are important. First, in the middle of a finely balanced system of karmic reward and punishment, which does bear interesting analogy with the medieval picture of merit and demerit and the satisfaction owing to the deity due to sin, we find an instance of a breaking of the circuit, where a single person's self-sacrifice can alleviate the karmic punishment due to another. The pursuit of karmic goodness engenders greater goodness that saves others. Analogically, this is Christ-like, although it is also deeply un-Christ-like in its requirement for repeated self-sacrifices from widows for their husbands. In Christ, a single sacrifice has taken place for the bad actions of all people past and to come, a single sati-like sacrifice in which all people are grabbed from the jaws of hell and released from sin. The drama of existence is the refusal or acceptance of this remarkable self-sacrifice.

Second, what of this practice's ecclesiological dimensions? These too are evident in the following that some satis gain. Such is the case with the recent young widow, Roop Kanwar, who died a sati in Rajput in 1987. (Between 1943 and 1987 there have been at least thirty satis in the Rajput/Shekavati region.)[16] Thousands of devotees of Kanwar have flocked to her

14. Ibid., 43r.4–5; and I. Julia Leslie, "Suttee or Sati: Victim or Victor?" in *Roles and Rituals for Hindu Women*, ed. I. Julia Leslie (London: Pinter, 1981) 185.

15. Leslie, *The Perfect Wife*, 43r.4–5; Leslie, "Suttee or Sati," 185.

16. Catherine Weinberger-Thomas, *Ashes of Immortality: Widow-Burning in India* (Chicago: University of Chicago Press, 1999) 182–85, who points out that the number is probably higher, given that this is the officially recorded number, plus two extra discovered in her fieldwork. This book is central for a deep understanding of the tradition that isn't simply negative, as is Leslie's work.

shrine to gain good merit through her salvific action. Rather than simply assimilate Kanwar to a saint and pilgrimage to her shrine in that manner, it is perhaps more analogically precise to see her as Christ-like here as she *is* seen as a *devi*, a manifestation of Kali, a goddess. In drawing upon the sacramental efficacy of her action, her devotees refuse to limit the extent of her blessings: they fall upon everyone: man, woman, or child who comes to her shrine. (I should say that this is currently an illegal practice, outlawed by the government of India; although from eyewitness reports the shrine still flourishes but only spasmodically.)

The analogy should not be pressed. If (and this is a very theoretical *if*—please note), if the Holy Spirit was acting in the heart of the free *sati* and through the practice of the institution of *sati*, we would witness an *inchoate* presence of Christ and his church, which would require the Catholic Church to carefully consider the institutional practice and see if it could be adapted into its own liturgical context. This is inculturation. It would also require the Catholic Church to mount an argument that the deepest longings behind this practice find a deeper satisfaction in Christ's breaking of the dharmic cycle, so that while the fruits of our actions still remain with us, just as the disruption of sin remains with the Christian, we are freed from the bad karma that we inherit and build up, if we are truly sorry, just as we are forgiven for our sins by Christ with true repentance. This is mission.

I have offered this example because it allows me to show how an intratextual reading can be transparently seen and reconfigured through an extra-textual reading. Some might find it objectionable in the way that some have found the letter to the Hebrews objectionable, which portrays the sacrificial system of the Second Temple as being superseded by Christ's sacrifice. I have also chosen this difficult example precisely because it shocks and deeply unsettles. It demands attention: is there a Christ-like pattern being generated here? I think a very ambiguous answer is generated: both yes and, more overwhelmingly, no.

I could have chosen an example that is far more attractive at an instinctive level. Throughout the religions this remarkable pattern of self-sacrifice for another is to be found. For example, we find it in the Buddha's self-sacrifice in feeding a hungry mother tiger with his own body so that she can nourish her five cubs, which are then reincarnated as five dharma disciples. The Buddha is moved by compassion in seeing this suffering and acts to alleviate it even though it is part of the cycle that one must break free from. I do not want to multiply examples, as each one requires substantial contextualizing and explanation, followed by a searching out for its Christ-likeness and church-likeness, and then an asking what we might learn from it, and how we might question it in the light of the gospel. While there is much to be learnt from this lovely story that deeply calls into question the long history of Christian use of the animal world in a way that has so often lacked compassion, it faces difficult questions as well. Can compassion be assimilated to love? Aloysius Pieris, the Sri Lankan Jesuit, answers with a resounding yes, and the ex-Buddhist and highly respected Buddhist scholar Paul Williams answers with a definite no.[17] Williams's answer does raise a raft of metaphysical questions that refuse easy transposition of terms from one cosmological and soteriological framework into another. So even the nicer example does not make things any easier.

Conclusion

The Holy Spirit is at work in the world religions. This Catholics can be sure of. Discerning and interpreting this reality is far more complex. At one level it is evident whenever truth, goodness, beauty, and self-sacrificial love are evident. At another level, these realities are only finally discovered and fully luminous in God, whose intra-Trinitarian truth, goodness, beauty, and love are revealed in the cross and the resurrection. Until the final resurrection, the question of discernment is both necessary and fraught, and I suspect that we may find Christ and his Church in places we Christians never expected or dreamt of.

---

17. See, for example, Aloysius Pieris, *Love Meets Wisdom: A Christian Experience of Buddhism* (Maryknoll, NY: Orbis, 1988); and Paul Williams, *Altruism and Reality: Studies in the Philosophy of the Bodhicaryavatara,* (Surrey: Curzon, 1998); and his further critique after his conversion to Roman Catholicism: *The Unexpected Way: On Converting from Buddhism to Catholicism* (Edinburgh: T. & T. Clark, 2002).

5

Dialogue between Muslims and Christians as Mutually Transformative Speech

David Burrell, CSC

The papacy continues to register symbolic valence, often more so for those who are not Catholic. A quick look at the acceleration of relations between Christians and Muslims within the scant two years since Regensburg contrasts dramatically with fourteen centuries of conflict or standoff. Many of us cannot help but attribute this dramatic turnabout to deep-flowing divine action in our current history: action starkly at variance with the prevailing Islamophobia in the West, evidenced in palpable fear in Europe and untutored prejudice in America. But let us first consider the unlikely chain of events since the professorial address at Regensburg, which the pope used to develop a recondite thesis about the intrinsic role which reason has played in developing the Christian faith over the centuries:[1] so far, a thoroughly Catholic view of the development of doctrine, with a side-long critique of "voluntarism" redolent of Radical Orthodoxy. But it was the aside that offended, ostensibly offered in homage to Professor Khoury, who had been a colleague of Professor Ratzinger at Regensburg. Not only does the aside offer contested views, but it is poorly constructed as well, with the lecturer quoting Khoury, who quotes the Byzantine emperor Paleologus (shortly before the fall of Constantinople), to bolster a thesis

---

1. The lecture can be found at the Vatican Web site: http://www.vatican.va/.

about Islam's insouciance towards reason, itself bolstered by citation of an early work by the distinguished French Isalmicist, Roger Arnaldez on Ibn Hazm, proposing that Iberian "hardline" thinker as the spokesperson for Islam.[2] In short, so many citations within citations that the lecturer's view of the matters in question was utterly obfuscated. Careless rhetorical construction could not but lead to utter distraction, yet when an intelligent theologian who is also pope distracts us, industrious speculators try to tell us what he meant by doing something so inept. So we were treated to inane Western commentators suggesting what he must have intended, while "friends of the court" invented astute reasons why a pope might have made such contentious statements—though we have seen that the concatenation of citations within citations makes it quite impossible to ascertain what the lecturer himself actually stated regarding the matters in question: the relevance of reason to Islam. So the most charitable comment would be that he made a gaffe, and the most salutary response of the pope should have been to admit just that.

Yet within a month thirty-eight Muslim scholars took the ball, reminding the lecturer of things he should have known—like medieval Christendom's reliance on Islamic thinkers to develop their own doctrinal positions, notably on creation—and reminding readers of the polemical cast of both Emperor Paleologus and Ibn Hazm.[3] The official Vatican response was lukewarm, but the pope himself offered a potent symbolic response on his visit to Istanbul, praying in a celebrated mosque. Yet other forces were at work, and a year after the initial Muslim response, a document appeared, endorsed by 138 Muslim thinkers, addressed to the pope, the archbishop of Canterbury, and other Christian leaders: "A Common Word." Capitalizing on the Qur'anic statement here rendered as "a common word between us," the document begins by reminding Christian leaders that Muslims and Christians make up more than half the world's population, and proceeds to celebrate what we hold in common: *love of God and love of neighbor.* Freely citing from Christian and Muslim Scriptures, the document challenges us all to reach for mutual

2. Arnaldez wrote his dissertation on Ibn Hazm, later published as Grammaire et théologie chez Ibnazm de Cordoue; essai sur la structure et les conditions de la pensée musulmane (Paris: J. Vrin, 1956).

3. Response of Muslim thinkers can be found at the Web site of the Yale Center for Faith and Culture: http://www.yale.edu/faith/.

understanding in the cause of peace.[4] Scarcely a month later, the Yale Center for Faith and Culture, spearheaded by Miroslav Volf and Joseph Cummings, gathered three hundred Christian signatories to a response printed as a full page advertisement in the *New York Times* (18 November 2007). Five months later, the Vatican inaugurated a Catholic-Muslim forum, to be jointly administered by five Muslim and five Catholic notables. Most recently, with the assistance of distinguished consultants, the archbishop of Canterbury issued a theologically astute response on July 14, 2008, as the Yale Center for Faith and Culture convened a gathering of Christian and Muslim leaders, including a broad representation of the signatories to "A Common Word," to probe the issue of love of God and neighbor in an explicitly comparative way.[5] Moreover, the way the Yale conveners facilitated a broad evangelical representation in this gathering, as well as in the earlier published response, is perhaps most telling for America. In the face of Islamophobia in America and pervasive fear in Europe over the very presence of Muslims, deep countercurrents emerge: the Spirit must be at work!

In fact, the "Common Word" Web site lists fifty-seven Christian responses to date, including an immediate response from the Vatican secretary of state to Prince Ghazi bin Muhammad bin Talal of Jordan, conveying Pope Benedict's enthusiastic praise for the initiative, notably for its focus on love of God and neighbor. We are trained to be critical of texts, but it is more telling to note the nearly miraculous fact of garnering signatures of so many notables across a widely diverse Muslim world. It would appear that Prince Ghazi's pellucid Islamic culture pervades the "Common Word" initiative from text to signatories. Let us try to ascertain what is at stake, as well as what is actually taking place, as much as we can.

Meaning and Truth; Dialogue and Proclamation

In encountering documents like "A Common Word," we shall see how dialogue, like any probing conversation, attends to *meaning* rather than

4. Online: http://www.acommonword.com/.

5. The response of the archbishop of Canterbury (composed with a distinguished group of consultants) can be found at the official Web site of *A Common Word*: http://www.acommonword.com/.

truth. This should be evident enough, but attempts to contrast 'dialogue' starkly with 'proclamation' have obscured this simple point, by implying that dialogue is radically deficient as a faith strategy since it stops short of proclaiming the truth. But what would it be to proclaim the truth? Would it be to make an assertion and then to insist that it was true, or as one wag put it, to stamp one's foot? In fact, of course, any properly formed assertion, actually stated, intends what is the case. Grammar is inherently ethical, which is why lying—deliberately stating what is not the case— is inherently wrong. Yet we know that our acceptance of what another says is often conditioned by the moral probity or veracity of the speaker. So "proclaiming the truth" of one's faith is better done than said, as the Amish community in Pennsylvania demonstrated to America by forgiving their children's killer. Merely stating one's faith convictions cannot in fact count as proclamation. What counts is witness; and while the fact of dialogue may give telling witness in certain situations, like in Israel/ Palestine, the intellectual endeavor of dialogue can at best be a means of sorting out awkward from promising ways of stating what we believe. Yet this is hardly a deficiency; it is simply what any conversation tries to do. Authentic proclamation is quite another thing, as the gospels remind us again and again.

John Henry Newman, Bernard Lonergan, and Nicholas Lash can each be invoked as witnesses to this crucial distinction. Newman reminds us (in *Grammar of Assent*) how sinuous is the path to arriving at truth, and how delicate are the balancing judgments involved.[6] Bernard Lonergan professedly acknowledges Newman's reflections when he parses Aquinas's insistence that truth can only be ascertained by way of judgment.[7] And Nicholas Lash's recent *Theology for Pilgrims* deftly exhibits the quality of dialectical reasoning that must attend reliable judgment.[8] In the spirit of Wittgenstein, the witness Lash's writing gives to constructive and critical dialogue offers a healthy antidote to current TV confrontations that leave listeners to "make up their own minds." One can almost hear Wittgenstein

6. Consult preferably Nicholas Lash's edition of John Henry Newman's *An Essay in Aid of a Grammar of Assent* (Notre Dame, IN: University of Notre Dame Press, 1979) for its illuminating introduction.

7. Bernard Lonergan, *Verbum: Word and Idea in Aquinas*, ed. Frederick E. Crowe and Robert M. Doran (Toronto: University of Toronto Press, 1996).

8. Lash, *Theology for Pilgrims* (Notre Dame IN: University of Notre Dame Press, 2008).

query: "I know how to make up my bed, but how might I make up my mind?" So whatever effective proclamation might be, it cannot be had without probing discussion and the conceptual clarification that dialogue can bring. Reduced to forthright assertion or downright insistence, it can be neither authentic nor effective. So there is no substitute for attending to meanings, as we attempt to minimize infelicitous expression in matters "pertaining to God and the things of God" (as Aquinas views theology). For the same thinker reminds us that our language *at best* can but "imperfectly signify God" (ST 1.13.3).

When the foil for philosophical theologians was the "village atheist," Jewish, Christian, and Muslim thinkers could attempt to refute their protagonist with arguments, notably regarding God's existence. And while the success of such arguments had always been contested, Catholics are enjoined (by Vatican Council I) to believe "that God, the source and end of all things, can be known with certainty from the consideration of created things, by the natural power of human reason" (1870). Now the very complexity of that statement invites prolonged discussion, but Denys Turner has recently offered a robust defense of it—that is, of our ability to generate a bona fide proof, *not*, of course, of the validity of any candidate.[9] He contends, in short, that it is not only true but must be accepted if our faith is to mean anything in the larger human arena—the very point of the Vatican statement. What is at stake is the very capacity of human reason to transcend its own limits by concluding to an incomprehensible result. Taylor's own supporting argument is complex and has been contested, but we can focus here on its central contention: the meaning of *reason*. So even the most rigorous proofs will turn crucially on interpretations of the key terms which allow us to discern their meaning relevant to the context. And in the fresh cultural context that is our own, as "village atheists" have been replaced by "other believers," this feature will predominate.

Even those Abrahamic believers who claim to have proved that God exists will never pretend to *prove* the truth of the revelation that animates their life and thought. For each of these traditions is grounded in an avowed presence of the divine in history, which could never be the result of ratio-

---

9. Turner, *Faith, Reason and the Existence of God* (Cambridge: Cambridge University Press, 2004); see my review in *Modern Theology* 21 (2005) 686–88, with further discussion in "Forward to Vatican I: Proving the Existence of an Unknowable God," *Yaarboek Thomas Instituut* (2005) 100–108.

nal deliberation, never captured in a timeless scheme: the gift of the Torah to Moses, the Word of God's taking flesh in Jesus, or the "coming down" of the Qur'an to the Prophet. And since the message communicated by the divine source regarding itself will be transmitted in human language, its meaning will always be a matter of commentary within each tradition. Moreover, precisely because of the slack that inevitably attends human language in speaking of the divine, thinkers operating within a tradition have often found space to interact with another tradition so as to enrich their own. What we know as interreligious dialogue has certainly been facilitated by the sea change wrought by the Vatican II document *Nostra Aetate*, but the practice of engaging one's own tradition by encounter with others has long been part of the creative assimilation of revelation that characterizes faith traditions. I have probed the ways Thomas Aquinas utilized the Jewish scholar Moses Maimonides as they both adapted the Islamic metaphysics of Avicenna, in an effort to offer a coherent account of free creation—a teaching shared among Jews, Christians, and Muslims in the face of formidable philosophical alternatives.[10]

More recently, in the main narrative of Pope Benedict's Regensburg address, he delineated the sustained role that rational inquiry has played in the ongoing development of Christian revelation. For now, let us turn to the sophisticated ways in which medievals interwove faith with reason to develop a discipline we have come to know as *theology*, as a way of modeling interfaith exchange into an apt vehicle for developing doctrine. Recall Aquinas's simple recommendations: should an apparent contradiction emerge between faith and reason, first determine whether the relevant interpretation of Scripture is a faithful one, then look to see whether the reasoning in question has been carried out responsibly. To appreciate the new context, however, we shall have to expand John Paul II's discussion of "faith and reason" [*Fides et ratio*] to embrace the variable of *culture*. For that encyclical explicitly notes how "reason itself, in accord with which Christians experience their faith, is soaked in the culture of the place nearest to it, and in its turn ensures that with the progress of time, its own nature [i.e., what we take to be *reason* itself] is bit by bit

---

10. See Burrell, *Knowing the Unknowable God: Ibn-Sina, Maimonides, Aquinas* (Notre Dame: University of Notre Dame Press, 1986); and Burrell, *Freedom and Creation in Three Traditions* (Notre Dame: University of Notre Dame Press, 1993).

transformed" (#71).[11] Yet since that prescient reminder is never developed within the text itself, it remains our task to delineate how the cultural shift in interfaith attitudes augurs new theological potential.

Each of the examples offered will illustrate the central role interpretation will play in sorting out contentious issues, to allow us to discern genuine from spurious conflict. Purported conflicts between faith and reason always required the same hermeneutic efforts, of course, but the task becomes far more complex when one juxtaposes entire traditions, each with internally conflicting histories of interpretation! So as experience has shown, most of the work will turn on discerning which interpretations are to be trusted, before attempting to understand what has been stated from the perspective we invariably bring to the discussion. Yet when carried out together with others whose faith is at issue, the very effort to clarify differences proves immensely illuminating, in fact allowing the proponents of each tradition to clarify their own assertions, as we shall see. Confirmed by the realization that no one can use purportedly neutral tools of logic to *prove* their own tradition, we will see why the fruits of dialogue can at best attain to a proper understanding of what one another *means,* leaving tactfully to one side why each believes their revelation to be *true.*

Three Neuralgic Issues

Let us explore three neuralgic issues, beginning with that of Trinity, to illustrate how interfaith exchange can now offer an apt vehicle for developing doctrine. Christian-Muslim disputations regularly opposed Muslim insistence on the unicity of God to a Christian Trinitarian presentation. Yet every student of the history of Christian thought knows that it took four to five centuries of christological controversies, plus another century of conceptual elaboration, to hone a "doctrine of trinity," precisely because of the *Shema*: "Hear, O Israel, God our God is one" (Deut 6:6). If Muslim teaching showcasing divine unity—*tawhid*—has been developed polemically over against a misunderstanding of the "threeness" of the one God, that should be perfectly understandable for Christians, given the

11. *Fides et ratio* can be found online at the Vatican Web site: http://www.vatican .va/.

time it took them to articulate "threeness" in God without prejudice to God's unity. Moreover, Islamic thought soon came to see how, as God's Word, the Qur'an must be coeternal with God, lest God be mute![12] So once we emphasize the Johannine expression of "Word" rather than the synoptic usage of "Son" in dialogue with Muslims, we will at once be able to converse with them less polemically yet also realize how thoroughly our baptismal formula refines the ordinary notion of *Son*. And rather than diminishing the presentation of our faith, we will have come to a more refined understanding of what we have long been affirming. The fact remains that our faith is indeed Trinitarian while theirs is not, yet the process of dialogue will have brought us to a better articulation of our respective understandings of *trinity* and of *unity* in God.

The next example comes as a corollary to the intradivine relations, called (in common parlance) persons yet utterly different from the distinct individuals we normally identify as persons. We are speaking of the mediating role of Jesus in effecting our relationship to God. Muslims insist that while the Prophet delivers the Qur'an, which presents us with the very Word of God, it is our response to God's very Word that effects an immediate relation with God. Given the gift of the Qur'an, there can be no need for a "mediator," nor should one think of Muhammad as one. On the other hand, Christian Scripture and theology speak in countless ways of Jesus Christ as "mediator between God and human beings." Now the ordinary use of *between* makes it sound as though Jesus operates in a space between the Creator and the creatures. Yet that would be an Arian view, explicitly repudiated in the early councils, so in orthodox Christian belief Jesus's mediation operates theandrically—that is, as something intrinsic to Jesus's divine-human constitution, so carefully elaborated in early councils from Nicaea to Chalcedon. So while the actions of Jesus can effect an immediate relation to God as Father, Jesus does not mediate as a "go-between." So the very feature of mediation which Muslims deny to the Prophet, thinking that to be Jesus's manner of mediating, represents a distortion of Christian thought, though one in fact proposed by

12. For a succinct statement of the eternal Qur'an, see Kenneth Cragg's learned introduction to his *Readings in the Qur'an* (Portland OR: Sussex Academic, 1999): "the Qur'an does not present itself as documenting what is other than itself. It is not about the truth; it is the truth . . . as a book already existing eternally" (18); for an illuminating discussion, see Yahya Michot, "Revelation," in *Cambridge Companion to Classical Islamic Theology*, ed. Tim Winter (Cambridge: Cambridge University Press, 2008) 185.

some Christians as well. One thinks of sixteenth-century debates between Protestants and Catholics, where the polemical edge doubtless distorted a more classical meaning of "mediation." For Catholics have elaborated a sense of 'mediator' to include ecclesial structures and personages, so that ordained persons "mediate" the saving power of God to the faithful. But just as Jesus could not be construed, thanks to the *Shema*, as a "being alongside God" (which is the meaning Muslims attach to *shirk*: something—either created or uncreated—on a par with the Creator), so Christians falsify their own faith if they conceive of Jesus's mediation (or, *a fortiori*, that of the church) as situated "between" the Creator and creatures. As the Word who is God, Jesus's mediation effects that immediate relation to God as Father, which Christians presume in their recurrent prayer: "Our Father."

The final example explores the polemical stance both Jews and Muslims take with regard to Christian teaching regarding "original sin." Here again, applying Aquinas's hermeneutical cautions, we find that there are widely divergent versions of "original sin" in diverse Christian lexicons, and one is never sure which one of them is at issue. The spectrum of meanings Christians attach to this teaching can be fairly represented between a characteristically Catholic view, captured in Chesterton's insistence that "original sin is the only empirically verified Christian doctrine" (or "Murphy's Law" in the moral order), to the most stark contention that its effects render our intellectual and voluntary faculties utterly dysfunctional. But these views all require that Adam's transgression somehow affect and infect us all by a path that remains obscure, as Rudi teVelde's delineation of Aquinas's attempt shows so clearly.[13] So they all focus on the universal human need for redemption, exemplified in and effected by Jesus's death on a cross. Now if this remains a sticking point for Muslims, an adequate way of articulating "the atonement" continues to elude Christian theology, which deems Anselm's account deficient on several counts but has yet to find a satisfactory formulation (though I find one in Sebastian Moore's *The Crucified Jesus is No Stranger*).[14] Yet we can all recognize how incapable are rational creatures of achieving their inbuilt

---

13. In Rik Van Nieuwenhove and Joseph Wawrykow, eds., *Theology of Thomas Aquinas* (Notre Dame: University of Notre Dame Press, 2005).

14. Sebastian Moore, *The Crucified Jesus Is No Stranger* (Mahwah NJ: Paulist, 1983).

goal of union with God, so some action on the Creator's part must make that possible—recalling Chesterton.

Now a closer look at the Muslim view of human beings' capacity for "drawing near to" God shows less difference between us than first appeared. Islamic thought takes the situation in the Hejaz before the Prophet's preaching the Qur'an, and readily applies it to the entire world: bereft of divine revelation, human beings are bound to wander aimlessly, seeking to fulfill their own desires and inevitably engaging in deadly combat, as we see every day! On this view, the Torah or the "Injil" [gospel, i.e., New Testament] serves the purpose for Jews or Christians that the Qur'an does for Muslims, since human beings left to themselves would never make it. So while Christianity focuses on the death and resurrection of Jesus, Muslims locate the redemptive act par excellence in the unmerited and serendipitous "coming down" of the Qur'an from God through the Prophet.[15] Human beings are invited to respond to this gift, and their everlasting redemption depends on the quality of that response. So this dynamic reinforces the fundamental analogy between Jesus and the Qur'an: as Christians believe Jesus to be the Word of God made human, Muslims believe the Qur'an to be the word of God made book. Each of these examples can show us how comparative inquiry will inevitably highlight dimensions of our own theological task, by accentuating items in our own traditions that need clarification and development.

Letting the Examples Culminate in an Exposition of Theological Grammar

Moving beyond examples to the grammar proper to theology, we can note the "play" of theological inquiry, rooted as it must be in practice, to display Aquinas's contention that our language, at best, will "imperfectly signify" divinity (ST 1.13.3). And if theological expression will ever be inadequate, theological inquiry will ever be comparative, always seeking the least misleading modes of expression. Yet that requires refinement of judgment, gained by weighing different expressions relative to each other, in an effort better to articulate what Augustine called "the rule of faith." Yet if there can be no adequate expression, we shall always be weighing

15. Cragg, *Readings in the Qur'an.*

candidates relative to each other. And once the idol of "pure reason" has been shattered, and we can learn to accept diverse ways of arriving at conclusions, we will also find that we can employ the skills learned in one tradition to follow reasoning in another. Traditions, in other words, are often found to be *relative to* one another in ways that can prove mutually fruitful rather than isolating. The traditions that prove to be so will be those that avail themselves of human reason in their development, as the patterns of stress and strain in their evolution will display their capacity for exploiting the resources of reason. (On this point, Pope Benedict was "spot on," as the thirty-eight Muslim scholars noted, yet for Muslim as well as Christian traditions!) In short, fears about "relativ*ism*" give way to the human fact that all inquiry takes place within a tradition. So just as medieval ways of resolving apparent conflicts between faith and reason turned on critical hermeneutics with regard to texts, together with critical assessment of the reasoning one is employing, so interfaith comparative inquiry will require skills of reading one set of texts in relation to another.

So where have we come? To an interim conclusion, using the skills we have developed to subvert the perfectly normal desire of each religious group to show it is superior to all comers, even though characteristic efforts to do so will invariably involve presenting the other in ways that can at best be contested for fairness and can at worst display brutal colonization. A final charitable look at the 2000 Vatican statement *Dominus Iesus* ("On the Unicity and Salvific Universality of Jesus Christ and the Church") can suggest a way of putting things less contentiously than that document did.[16] It purports merely to proclaim abiding Christian truth, yet recalling our earlier discussion of "proclaiming truth," article 2 of the document effectively derails that intent. After expressing the elements of Christian faith in the words of the Nicene Creed in article 1, the authors go on to claim, with disarming self-assurance, that "in the course of the centuries, the Church has proclaimed and witnessed with fidelity to the Gospel of Jesus." Proclaimed, yes; but witnessed with fidelity? If this were true, past centuries would have been radically different and our own century surely unrecognizable. Indeed, a contestable assertion can fault an entire document. Nor is this a minor flaw, for this claim to have witnessed

16. See *Sic et Non: Encountering Dominus Iesus*, ed. Stephen J. Pope and Charles Hefling (Maryknoll, NY: Orbis, 2002).

faithfully throughout the centuries, so out of touch not only with history but also with present-day reality, can only make our proclamations arrogant and monopolistic. Indeed, ethical humility and intellectual humility are intimately related, as proclamation is to witness, as we have seen in the Amish example.[17]

So Christian theology must always begin, as does Christian worship, with a *mea culpa* and a *Kyrie eleison*. Its focus is proclamation, yet substantial moral failures of the Christian community will inevitably mute the truth claims we may make, as Pope Benedict has acknowledged in asking forgiveness for clerical abuse. Had the Christian community, including its officials, offered better witness to Jesus, claims about the importance of the Church in God's saving plan and activity could find a more receptive audience. (These words are adapted from Dan Madigan's reflections on a discussion in which we both participated.) Yet our discussion of the effects of interfaith dialogue, in this case with Muslims, can offer an alternative way of expressing the distinctiveness of Christianity, and do so in a fashion that might be intelligible to others: that our revelation is in a person. Preceded by an appropriate *mea culpa* regarding our collective ability as "Christians" to follow that same Jesus (as John Paul II did during Lent in the same year 2000), we can simply remind ourselves that Christians believe that Jesus is the Word of God made human, while Muslims believe that the Qur'an is the word of God made book. These parallel formulae express profound difference as well as structural similarity, and recalling them can advance ecumenical interests as well as our own self-understanding as Christians. So the practice of dialogue can serve to affect, for the better, our attempts at proclamation as well. As our own sense of who we are develops in the face of generous Muslim initiatives like "A Common Word," we will come to appreciate how much we need one another to appreciate as well as to give witness to what we have received from God.

17. I have adapted this last observation from Dan Madigan's comments on an observation I made to an interfaith gathering at Tantur Ecumenical Institute (Jerusalem) in 2006, whose proceedings, edited by James Heft, will be published by Oxford University Press.

Part III
Muslim Perspectives

Part II

Mission Perspectives

6

Discerning a Qur'anic Mandate for Mutually Transformational Dialogue

Asma Afsaruddin

It is generally recognized among Muslims that they are encouraged to engage in honest and respectful dialogue with the People of the Book (mainly Jews and Christians), who are recognized as fellow monotheists with both similar and different religious beliefs and teachings. While similar teachings concerning ethical values, for example, create common ground, differences in doctrine and beliefs invite sensitive and carefully crafted discussions that do not give offense or cause polarization. Interfaith dialogue can be both a minefield and a richly rewarding learning experience, depending on the approach of the interlocutors involved.

For Muslims, the incentive to seek interfaith dialogue is based on Qur'anic imperatives, the practice of the Prophet Muhammad, and the examples set by early Muslims. Muslims often refer to examples from the early history of Islam that establish valuable normative precedents for them in this regard. One such frequently quoted example is the Prophet's encounter with a Christian delegation from Najran in the year 630 in Medina. This group of sixty men was received kindly by the Prophet, with whom they are said to have engaged in frank discussion regarding the doctrines and beliefs of their respective religions. At the end of the vigorous discussion in which both sides agreed to disagree on key doctrinal issues, the Christian delegation concluded a pact with the Prophet, according to which they were granted full protection of their churches and their possessions in return for the payment of taxes. They were also allowed to pray in the mosque at Medina over the protests of some.[1]

Another positive example of interreligious encounters in the early period is afforded by the second caliph 'Umar's interactions with the Christians of Jerusalem. In 638, upon the surrender of the city to Muslim forces, 'Umar concluded an agreement with the inhabitants of the city that allowed them considerable freedom in the practice of religion.[2] A practically identical agreement was drawn up with the inhabitants of Ludd in Palestine.[3]

While interfaith encounters may lead to such positive interactions, they are, however, also fraught with the possibility of rancorous exchanges and counterproductive consequences when engaged in for the wrong reasons (for example, to establish the dominance of one community over another) or by inexperienced and ill-informed people. Two questions then that may be fruitfully asked in this context are as follows: First, how may we establish a general protocol of respectful and honest interfaith dialogue that is mutually beneficial and illuminating? And second, what sources should be invoked to establish the authoritative nature of both dialogue itself and its methodology? For Muslims the answer to both questions lies in the revealed text of the Qur'an. The Qur'an after all is fundamentally concerned with Muslim relations with the other Abrahamic communities, to which Islam is organically and historically related. There are a number of verses that specifically deal with the mechanics of inter-Abrahamic dialogue and the fostering of peaceful relations with the People of the Book; some verses go beyond addressing only the Abrahamic communities and counsel respect for the religious sensibilities of all, including idol

1. Martin Lings, *Muhammad: His Life Based on the Earliest Sources* (Cambridge: Islamic Texts Society, 1995) 326.

2. For the terms of this agreement, see Thomas Walker Arnold, *The Preaching of Islam: A History of the Propagation of the Muslim Faith* (New York: Scribner, 1913) 56. It is further reported that 'Umar visited the holy places in Jerusalem in the company of the patriarch of Jerusalem. When the time for prayer came, the patriarch graciously invited the caliph to offer his prayers in the Church of the Resurrection. 'Umar declined, saying that if he were to do that, later Muslims might wrongfully claim the church as their own place of worship; see ibid., 57.

3. These accounts are recorded by the ninth-century historian al-Tabari in his widely consulted universal history; see his *Ta'rikh al-umam wa 'l-muluk* (Beirut: Dar al-kutub al-islamiyya, 1997) 2:449.

worshipers. Despite the obvious significance of these verses for interfaith and intercultural relations, they have not previously been subjected to a close and detailed study. With a resurgent interest in interreligious conversations in the contemporary period, it is precisely these kinds of verses and their explications that should be the focus of our attention.

This chapter is therefore primarily devoted to a study of the exegeses of four sets of Qur'anic verses that allow for the extrapolation of preliminary guidelines concerning dialogic encounters between Muslims and non-Muslims. These verses are: Qur'an 29:46, 41:34–35, 3:64, and 6:107–8. This study will begin by selectively focusing on the relevant exegeses of these verses through a broad span of time to determine how some of the most prominent Muslim scholars have understood their meanings and their application to relations with primarily the People of the Book but also to non-Muslims in general. The first three groups of verses deal with Muslim interactions with Jews and Christians specifically while the last set is concerned with relations with non-Scripturaries. The study will conclude with a reflection upon the further implications of these exegeses for fostering better interfaith understanding between Muslims and their dialogue partners today and the possibility of their mutual transformation through such encounters in the contemporary period.

Exegeses of Qur'an 29:46

This verse states "Do not dispute with the People of the Book save with what is better; except for those who do wrong among them, and say [to them]: 'We believe in that which was revealed to us and revealed to you, and our God and your God is one, and we submit to Him.'"

This has been understood to be the quintessential verse advocating a protocol of dialogue for Muslims, particularly with adherents of the Abrahamic religions. The earliest extant commentary on this verse is that of Mujahid b. Jabr (d. 720). In his brief but significant exegesis, Mujahid understands the first part of the verse as counseling Muslims "to speak [of] goodness (*khayran*) when they [sc. the People of the Book] utter what is wrong/evil (*sharran*)." "Those who do wrong among them" is glossed as those among the People of the Book who speak falsehood concerning God, for instance, ascribing partners to him, or those who cause harm to the Prophet Muhammad. Mujahid lists a variant exegesis emanating from Sa'id b. Jubayr that this phrase refers to those among the People of the Book who have not signed a treaty with the Muslims and consequently engage in hostilities against them.[4]

The famous exegete Muhammad b. Jarir al-Tabari (d. 923) comments that this verse is specifically directed at Jews and Christians who are the People of the Book. As for the critical phrase in the verse "save with what is better" (*illa bi-'llati hiya ahsan*), al-Tabari remarks that it means, "except for what is good or fine speech" (*illa bi-'l-jamil min al-qawl*). This, he explains further, is a reference to "an invitation to God by means of His verses/signs (*bi-ayatihi*), and drawing attention to His proofs (*hujajihi*)." "Those who do wrong" among the People of the Book are those among them who ascribe partners to God, including Christians, who maintain that Jesus was the son of God and refuse to submit to Muslim authority. They must be fought against until they agree to pay the poll tax (*jizya*).[5] It is highly revealing of his time that al-Tabari spends more time explicating who the wrongdoers are among the People of the Book and the consequences they must face than on fully exploring the implications of the phrase "save with what is better." Tellingly, he does not seek to amplify further the common ground delineated by the Qur'an when it states in this verse that righteous Jews and Christians worship and submit to the one and same God. Al-Tabari's brief explanation that "save with what is better" refers to "good or fine speech" (*al-jamil min al-qawl*) is clearly set in the context of attempting to convince the People of the Book of the truth of Islam. I think we are justified in concluding that al-Tabari does not have in mind interfaith dialogue as we would understand it today, but rather proselytization among the People of the Book.[6]

Some of the later post-Tabari exegetes, however, offer more nuanced and less confessional approaches to this verse. For example, al-Zamakhshari (d. 1144) glosses *ahsan* in this verse as "what is offered of gentleness (*bi-'l-lin*) in response to roughness (*al-khushuna*); of equanimity (*bi-'l-*

---

4. Mujahid b. Jabr, *Tafsir Mujahid*, ed. Abu Muhammad al-Asyuti (Beirut: Dar al-kutub al-'ilmiyya, 2005) 205.

5. Al-Tabari, *Jami' al-bayan fi ta'wil al-qur'an* (Beirut: Dar al-kutub al-'ilmiyya, 1997) 10:149–50.

6. The eleventh-century exegete al-Wahidi (d. 1076) similarly understands "what is better" as a reference to "the Qur'an and invitation to God through His verses/signs and drawing attention to His proofs"; see his *al-Wasit fi tafsir al-qur'an al-majid* (Beirut: Dar al-kutub al-'ilmiyya, 1994) 3:422.

kazm) to anger; and of forbearance (*bi-'l-anat*) in the face of vehemence or violence (*al-sawra*)." Here he references Qur'an 41:34, which we will be discussing next, to lend support to his interpretation. He similarly offers a nonconfessional understanding of "those who do wrong among the People of the Book," commenting that they are those who are "excessively hostile and obstinate, refusing to accept good counsel (*al-nush*), and with whom gentleness and compassion (*al-rifq*) are of no avail." Such people are to be dealt with sternly.[7] It is worthy of note that in al-Zamakhshari's understanding, those who do wrong among the Scriptuaries are so considered not on account of theological error on their part, but on account of their bad manners and hostile attitude.

Al-Zamakhshari goes on to list the variant interpretations of other exegetes, some of whom were of the opinion that this phrase referred to those Jews and Christians who ascribed partners to God or made other theologically erroneous statements regarding him. Others, however, maintained that it referred to a contingent among these Scriptuaries who had physically harmed the Prophet or to those who refused to submit to Muslim authority. The most polemical interpretation is attributed to Qatada b. Di'ama (d. 736), an early exegete and jurist from the second generation of Muslims (*tabi'i*), who averred that this verse was abrogated by Qur'an 9:29, which allows Muslims to fight against those among the People of the Book who refuse to pay the poll tax.[8]

It is in the commentary of Fakhr al-Din al-Razi (d. 1210) that we begin to discern the fuller potential of this verse in the context of interfaith dialogue. Al-Razi mentions at the outset that according to certain unnamed exegetes, the first part of the verse "Do not dispute with the People of the Book except with what is better" means "Do not dispute with them with the sword even if they refuse to accept Islam (*wa-in lam yu'minu*) except when they resort to wrong-doing or oppression and take up arms (*illa idha zalamu wa-haarabu*)." His own opinion is that this verse counsels Muslims in general to deal gently with the People of the Book because of the religious tenets they share with the former. Jews and Christians after all also have faith in the one God, believe in the revelation

---

7. Al-Zamakhshari, *al-Kashshaf 'an haqa'iq ghawamid al-tanzil wa-'uyun al-aqawil fi wujuh al-ta'wil*, ed. 'Adil Ahmad 'Abd al-Wujud and 'Ali Muhammad Mu'awwad (Riyad: Maktabat al-'Ubaykan, 1998) 4:553.

8. Ibid.

of books, in the sending of messengers, and in the final resurrection. Each of these articles of belief is designated a *husn* ("a goodness") by al-Razi. Where the People of the Book are lacking, he continues, is in their failure to acknowledge the mission of the Prophet Muhammad, despite the fact that their Scriptures contain references to him. In acknowledgment, however, of the aggregate goodness (*ihsanihim*) of the People of the Book, Muslims should debate with them with what is better/best. Al-Razi leaves undefined here the precise nature of "what is better/best." But since he next proceeds to say that Muslims should not treat the opinions of Jews and Christians lightly or ascribe error to their ancestors, as they might— or perhaps should—in the case of polytheists, then we may assume that "what is better/best" is a reference to the adoption of such conciliatory and respectful modes of conversation across faith lines. Al-Razi specifically points to the self-defeating nature of arguments about the merits of the various prophets and religious leaders within the Abrahamic tradition. He remarks that that is the equivalent of wrangling over the merits of various political leaders and kings (*al-ru'asa' wa-'l-muluk*), which can only lead to factionalism and hostility. The best, peaceful resolution is achieved when one is able to point out that the two kings or chiefs who are the objects of the wrangling are themselves in agreement with one another. Here al-Razi references a statement of the Prophet in which he asserts that all the prophets through time have believed in one another, including in Muhammad (implying that they had prior knowledge of his mission), and thus the People of the Book are wrong in showing partisan attachment to their prophets to the exclusion of others. Therefore, even though Jews and Christians are far superior to the polytheists on account of their adherence to laudable religious tenets, they are clearly remiss in this regard, which draws them dangerously close to unbelief.[9]

Notwithstanding this final caveat, we have on the whole in al-Razi's exegesis the articulation of a thoughtful, reasoned protocol of dialectics between Muslims and the People of the Book, which, while stressing commonalities, also candidly acknowledges the differences between them. Acknowledgment of these differences is not meant to generate disrespect for these Abrahamic interlocutors or the imputation of fundamental error to them. Although al-Razi does not state this explicitly, his

9. Fakhr al-Din al-Razi, *al-Tafsir al-kabir* (Beirut: Dar ihya' al-turath al-'arabi, 1999) 9:63–64.

line of reasoning implies that the common ground that may be retrieved between Muslims and the People of the Book on the basis of this verse is broader than the points of contention between them; it is this common ground that serves as a more fruitful point of departure for interfaith encounters.

The fourteenth-century exegete Ibn Kathir (d. 1373) points to the existence of two distinctive schools of thought in regard to this verse. One school led by, once again, Qatada and others asserted that this verse was abrogated by the sword verse (Qur'an 9:29), and there could no longer be debates with the People of the Book. They were left with three choices: acceptance of Islam, payment of *jizya*, or fighting ("the sword"). The other school (which included Ibn Zayd) maintained that this verse was unabrogated and remained in force for those who wished to gain insight (*al-istibsar*) into the religion of the People of the Book and debate with them with what is better so that there might be greater benefit in it. It is significant that insight and discernment, as signified by the Arabic word *al-istibsar* here, are regarded as essential accompaniments to fruitful beneficial dialogue by Ibn Zayd and others. This equation is borne out by another Qur'anic verse (16:125), which exhorts Muslims to "Invite to the path of your Lord with wisdom and good counsel." Rules of interfaith engagement may further be derived from Qur'an 20:44, continues Ibn Kathir, in which God counsels Moses and Aaron when they were being dispatched to the Pharaoh "to say to him words of gentleness so that he may reflect or be fearful [of God]."[10] For this school of thought, gentle and reflective speech to one another in the course of such interreligious dialectics represents "that which is better" mentioned in this verse.

As for those who do wrong, they are those among the People of the Book who veer away from the truth and deny clear proofs out of obstinacy and arrogance and resort to fighting to uphold what was forbidden them.[11] Although it might be suspected that Ibn Kathir construes their wrongdoing to ultimately mean stubborn rejection of Islam, the lack of theological language in defining this wayward contingent from among the People of the Book more persuasively suggests that it is rather their roughness of behavior and hostile attitude towards Muslims that is the object of denunciation, rather than their religious beliefs as such.

10. Ibn Kathir, *Tafsir al-qur'an al-'azim* (Beirut: Dar al-jil, 1990) 3:401.
11. Ibid.

Exegeses of Qur'an 41:34–35

This verse states, "Repel [evil] with what is better, then the one between whom and yourself enmity prevails will become like your friend. But none achieves it [this state of affairs] except for those who are patient and of great fortune."

Among the exegetes we just surveyed in relation to Qur'an 29:46, only al-Zamakhshari cross-references Qur'an 42:34 in the course of his discussion. Yet an obvious connection exists between these two verses because of the identical phrase "with what is better" (*bi-'llati hiya ahsan*) used in both. Qur'an 41:34 further explicitly states that the likely and desirable outcome of warding off evil with what is better than it, is reconciliation among enemies and the winning of friends. Compared with Qur'an 29:46, the applicability of this verse is not restricted to the People of the Book only but potentially concerns all humanity. Despite the obvious link between these two verses, most of our premodern exegetes appear not to have had great interest in probing this link to shed further light on the meaning(s) of *ahsan* in the context of interfaith relations that extend beyond the Abrahamic religions, and in regard to interpersonal relations as well.

For example, Muqatil, in the first half of the eighth century, understands these verses in a narrow historical sense. He says these verses refer to Abu Lahab and his persecution of Muhammad so that the Prophet came to harbor a great dislike for his tormentor. Qur'an 41:34 counseled him to forgive and pardon Abu Lahab so that his enemy may become transformed into a close friend and ally. The next verse states that only those who show forbearance by suppressing their anger may attain to these good deeds—here good deeds are glossed as forgiveness and clemency (*al-'afu wa-'l-safh*). And only they will attain to the bounteous blessings of paradise, continues Muqatil, which is the meaning of "a great portion" or "fortune," referred to in this verse (*hazz 'azim*). God had thus exhorted the Prophet to be forbearing in the face of injury and to pray for refuge from Satan in the case of Abu Jahl.[12]

Al-Tabari understands Qur'an 41:34 to contain a more general injunction for the Prophet to counter the ignorance (*jahl*) of his adversaries

---

12. Muqatil b. Sulayman, *Tafsir*, ed. 'Abd Allah Mahmud Shihata (Beirut: Mu'assasat al-ta'rikh al-'arabi, 2002) 3:743.

with clemency (*hilm*) and to disarm those who wish him harm through forgiveness and forbearance. According to Ibn 'Abbas, this verse commands all believers (*mu'minin*) to be forbearing when provoked to anger and practice magnanimity and forgiveness (*al-hilm wa-'l-'afu*) in the face of injury. When they do so, God protects them from the machinations of Satan and their enemies relent and become transformed into intimate friends. (Other early exegetes, like 'Ata' b. Abi Rabah [d. 732] and Mujahid [d. 720],[13] were of the opinion that the verse required Muslims to respond with greetings of peace [*al-salam*] to those who caused them injury, in explanation of the phrase "with that which is better.") Al-Tabari then proceeds to restrict the applicability of this verse by commenting that God had commanded the Prophet to extend such forbearance and forgiveness to his hostile relatives so that they would become his dedicated and compassionate companions. He specifically glosses *al-hamim* as *al-qarib* or "relative."[14] These verses thus signify both a general injunction to all believers and a more particularist meaning rooted in a specific cause of revelation.

As for Qur'an 41:35, al-Tabari continues, it affirms that only those who show considerable forbearance in the face of wrongdoing and tribulations are able to ward off evil with goodness: "Those who attain to a great portion" are the fortunate ones (*dhu jadd*), according to the exegete al-Suddi (d. 745), while others, like the Companion Ibn 'Abbas, said that *hazz 'azim* specifically referred to paradise. In this connection, Qatada b. Di'ama is said to have related an anecdote regarding Abu Bakr (d. 634), the first caliph, who was once cursed by a man in the presence of Muhammad. At first Abu Bakr reacted with forbearance and restraint, but then he retorted heatedly, which caused the Prophet to get up and leave. When Abu Bakr pursued him and wished to know the reason for his abrupt departure, Muhammad explained that when the former had exercised self-restraint, an angel supported him, but when he retaliated the angel left and Satan took his place. "And I did not wish to sit in the company of Satan, O Abu Bakr!" remarked the Prophet.[15]

---

13. Mujahid's extant published *tafsir*, referred to in note 1 above, has not preserved his exegesis of this verse.

14. Al-Tabari, *Jami'*, 11:111.

15. Ibid., 11:111–12.

Al-Zamakhshari notably illustrates the difference between *hasana* and *ahsan* by offering concrete examples of what constitutes "that which is better" in the face of wrongdoing. An act of goodness (*hasana*) in such a situation is to forgive the wrongdoer. To carry out that which is better (*wa-llati hiya ahsan*) is to respond with an act of goodness or charity to specifically counter or nullify the original injury and thus to go beyond simple forgiveness. Thus, he counsels, if an adversary "were to revile you, praise him; if he were to kill your son, then ransom his son from the hands of his enemy; if you were to carry this out, your inveterate enemy will become transformed into a sincere friend full of good will towards you."[16] Only the people of forbearance and patience (*ahl al-sabr*) attain to this and reap goodness (*khayr*) as result. Al-Zamakhshari cites Ibn 'Abbas who glossed "with that which is better" as "forbearance when angered, magnanimity in the face of ignorance, and pardon in the face of injury" and understood *al-hazz* in this verse to refer to reward or recompense (*thawab*) for a good deed. Al-Zamakhshari notes that the famed successor and pious scholar al-Hasan al-Basri, however, had understood *hazz* to be a reference to paradise. The specific referent in this verse, concludes al-Zamakhshari, is Abu Sufyan b. Harb, who had been a trenchant foe of the Prophet but then became a sincere ally.[17] Like al-Tabari, al-Zamakhshari also points to the possibility of deriving a broad moral injunction from this verse, while bearing in mind the more limited historical context of the verse.

Al-Razi corroborates the understanding of some of his predecessors in regard to these verses but also offers us some rather fresh and original perspectives. He defines *al-hasana* in Qur'an 41:34 as a reference to the Prophet's summons to "the true religion" (*al-din al-haqq*), his patience in the face of the unbelievers' ignorance, his avoidance of retaliation, and refusal to be perturbed by them [sc. unbelievers]." It's antonym, *al-sayyi'â*, is defined as the harshness displayed by unbelievers, particularly in their speech, and the two, he asserts, cannot be equivalent. The verse promises that Muhammad's *hasana* will be the basis of his glorious status in this world and his reward in the next and counsels that the wrongdoing of his

16. Al-Zamakhshari, *Kashshaf*, 5:383.

17. Ibid. Abu Sufyan is a more plausible referent in this verse since Abu Lahab until his death maintained his virulent opposition to Muhammad.

adversaries should not distract him from the commission of these good acts.[18]

As for the phrase "repel with that which is better," it commands the Prophet to ward off the ignorance and foolishness of the ignorant by the best means—by unflaggingly bearing with patience their evil nature, not reacting in anger to their insolence, and by refraining from physical retaliation in return for their injury. It is possible that they will thereby become ashamed of their reprehensible behavior and abandon their repugnant acts, and their feelings of animosity will become transformed into affection and goodwill. Al-Razi cites the well-known lexicographer al-Zajjaj (d. 923), who commented, like previous exegetes, that only those who are patient and forbearing in the face of trials and tribulations, who suppress their anger, and who forego retaliation will attain to the great portion or fortune promised in this verse.[19]

Worthy of note is al-Razi's understanding of the locution "those who attain to a great portion/fortune," as those who have acquired many "cognitive excellences" (*al-fada'il al-nafsaniyya*) and reached a high level of "spiritual potential" (*al-quwwa al-ruhaniyya*), on account of the fact that their psyches are not perturbed by a preoccupation with exacting vengeance and retaliation. Such perturbances, he says, are the result of external causes to which the weak psyche is susceptible, and that the strong psyche successfully resists. Al-Razi acknowledges the more common understanding of "a great portion" as a reference to a large share of reward in the hereafter for those who are forbearing, and concedes that this is a possible explanation.[20]

Ibn Kathir offers a very brief exegesis of these two verses, affirming like most of the previous exegetes, that "repel with what is better" means that one should ward off the harm of the wrong-doer through acts of goodness (*ihsan*), who is thereby transformed into an affectionate friend and sincere ally. Only those who are patient and practice forbearance—which, according to 'Ali b. Abi Talha, involves restraining one's anger, magnanimity in the face of ignorance, and forgiveness of injury—attain to abundance of happiness in this world and the next, are protected by

18. Al-Razi, *Tafsir*, 9:564.

19. Ibid., 9:565.

20. Ibid.

God from the machinations of Satan, and convert their enemy into a bosom friend.[21]

Exegeses of Qur'an 3:64

This verse states, "Say, O People of the Book, let us come to a common word (*kalimat sawa'*) between us and you that we will not worship but the one God nor ascribe any partner to Him or that any of us should take others as lords besides the one God. If they should turn their backs, say: 'Bear witness that we submit to God (*muslimun*).'"

This verse, which has received considerable attention in recent times,[22] is concerned primarily with Muslim relations with Jews and Christians. Some of our exegetes reflect upon whether this verse deals exclusively with Jews or with Christians or both together, and what exactly the Arabic word *sawa'* occurring in this verse signifies.

In his brief commentary, Muqatil glosses *kalimat sawa'* as "a word of justice, which is sincerity" (*kalimat al-'adl wa-hiya al-ikhlas*) to be agreed upon by Muslims and the People of the Book that they will worship but the one God and not ascribe partners to Him. Muqatil understands this verse to be directed at Christians, since he says it specifically implies that these People of the Book regard Jesus as a deity (*rabban*). If they should turn away at that, it means that they have disavowed monotheism, and Muslims are instructed to assert that they have submitted to God.[23]

Al-Tabari glosses *ahl al-kitab* as a reference to both Jews and Christians (*ahl al-tawrat wa-'l-injil*), who are summoned to "a word of justice between us and you." He records the variant opinion of Qatada and others, who thought that the verse refers only to the Jews of Medina while others, like al-Suddi and Ibn Zayd, were of the opinion that the verse was directed towards the Christian delegation from Najran exclusively. The "word of justice" means that "we should believe in the unicity of God and

21. Ibn Kathir, *Tafsir*, 4:103.

22. "A Common Word," invoking Qur'an 3:64, was the title given to a letter signed initially by 138 Muslim scholars and clerics in 2006 addressed to the major Christian leaders of the world. The letter emphasized love of God and of neighbor as the central tenets common to both Muslims and Christians.

23. Muqatil, *Tafsir*, 1:281.

not worship anyone else; repudiate (*nabra'*) all other beings as objects of worship except Him," and that we should not ascribe any partner to Him, comments al-Tabari. The locution "that any of us should take others as lords besides the one God" is understood to mean that one should not obey any human in matters that contravene God's commandments, or exalt one another by prostrating before another as one prostrates before God. If they should retreat from that, the believers (*al-mu'minun*) should assert that they are Muslims.[24]

Al-Zamakhshari similarly points out the different interpretations of *ahl al-kitab*, variously understood to be a reference to the Christians from Najran, to the Jews of Medina, or to both communities. "Common" (*sawa'*) refers to what is "[deemed] upright by us and you, regarding which the Qur'an, the Torah, and the Gospel do not differ." The "word" or "statement" (*kalima*) is elaborated upon by the verse itself: "that we worship none but God and not ascribe partners to Him and that none of us should take others as lords besides the one God." If the People of the Book disregard this summons, continues al-Zamakhshari, then Muslims are free to assert that only they have truly submitted to God.[25]

In contrast to what has now become the standard commentary on Qur'an 3:64, al-Razi in the late twelfth century offers us a refreshingly new reading of this important verse. In summary, he understands this verse to be concerned specifically with the Christians of Najran. Its revelation occurred after the Prophet had engaged in a vigorous debate with these Christians and had apparently frightened them to a certain extent with the fervor of his arguments and his call for mutual imprecation (*al-mubahala*), after which they opted to pay the poll tax. Al-Razi comments that it is as if God was saying to Muhammad in this verse, "Give up this manner of speaking and adopt another which the sound intellect and upright disposition recognizes as speech founded upon fairness and justice (*al-insaf*)." So the Prophet abandoned disputation with the Christians of Najran and instead, as the verse exhorted him, summoned them to arrive at a common word or statement based upon fairness between them with no preference shown towards anyone at the expense of the other. The

24. Al-Tabari, *Tafsir*, 3:300–302.
25. Al-Zamakhshari, *Kashshaf*, 1:567.

statement is, as given in the verse, "that we worship none but God and do not ascribe partners to Him."[26]

The conciliatory nature of this verse directed towards the Christians of Najran is indicated by the appellation *ahl al-kitab* for them, says al-Razi. He says that this is so because it is the best of appellations and the most perfect of titles, for it has made of them "worthy of the Book of God" (*ja'alahum ahlan li-kitab allah*). Its equivalents are the titles conferred upon those who have memorized the Qur'an, such as in the address, "O the bearer of the Book of God" (*ya hamil kitab allah*) and upon the exegete of the Qur'an, "O commentator upon the Speech of God" (*ya mufassir kalam allah*). Such sobriquets coined in conjunction with "the Book [of God]" (*al-kitab/kitab allah*) are intended to honor those who are so addressed and to cultivate their good will, and to persuade people to abandon the path of disputation and obstinacy and embark instead on a quest for fairness and justice. Al-Razi understands the command *ta'alu* ("come") as "derived from *al-ta'ali*, which is an elevation from low ground to a high place."[27] The implication is that the Christians are being invited to a higher [moral] ground by the Prophet.

"A common word" is further understood by al-Razi to refer to "a word that embodies fairness or equality between us," and no one is accorded any preference. *Al-sawa'* is specifically "justice and fairness" (*al-'adl wa-'l-insaf*). Fairness (*al-insaf*) furthermore implies equality, says al-Razi, because it implies equal sharing (*nisf*) and thus avoiding oppression of oneself and of others, which involves getting more than your equal share. "A common word" is a word that is just, upright, and egalitarian. The common word specifically referred to in this verse is that "we will worship no one but God nor ascribe any partner to him and not take each other as lords other than God."[28]

Al-Razi then does go on to document what he describes as the erroneous beliefs of Christians, particularly their trinitarian conception of God and their tendency to exalt and obey their priests uncritically, which, according to him, seriously undermines their adherence to the "common word." Despite this critique of specific Christian tenets and practices, al-Razi's commentary is remarkable nevertheless for its emphasis on estab-

26. Al-Razi, *Tafsir*, 3:251.

27. Ibid.

28. Ibid., 3:252.

lishing common ground between Muslims and Christians on the basis of this verse, and for its insistence that such common ground is best established by approaching one another with civility, goodwill, and respect, forsaking the desire to vanquish the other through harsh or clever arguments.[29] In their comments on this verse, Ibn Kathir[30] and Muhammad 'Abduh[31] essentially replicate much of what is stated by al-Razi and their views need not be repeated here.

Exegeses of Qur'an 6:107–8

This verse states "Had God willed, they would not be idolaters; but We have not appointed you [addressing the Prophet] a watcher over them, nor are you their guardian. Do not abuse to whom they pray apart from God, or they will abuse God in retaliation without knowledge."

Muqatil in his brief exegesis of Qur'an 6:107 states that if God had so willed, he would have prevented the Meccans from being polytheists. But he has not appointed the Prophet their guardian nor is he their guardian if they refuse to believe in the one God. It is telling that Muqatil next asserts that the sword verse (Qur'an 9:5) abrogates this verse. As for Qur'an 6:108, it informs us that the early Muslims used to curse the idols of the pagan Meccans, and God forbade them from doing so lest the pagan Meccans curse God in their ignorance.

Al-Tabari similarly comments that Qur'an 6:107 affirms that if God had willed, the people of Mecca would have not disbelieved in God and his messenger, but Muhammad was sent only as an emissary and summoner to people and not as an overseer of their actions or as one who was responsible for their maintenance and welfare. The next verse forbids Muslims from reviling the idols of the polytheists, for that would cause them to revile God in their ignorance, as has been reported by Ibn 'Abbas, Qatada, and others. According to the early exegete al-Suddi, the occa-

29. Ibid., 3:252–53.

30. Ibn Kathir, *Tafsir*, 1:351. Ibn Kathir also lists a different referent for this verse on the authority of Ibn 'Abbas reporting from Abu Sufyan: Khosroes, the king of Persia, to whom Abu Sufyan carried a letter of summons from the Prophet.

31. Rashid Rida, *Tafsir al-qur'an al-hakim* (Beirut: Dar al-kutub al-'ilmiyya, 1999) 3:268–71. At 3:270, 'Abduh/Rida mentions that this verse occurred in the letter sent by the Prophet to Heraclius, the patriarch of Rome, inviting him to accept Islam.

sion of the revelation of this verse was the final illness of Abu Talib, the Prophet's uncle, when some of the prominent pagan Meccans entreated Abu Talib to make his nephew repudiate Islam. Muhammad refused to do so, famously stating that if they were able to bring down the sun and place it in his hand, he would still not abandon Islam. At that the pagan Meccans demanded that the Prophet at least refrain from cursing their gods, or they would curse him and "the one who commands you." Then occurred the revelation of this verse.[32]

Similar commentaries are given by al-Zamakhshari,[33] al-Razi,[34] and Ibn Kathir.[35] Al-Zamakhshari notably provides a rationale for why this early practice of reviling idols was proscribed, in answer to the possible query that this proscription appears to be contrary to the general ethical injunction to prevent what is objectionable (*al-nahy 'an al-munkar*); and polytheism, one may aver, is certainly objectionable from the Islamic perspective. The answer is that if an otherwise-moral act were to result in a greater wrong, then it is no longer to be considered a moral act but something that should be interdicted.[36] A similar rationale is given by al-Razi in response to the same hypothetical question.[37]

The modern exegete Muhammad 'Abduh (d. 1905) reproduces many of the essential points made by his premodern predecessors in connection with these two verses. But he goes further than his predecessors in asserting that Qur'an 6:107 makes clear that God, despite being the Guardian and Overseer of humanity, does not force humans to believe in and obey him. If he were to do so, humans would no longer be humans but become a different species; that is to say, humans by virtue of their humanness have freedom of choice in religious matters. This is therefore doubly true of the Prophet who was not sent as the guardian of humans. All the prophets through time, continues 'Abduh, have been "summoners not overseers; guides not tyrants, obligated to not restrict even by an inch the God-given freedom of humans in matters of faith." He dismisses Ibn 'Abbas' reported opinion that this verse had been abrogated by the sword

32. Al-Tabari, *Jami'*, 5:304–5.

33. Al-Zamakhshari, *Kashshaf*, 2:385.

34. Al-Razi, *Tafsir*, 5:108–11.

35. Ibn Kathir, *Tafsir*, 2:156.

36. Al-Zamakhshari, *Kashshaf*, 2:385.

37. Al-Razi, *Tafsir*, 5:110.

verse, saying this is not the opinion of the majority. This verse may have been revealed before the Medinan period when the Prophet became the ruler of the Muslim polity, but its equivalent exists in Qur'an 9:79, which is Medinan: "Whoever believes in the Messenger has obeyed God, and whoever turns his back, we have not sent you as a guardian (*hafizan*) over them."[38]

'Abduh further asserts that this verse must be understood as containing a general prohibition against reviling any one's religion or shade of belief. Thus Muslims may not insult Christians and vice versa, Sunnis may not revile the Shi'a and vice versa, and so forth. Those who revile other people do so, he says, out of "love for one's self and culpable ignorance."[39] 'Abduh makes a distinction between valid criticism and gratuitous insult intended to give offence. Therefore one may describe the idols of the polytheists as "neither causing harm nor benefit, or capable of drawing near and interceding," which is a merely descriptive account and in itself not offensive and therefore not proscribed. However, like a number of his predecessors, he maintains that even if this valid criticism were to cause greater harm, then one should refrain from it.[40]

It is noteworthy that 'Abduh quotes Qur'an 29:46 in this context. By invoking this verse here, he is clearly implying that the injunction contained in it to debate with the People of the Book with what is better has a broader applicability to all interreligious and intrareligious conversations. Considered together, these two verses—Qur'an 6:108 and Qur'an 29:46—create for him a moral imperative to conduct dialogue with all religious groups with congeniality and without recourse to offensive and harsh language.[41]

Conclusion

The Qur'anic verses I discussed were selected for their relevance to relations between Muslims and non-Muslims. From a contemporary vantage point, most of the premodern exegetes I surveyed appear not to do

38. Rashid Rida, *Tafsir*, 7:548–49.
39. Ibid., 7:549.
40. Ibid., 7:551–52.
41. Ibid., 7:550.

full justice to the wide-ranging implications of this verse for interfaith dialogue, and a few even tend to undermine the irenic potential of these verses. Thus in his commentary on Qur'an 29:46 which many of us today tend to privilege as promoting, even mandating, courteous and respectful interfaith encounters, al-Tabari disappointingly reads into it an unequal relationship between Muslims and the People of the Book and the requirement of the former to instruct the latter in "correct" doctrine.

It can be argued that this indictment is somewhat unfair because al-Tabari's historical circumstances were not conducive to the kind of open and honest interfaith dialogic conversations that are possible today. In different periods, other exegetes, like al-Zamakhshari and al-Razi, for example, would discern in this verse and in others a more irenic and universal injunction to cultivate gentler respectful relations among religious communities. Al-Zamakhshari's and Razi's views are more strikingly congenial to us. After all, easier physical and intellectual access to other people's cultures and thought has made many of us in the twenty-first century more receptive to different ways of looking at the world and to interaction with one another on an egalitarian basis. The constellation of verses I examined above could therefore provide the interpretive stimulus today for the emergence of a genuine pluralism in Muslim ethical and moral thinking vis-à-vis other religions and peoples.

And we see this hermeneutic process already underway to a certain extent in a number of academic and popular venues. A case in point is provided by the recent exegesis of the Qur'anic phrase *kalimat sawa'* in the "Common Word" statement issued by 138 Muslim scholars and clerics addressed to Christians in 2007. All the exegetes we surveyed are in agreement that this phrase is primarily a reference to "a word of justice," which in itself is open to interpretation. Justice is thus variously interpreted as "sincerity" by Muqatil, as "upright" and as an assertion of the oneness of God by al-Tabari and al-Zamakhshari; as "fair" and "equitable" by al-Razi, Ibn Kathir, and Muhammad 'Abduh. With interpretive creativity, the signatories to the "Common Word" statement may be regarded as having distilled these various significations of justice into the pithy commandment "Love God and your neighbor." What after all could be more upright, sincere, and common than this commandment which resonates immediately with Abrahamic communities and, reaching even further, with all religious and ethical people? Such interpretive discernment in the context of dialogue is born of deep reflection on the whys and wherefores of interfaith encounters and necessity. In our fractious and fragile post–September 11 world, a common word must of necessity be not just a "good word" but a "better word" that establishes commonalities, heals relations, and offers the prospect of much more than was previously imaginable in interpersonal and intercommunal relations. "Repel evil with what is better," adjures the Qur'an; the "better" in this case, as movingly explained by al-Zamakhshari, means going the extra mile in abnegating one's self and doing good to the other, so that we may become inclined to praise our enemies when they revile us or save the life of their child when they take the life of our own. "But none attains to it [sc. to such a state of self-abnegation and selfless offering of charity in the face of harm]," continues Qur'an 41:35, "except for those who are forbearing and of great fortune."

Not all exegetes, as we saw, counseled such a spirit of forbearance and forgiveness towards those non-Muslims who caused Muslims harm. Some specifically asserted that these conciliatory verses had been abrogated by later revelations contained in Qur'an 9:5 or 9:29, the so-called sword verses, which when historically decontextualized could be understood (and so has been) to permit fighting against non-Muslims merely on account of their theological differences with Muslims. As noted by Muhammad 'Abduh, this position of the pro-abrogation school of thought is revealed to be self-serving and rather arbitrary, for it ignores other verses in the same Qur'anic chapter, and which are therefore also late revelations, that counsel Muslims to take no punitive action against those who refuse to accept Islam.[42] As the exegeses of most of the commentators surveyed above demonstrates (notably al-Razi's insightful commentary on the term *ahl al-kitab*), the Qur'an displays affection and approval for righteous Jews and Christians and counsels Muslims to establish peaceful and respectful relations with non-Muslims in general who show no inclination for accepting Islam but who are otherwise amiable towards Muslims and cause them no harm.[43] Non-Muslims who perpetrate acts of injustice and resort

42. For example, Qur'an 9:6 states, "If anyone of the idolaters seeks your protection (addressing Muhammad), then protect him so that he may hear the word of God, and afterward transport him to a place of safety."

43. Thus Qur'an 60:8 states, "God does not forbid you from being kind and equitable to those who have neither made war on you on account of your religion nor driven you from your homes. God loves those who are equitable."

to physical hostility towards Muslims *qua* Muslims—that is, violently encroach upon the right of Muslims to practice their religion freely, and who remain intractable in their violent opposition to Muslims despite the conciliatory efforts of the latter, merit a different treatment, however. A number of Qur'anic verses grant Muslims the right to retaliate in self-defense in such cases, the discussion of which is beyond the purview of this article.[44] Such physical self-defense is an important manifestation of the overall struggle—*jihad*—to uphold what is good and right over what is bad and wrong incumbent on every believer.[45]

Finally we may ask: what does the Qur'an intend by encouraging dialogue, particularly among the Abrahamic faiths? Dialogue for its own sake is a laudable activity—it promotes goodwill, trust, and conviviality, always a better alternative to mutual distrust and hostility. Respect should be extended to non-Abrahamic communities as well, as clearly asserted in Qur'an 6:107–8, which elicits respect for Muslims in turn. Dialogue conducing to mutual understanding and knowledge is even better—it is a step beyond the establishment of respect and trust, for knowledge of one another leads to enduring and positive changes, cognitively and concretely, in one's attitudes and interactions with the "other." Some exegetes in our survey noted this beneficial consequence of interfaith encounters. Ibn Zayd, for instance, as reported by Ibn Kathir, highlighted the insight (*istibsar*) to be gained by Muslims in respectfully engaging particularly the People of the Book in conversation and attempting thereby to find common ground among fellow monotheists.

Moving beyond the Abrahamic communities, a more general injunction to engage with all peoples everywhere, irrespective of faith, ethnicity, culture, etc., so that mutual knowledge and understanding will ensue is contained further in another verse from the Qur'an (49:13), which states, "O humankind! We have created you from a male and a female, and made

---

44. For example, Qur'an 22:39–40, which states, "Permission is given to those who fight because they have been oppressed, and God is able to help them. These are they who have been wrongfully expelled from their homes merely for saying 'God is our Lord.' If God had not restrained some people by means of others, monasteries, churches, synagogues, and mosques in which God's name is mentioned frequently would have been destroyed. Indeed God comes to the aid of those who come to His aid; verily He is powerful and mighty."

45. See, for example, my monograph, *Striving in the Path of God: Jihad and Martyrdom in Islamic Thought and Praxis*, in progress.

you into nations and tribes, that you might get to know one another. The noblest of you in God's sight is the one who is most righteous." This verse clearly advocates that humans should proactively get to know one another (Ar. *li-ta 'arafu*), irrespective of backgrounds, and reminds us that individuals find esteem before God only on the basis of piety. On account of length constraints, we cannot engage in a detailed analysis of this verse, but it is clearly relevant to a holistic discussion of Qur'anic perspectives on dialogic encounters. Because of the more parochial circumstances of their own time, medieval exegetes tended to gloss the verb *ta'arafu* in this verse to mean "learning about each other's tribal and similar affiliational backgrounds in order to establish bonds of kinship and affection." In explanation of *ta'arafu*, al-Tabari, for example, glosses it as commanding people to get to know one another so that they may discover their bonds of kinship. He warns that knowledge of such kinship is not meant to induce any sense of superiority but rather "to bring you closer to God, for indeed only the most pious among you is the most honorable."[46] Ibn Kathir, in his exegesis of this term, cites a *hadith* in which the Prophet states, "Learn about each other's pedigrees so as to establish your bloodties, for it is such ties which lead to love among people."[47]

Today we can expand the exegetical purview of the verb *ta'arafu* to extend to not just our blood-relatives but all the coresidents of the global village we are now beginning to regard as our shared home, thus realizing more fully the pluralist potential of this verse. In our contemporary circumstances, Qur'an 49:13 may be understood as representing the overall objective of our interfaith and intercultural conversations—to broaden the common ground we inhabit as human beings and to learn about one another as inhabitants of different countries, cultures, and faith communities, with an appreciation for these differences that enrich our lives. Such a dialogic process also leads to self-disclosure and self-understanding, a necessary correlate of this process of mutual illumination and transformation. Finally, dialogue is ultimately about the dissolution of epistemological and cognitive boundaries that separate us from one another—and thus ultimately from God.

46. Al-Tabari, *Jami' al-bayan*, 11:398.
47. Ibn Kathir, *Tafsir*, 4:218.

7

Dialogue and Discernment in the Qur'an

Mustafa Abu Sway

> And do not dispute with the People of the Book except by what is
> best, except those of them who act unjustly, and say: We believe in
> that which has been revealed to us and revealed to you, and our
> God and your God is One, and to Him do we submit.[1]

This paper explores the possibility of truth and goodness in Jewish
and Christian Scriptures, as expressed in the Islamic worldview, which
is based on two primary sources, the Qur'an and the traditions of the
Prophet Muhammad. This is to say that certain literature such as Rumi's
poetry, despite its recent popularity in the West, is not representative
of Islam per se. Muslim participants in interfaith dialogue who restrict
their contribution to readings from Rumi's poetry or any other nonrepresentative literature[2] are depriving the other participants the chance to

---

1. Qur'an 29:45.

2. Representative literature (i.e., normative sources of the Islamic worldview) includes
the Qur'an, and the most authentic compendia of hadith, Sahih Al-Bukhari and Sahih
Muslim. Other compendia of hadith, such as Sunan Abu Dawud, Sunan Al-Tirmidhi,
Sunan Al-Nasa'i, and Sunan Ibn Majah do include sound prophetic traditions and other
less than sound traditions that are known to scholars of hadith. While it is almost impossible to list all specific titles of nonrepresentative literature, such literature does include
poetry, fiction, history books, biographies, and many Sufi works, to name a few kinds.
Islamic literature such as books of Tafsir (i.e., exegesis of the Qur'an) falls somewhere in
between—not everything included in Tafsir is representative, especially when it includes
Israeliyat.

know the core theological issues in Islam. A serious interfaith dialogue will highlight commonalities without ignoring serious differences. This approach is different than the all-embracing, thematically eclectic and politically correct dialogue as found in some circles that deliberately drop the Islamic sources.

Islam essentially embodies and augments the history of revelation, recognizes all prophets and their original messages, and not necessarily the postrevelational theological constructs that emerged afterwards. In the interest of serious interfaith dialogue, a few examples of difficult theological issues and differences between Islam, on the hand, and Judaism and Christianity, on the other, are discussed below.

Islam constitutes the last phase in the history of divine revelation, beginning with Adam,[3] and ending with the Prophet Muhammad, who is described in the Qur'an as the "Seal of the Prophets."[4] The word "Islam" is used in two senses: the most common use refers to the religion revealed to the Prophet Muhammad, and the second refers to the history of revelation as a history of Islam, where all the prophets are considered Muslims, surrendering their will to God:

> And strive hard in [the way of] Allah, [such] a striving a is due to Him; He has chosen you and has not laid upon you any hardship in religion; the faith of your father Ibrahim; He named you *Muslims* before and in this, that the Messenger may be a bearer of witness to you, and you may be bearers of witness to the people; therefore keep up prayer and pay the poor-rate and hold fast by Allah; He is your Guardian; how excellent the Guardian and how excellent the Helper![5]

Two of the Islamic articles of faith cover belief in all prophets and belief in their revealed books, on equal footing: "The messenger believes in what has been revealed to him from his Lord, and [so do] the believers; they all believe in Allah and His angels and His books and His messengers; We make no difference between any of His messengers; and they say: We hear and obey, our Lord! Thy forgiveness [do we crave], and to Thee is the

---

3. "Then Adam received from his Lord words [of revelation], and He relented toward him . . ." Qur'an 2:37.

4. Qur'an 33:40.

5. Qur'an 22:78.

eventual course."[6] All previously revealed messages, because they all come from the same divine source, have also identical theological content with that of the Qur'an: "And verily We have raised in every nation a messenger, [proclaiming]: Serve Allah and shun false gods . . ."[7] Another verse that declares Islam as being the same religion that was revealed before connects the vocation of Muhammad as a prophet to that of Noah, Abraham, Moses, and Jesus, who are considered in Islamic literature as the prophets of "firm resolution,"[8] as far as conveying their message is concerned: "He has ordained for you that religion which He commended unto Noah, and that which We revealed to you [Muhammad], and that which We commended unto Abraham and Moses and Jesus, saying: Establish the religion, and be not divided therein . . ."[9] This inclusive and organic relationship between all prophets is reflected in a tradition that was reported by Abu Hurayra, one of the Prophet's prominent companions. He said:

> The Messenger of Allah—May His peace and blessings be upon him—said: "Verily, my relationship with the prophets who preceded me is similar to a man who skillfully built a beautiful house and perfected it, except for the place of one brick [that was left empty] in one of the corners. People visited [this house], marveled at its beauty and said: "Why not put the brick [in its place]." The Prophet said: "I am that brick and I am the Seal of the Prophets."[10]

This tradition shows that all prophets were part of the same structure, which was brought to completion and perfection with the last phase of revelation: "This day have I perfected your religion for you and completed My favor on you, and chosen for you Islam as a religion . . ."[11] Islam, therefore, is the only religion accepted in the Qur'an: "And whoever desires a religion other than Islam, it shall not be accepted from him, and in the hereafter he shall be one of the losers."[12] There is no doubt that the followers of earlier prophets (as long as they were faithful to the teachings

6. Qur'an 2:285.

7. Qur'an 16:36.

8. Qur'an 46:35.

9. Qur'an 42:13.

10. Muhammad Ibn Ismail Al-Bukhari, *Sahih*, Hadith #3271; online: http://hadith.al-islam.com.

11. Qur'an 5:3.

12. Qur'an 3:85.

of their Prophets, and unless a new prophet was raised amongst them which necessitates believing in him and the new message, if there is a new one) are considered true submitters to God. This might help in explaining the following verse: "Surely those who believe, and those who are Jews, and the Christians, and the Sabians, whoever believes in Allah and the Last day and does good, they shall have their reward from their Lord, and there is no fear for them, nor shall they grieve."[13] While theology, in stressing monotheism, was always identical in all originally revealed messages, the Law (i.e., *Shari'ah*) is acknowledged as being different:

> And We have revealed to you the Book with the truth, verifying what is before it of the Book and a guardian over it, therefore judge between them by what Allah has revealed, and do not follow their desires [to turn away] from the truth that has come to you; for every one of you did We appoint a *law* (*shir'ah*) and a way, and if Allah had pleased He would have made you [all] a single people, but that He might try you in what He gave you, therefore strive with one another to hasten to virtuous deeds; to Allah is your return, of all [of you], so He will let you know that in which you differed.[14]

The essential story of humanity is that of God creating a viceregent on earth.[15] Every human being has the potential to be a caliph in the original sense of the word *khalifah*, which has to do with what is positive, according to revelation. Life on earth is nothing but a transit station situated between the expulsion from the garden and the Day of Judgment. And, as long as one is on earth, one should be at the service of humanity at large. The Prophets help in guiding humanity to a proper and favorable return.

Belief in All the Prophets

It is part of the Islamic creed to believe in all twenty-five prophets mentioned in the Qur'an; many of them are mentioned in the following verses:

13. Qur'an 2:62.

14. Qur'an 5:48.

15. "And Behold, thy Lord said to the angels: 'I will create a viceregent (*Khalifah*) on earth . . .'" (Qur'an 2:30).

> That is Our argument. We gave it unto Abraham against his folk. We raise unto degrees of wisdom whom We will. Lo! thy Lord is Wise, Aware. And We bestowed upon him Isaac and Jacob; each of them We guided; and Noah did We guide aforetime; and of his seed [We guided] David and Solomon and Job and Joseph and Moses and Aaron. Thus do We reward the good. And Zachariah and John and Jesus and Elias, each one [of them] was of the righteous. And Ishmael and Elisha and Jonah and Lot, each one [of them] did We prefer above [Our] creatures, With some of their forefathers and their offspring and their brethren; and We chose them and guided them unto a straight path.[16]

When a story of a prophet is mentioned in the Bible, but not in the Qur'an, Muslim theologians could neither confirm it nor deny it, unless it contradicts an established Islamic theological principle such as prophets' being infallible (they could make judgmental mistakes, but could not commit grave sins), or an established story in the Qur'an. The latter position is rooted in the Qur'anic position that the previous revelations suffered from various forms of human editing, and that in the prophetic tradition[17] it is possible to convey the narratives of the children of Israel without confirming the truth of the story if it is not confirmed in the Qur'an. This latter position allowed room for the emergence of a body of literature comprising the stories of People of the Book, called *Israeliyat*. These stories infiltrated many Islamic sciences, such as the exegesis of the Qur'an. Israeliyat led to many studies that led to a modern process to de-Israelize Islamic literature.

The issue of previous revelation suffering from human editing and from the vagaries of transmission proved to be a point of contention in interfaith circles. The changes took many forms, oral[18] and written: "Woe, then, to those who write the book with their hands and then say: This is from Allah, so that they may take for it a small price; therefore woe to them for what their hands have written and woe to them for what they earn."[19] The raison d'être for sending prophets, one after the other, was to confirm divine revelation, especially when the prophets were rejected:

16. Qur'an 6:83–87.

17. "Report [the stories] of the Children of Israel, without guilt." Abu Dawud, *Sunan*, Hadith #3177. Online: http://hadith.al-islam.com.

18. Qur'an 4:46.

19. Qur'an 2:79.

"Then We sent Our messengers one after another; whenever there came to a people their messenger, they called him a liar, so We made some of them follow others and We made them stories; so away with a people who do not believe!"[20]

An example of an important difference in the narrative of a story that is mentioned in the Bible and the Qur'an is that of the angels who visited Abraham on their way to punish the people of Lot. They took anthropomorphic forms, but their angelic nature did not change. Abraham offered them hospitality; they ate the food in the Bible: "And Abraham ran to the herd, and fetched a calf tender and good, and gave it to a young man; and he hurried to dress it. And he took butter, and milk, and the calf which he had dressed, and set it before them; and he stood by them under the tree, and they did eat."[21] They refrained from eating in the Qur'an: "And Our messengers came unto Abraham with good news. They said: Peace! He answered: Peace! and delayed not to bring a roasted calf. And when he saw their hands reached not to it, he mistrusted them and conceived a fear of them. They said: Fear not! Lo! we are sent unto the folk of Lot."[22] How to deal with contradicting stories (and they are many)? Understandably, the Qur'an presents itself as having the upper hand vis-à-vis previous revelations:

> And We have revealed to you the Book with the truth, verifying what is before it of the Book and a *guardian* over it, therefore judge between them by what Allah has revealed, and do not follow their desires [to turn away] from the truth that has come to you; for every one of you did We appoint a law and a way, and if Allah had pleased He would have made you [all] a single people, but that He might try you in what He gave you, therefore strive with one another to hasten to virtuous deeds; to Allah is your return, of all [of you], so He will let you know that in which you differed.[23]

There is a Christian postrevelational theological construct that interprets the "three" men (i.e., angels) in the same story as alluding to the three persons of the Trinity. The Qur'an, in this case, has an absolute rejection of these theological constructs and an extensive refutation of the concept

20. Qur'an 23:44.
21. Genesis 18:7–8 (AKJV).
22. Qur'an 11:69–70.
23. Qur'an 5:48.

of the Trinity and the Sonship of Jesus Christ, temporal or eternal.[24] To begin with, as a part of the notion of the oneness of God, and because only God knows Himself, nothing could be said about the essence of God except that which is revealed. The Qur'an addresses the essence of God in negation, for it is not possible for humanity to go beyond that: "there is nothing whatever like unto Him."[25] As far as Jesus Christ is concerned, he is the word of God to Mary, the only woman to be mentioned by name in the Qur'an. Chapter 19 is named after her, and she was chosen over all women on earth:

> And when the angels said: O Mary! Lo! Allah hath chosen thee and made thee pure, and hath preferred thee above [all] the women of creation. O Mary! Be obedient to thy Lord, prostrate thyself and bow with those who bow [in worship]. This is of the tidings of things hidden. We reveal it unto thee [Muhammad]. Thou wast not present with them when they threw their pens [to know] which of them should be the guardian of Mary, nor wast thou present with them when they quarreled [thereupon]. [And remember] when the angels said: O Mary! Lo! Allah giveth thee glad tidings of a word from him, whose name is the Messiah, Jesus, son of Mary, illustrious in the world and the Hereafter, and one of those brought near [unto Allah].[26]

Jesus Christ, who is also described as the Messiah in the Qur'an, performed miracles by leave of God:

> When Allah saith: O Jesus, son of Mary! Remember My favour unto thee and unto thy mother; how I strengthened thee with the holy Spirit, so that thou spakest unto mankind in the cradle as in maturity; and how I taught thee the Scripture and Wisdom and the Torah and the Gospel; and how thou didst shape of clay as it were the likeness of a bird by My permission, and didst blow upon it and it was a bird by My permission, and thou didst heal him who was born blind and the leper by My permission; and how thou didst raise the dead by My permission; and how I restrained the Children of Israel from (harming) thee when thou camest unto

---

24. See the following verses from the Qur'an for the rejection of the "sonship": 2:116; 10:68; 17:111; 18:4; 19:88–92; 21:26; 39:4; 72:3; 112:1–4.

25. Qur'an 42:11.

26. Qur'an 3:42–45.

them with clear proofs, and those of them who disbelieved ex-
claimed: This is naught else than mere magic.[27]

Ultimately, Jesus Christ, who said about himself in the Qur'an: "And peace
on me on the day I was born, and on the day I die, and on the day I am
raised to life,"[28] was raised from among his people when they plotted harm
against him; it appeared as if they have crucified him, but he was not:

> And because of their saying: We slew the Messiah, Jesus son of
> Mary, Allah's messenger—they slew him not nor crucified him,
> but it appeared so unto them; and lo! those who disagree concern-
> ing it are in doubt thereof; they have no knowledge thereof save
> pursuit of a conjecture; they slew him not for certain. But Allah
> took him up unto Himself. Allah was ever Mighty, Wise. There
> is not one of the People of the Scripture but will believe in him
> before his death, and on the Day of Resurrection he will be a wit-
> ness against them.[29]

God created Jesus Christ, and if being born without a father is difficult
for people to accept, the Qur'an refers to the example of Adam; he neither
had a father, nor a mother: "Lo! the likeness of Jesus with Allah is as the
likeness of Adam. He created him of dust, then He said unto him: Be! and
he is."[30] To attribute any divine attribute to anything or anyone, other than
God, is an act of disbelief:

> Certainly they disbelieve who say: Surely Allah is the third [per-
> son] of the three; and there is no god but the one Allah, and if they
> desist not from what they say, a painful chastisement shall befall
> those among them who disbelieve.[31]

> . . . and the Christians say: The Messiah is the son of Allah; these
> are the words of their mouths; they imitate the saying of those who
> disbelieved before; may Allah destroy them; how they are turned
> away![32]

27. Qur'an 5:110.
28. Qur'an 19:33.
29. Qur'an 4:157–159.
30. Qur'an 3:59.
31. Qur'an 5:73.
32. Qur'an 9:30.

All three—God, the spirit of the holy,[33] and Jesus Christ—are mentioned in the same verse in the Qur'an as separate entities:

> Of those messengers, some of whom We have caused to excel others, and of whom there are some unto whom Allah spoke, while some of them He exalted [above others] in degree; and We gave Jesus, son of Mary, clear proofs [of Allah's Sovereignty] and We supported him with the spirit of the holy . . .[34]

Another example of change is that of the Prophet David's Zabur, which is usually translated as "Psalms": "Surely, We revealed to you as We revealed to Noah and the prophets after him, as We revealed to Abraham and Ishmael and Isaac and Jacob and the tribes, and Jesus and Job and Jonah and Aaron and Solomon, and as We imparted unto David the *Psalms*."[35] This is a problematic translation because it conveys the message as if Muslims believe in the existing Psalms, with all its contents. I do not need to go further than the following disturbing example that should not have been considered as Scripture:

> O Daughter of Babylon, doomed to destruction,
> happy is he who repays you for what you have done to us
>
> *he who seizes your infants*
> *and dashes them against the rocks.*[36]

Dashing infants against the rocks cannot be construed as divine revelation. It is a clear violation of one of the Ten Commandments. Such violence is incompatible with what God wants from humanity. This is not a theological position that is detached from reality; I did single out this example from Psalms because of the hundreds of Palestinian children who were killed right after Christmas (2008) in Gaza. I am reluctant to call it post-Gazacaust theology, but that is where my thoughts are at this stage in my life. There are, on the other hand, parts of biblical revelations that are included in the Qur'an, such as the following verses:

---

33. Almost everyone else, including Yousef Ali, Pickthal, and Shakir, translate "*ruh al-Qudus*" as the holy spirit.

34. Qur'an 2:253.

35. Qur'an 4:136.

36. Psalm 137:8–9.

> On that account: We ordained for the Children of Israel that if any one slew a person—unless it be for murder or for spreading mischief in the land—it would be as if he slew the whole people: and if any one saved a life, it would be as if he saved the life of the whole people. Then although there came to them Our messengers with clear signs, yet, even after that, many of them continued to commit excesses in the land.[37]

The Gospel, from an Islamic perspective, confirms the Torah, and the Qur'an confirms both:

> And We caused Jesus, son of Mary, to follow in their footsteps, confirming that which was [revealed] before him in the Torah, and We bestowed on him the Gospel wherein is guidance and a light, confirming that which was [revealed] before it in the Torah—a guidance and an admonition unto those who ward off [evil].[38]

> Say: O people of the Book! you follow no good till you keep up the Torah and the Injil and that which is revealed to you from your Lord; and surely that which has been revealed to you from your Lord shall make many of them increase in inordinacy and unbelief; grieve not therefore for the unbelieving people.[39]

People of the Book

The very description of "People of the Book" ensures a special status in the Islamic worldview. What I have deciphered for many years is that this categorization softens the otherness of Jews and Christians, which prompted me to advance an Islamic theology of soft-otherness. There are several positive aspects associated with the legal implication that include different forms of socializing between both sides:

> This day [all] the good things are allowed to you; and the food of those who have been given the Book is lawful for you and your food is lawful for them; and the chaste from among the believing women and the chaste from among those who have been given

37. Qur'an 5:32.
38. Qur'an 5:46.
39. Qur'an 5:68.

the Book before you [are lawful for you]; when you have given them their dowries, taking [them] in marriage, not fornicating nor taking them for paramours in secret; and whoever denies faith, his work indeed is of no account, and in the hereafter he shall be one of the losers.[40]

One might explore the hundreds of instances in the Qur'an that reinforce the relationship with the People of the Book. A major story of the Qur'an is that of the children of Israel, including the Prophet Moses, who is mentioned by name 139 times, while, for comparison, the name of the Prophet Muhammad is mentioned only four times.

One of the most important aspects of the People of the Book's life in the Islamic state is that they were autonomous. (They still retain their independent religious courts in many parts of the Muslim world today.) In the Covenant of Medina, which the Prophet concluded with the Jewish tribes of Medina and its surroundings, the Jews, beginning with the Jewish tribe of Banu 'Awf, formed one "Ummah" with the Muslims.[41] Nevertheless, the covenant granted them freedom of religion and the right to be economically independent. Indeed, the People of the Book are required in the Qur'an to live according to their own laws: "Say O People of the Scripture! Ye have naught [of guidance] till ye observe the Torah and the Gospel and that which was revealed unto you from your Lord. That which is revealed unto thee [Muhammad] from thy Lord is certain to increase the contumacy and disbelief of many of them. But grieve not for the disbelieving folk."[42] While "People of the Book," as a category, covers both Jews and Christians, it should be noted that according to the Qur'an they are not equidistant from Muslims:

Thou wilt find the most vehement of mankind in hostility to those who believe [to be] the Jews and the idolaters. And thou wilt find the nearest of them in affection to those [Muslims] who believe [to be] those who say: Lo! We are Christians. That is because there are among them priests and monks, and because they are not proud. When they listen to that which hath been revealed unto the messengers, thou seest their eyes overflow with tears because of their

40. Qur'an 5:5.

41. Ibn Hisham, *Al-Sirah Al-Nabawaiyyah* (Al-Mansurah: Maktabat Al-Iman, 1995) vol. 2, 98.

42. Qur'an 5:68.

recognition of the Truth. They say: Our Lord, we believe. Inscribe us as among the witnesses.[43]

Those non-People of the Book, nonmonotheistic religions, such as Hinduism and Buddhism, are considered cases of polytheism and pantheism, respectively. One of the major criteria for acceptance remains whether God is transcendent (nothing is like unto Him) without associating anyone or anything with Him. Association (i.e., *shirk*) is the only unforgivable sin in the Qur'an.[44]

Is Previously Revealed Law Applicable to Muslims?

This is an important question that is asked in Islamic philosophy of law (i.e., *Usul Al-Fiqh*). Muslim scholars differed in their positions when answering this question, with the position of many scholars stating that unless the previously revealed law is abrogated, the law is still applicable when confirmed in the Qur'an. According to Abdul-Wahhab Khallaf, "For most of the scholars of the Hanafi school of jurisprudence, and some scholars of the Maliki and the Shafi`i schools, it becomes a law for us, and we have to follow it and implement it, as long as it has been narrated to us, and as long as there is nothing in our law that abrogates it, for it is amongst the divine laws that Allah has revealed through His messengers."[45] Fasting, in the Qur'an, for example, is made imperative in the light of fasting among the followers of previous prophets: "O you who believe! Fasting is prescribed for you, as it was prescribed for those before you, so that you may guard [against evil]."[46] One legal aspect that has been abrogated for Muslims is Sabbath, though the Qur'an does mention that the children of Israel who violated the Sabbath were met with divine punishment: "The Sabbath was ordained only for those who differed about it,

---

43. Qur'an 5:82–83.

44. "Surely Allah does not forgive that anything should be associated with Him, and forgives what is besides that to whomsoever He pleases; and whoever associates anything with Allah, he devises indeed a great sin." Qur'an 4:48.

45. Abdul-Wahhab Khallaf, `*Ilm Usul Al-Fiqh* (Istanbul: EDA Nesriyat, 1968) 94.

46. Qur'an 2:183.

and most surely your Lord will judge between them on the resurrection day concerning that about which they differed."[47]

The Modern Scene

Dialogue is employed as a tool that could establish social cohesion and healthy relationship between the nations; between the North and the South, the East and the West; between Judaism, Christianity, and Islam, and between them and other religions as well. Dialogue aims at peaceful *convivencia* that respects the right to be different. This paradigm, comprising interfaith and civilizational dialogue is the antithesis of wars and conflicts. One should highlight the fact that this paradigm cannot be implemented in the shadows of imperialism or under direct colonial rule. Participation in dialogue should be based on equality and should not be used to patronize the other!

The Islamic worldview presents humanity as a family united through the same parents, rich with commonalities, and yet has many differences. Though many of these differences are postrevelational constructs created by human beings, the Qur'an recognizes that some of these differences are positively created by God, and, therefore, they command a pluralistic paradigm: "O mankind! Lo! We have created you male and female, and have made you nations and tribes *that you may know one another*. Lo! the noblest of you, in the sight of Allah, is the best in conduct/piety. Lo! Allah is Knower, Aware."[48] This verse is clear in dismissing superiority because of natural differences, the kind of ideology found in Nietzsche's concept of *Übermensch* in *Thus Spoke Zarathustra*, which was interpreted as aiming at biological superiority. There is no dialogue with supremacists who will ultimately translate their ideology, if they have the power, into ethnic cleansing. Claims of natural superiority are contrary to God's plan for humanity. God did not create a hierarchy of human beings based on their physiological functions or physical appearances, and there is definitely no divine reward for the natural things that are created by God. There is no reward for being male, and there is no reward for being white.

47. Qur'an 16:124.
48. Qur'an 49:13 (italics added).

Rather than being preoccupied with appearances, people are invited to "know one another." Knowing the other is possible through engaging the other in dialogue. Speaking in the name of the other, as in Orientalism, could at times deliberately create misinformation and stereotyped images, especially when speaking from a Eurocentric position that does not reconcile itself with the possibility of a wholesome existence outside its terms of reference.

"That you may know one another" was raised as a slogan representing *convivencia* by Muslim scholars and intellectuals who were alarmed by Samuel Huntington's clash-of-civilizations, an end-of-the-cold-war scenario that promoted cultural differences as the source of conflicts between the civilizations, rather than real economic and political interests. Clashes are not inevitable; they are imposed upon history. Conflicts reflect the dark side of human creativity. There is no lack of Islamophobes who continue to present Islam as the enemy par excellence. It is in their personal interest to keep their societies and the world polarized. This egalitarian ethos that does not give credit to ethnic or natural differences has been confirmed in the following tradition of the Prophet Muhammad: "O People! Verily your Lord is one, and your father is one. Neither an Arab is better than a non-Arab nor a non-Arab over an Arab. And no white over black and no black over white, except for piety. . ."[49] The Qur'an does not neutralize natural phenomena, it celebrates them: "And of His signs are the creation of the heavens and the earth, and the difference of your languages and colors. Lo! Herein indeed are portents for people of knowledge."[50] This verse proves that racial differences do not constitute a criterion for legitimate hierarchy. The respect for the other as is, regardless of her ethnic or cultural background, constitutes a firm foundation for social behavior in Islam.

God and Dialogue

God is Omnipotent, and he has the power to force his creatures to do whatever he wills. Nevertheless, on more than one occasion in the Qur'an, he chose to have a dialogue with the angels, Satan, and Adam. The first

49. Ahmad Ibn Hanbal, *Musnad*, Hadith #22391; online: http://hadith.al-islam.com.

50. Qur'an 30:22.

story in the Qur'an begins with a dialogue in which God speaks with the angels: "And when your Lord said to the angels, I am going to place in the earth a viceregent, they said: Wilt Thou place in it such as shall make mischief in it and shed blood, and we celebrate Thy praise and extol Thy holiness? He said: Surely I know what you do not know."[51] The dialogue with the angels continues after the creation of Adam until they recognize that their knowledge is limited to that which God has taught them; then the dialogue continues with Adam: "He said: O Adam! inform them of their names. Then when he had informed them of their names, He said: Did I not say to you that I surely know what is unknown to you in the heavens and the earth and [that] I know what you manifest and what you hide?"[52] The dialogue is extended to Satan; the angels were commanded to respect Adam by prostrating to him; they obeyed, Satan refused: "[God] said: What hindered you so that you did not prostrate when I commanded you? [Satan] said: I am better than he: Thou hast created me of fire, while him Thou didst create of dust. He said: Then get forth from this [state], for it does not befit you to behave proudly therein. Go forth, therefore, surely you are of the abject ones."[53] Satan was given respite until the Day of Judgment continuing the temptation. Dialogue, therefore, is one way of countering Satan.

The Prophetic model also emphasized dialogue. The very nature of his vocation as a prophet, which requires conveying the message of Islam to all people, led the Prophet Muhammad to visit Bayt Al-Madaris (i.e., Beit Hamidrash) to have dialogue with the Jews.[54] He also welcomed the delegation of the Christians of Najran, a region in the southwestern part of the Arabian Peninsula, in the mosque of Medina. Theological differences between Muslims and Christians in Arabia were never translated into any conflicts. This Prophetic model of *convivencia* manifested itself historically in several places including Palestine and Andalusia.

The moral of these stories stresses the importance of dialogue, for there is something good in dialogue, even with the enemies, provided that dialogue itself is not a substitute for restitution, where injustices prevail,

51. Qur'an 2:30.

52. Qur'an 2:33.

53. Qur'an 7:12–13.

54. Ibn Hisham, *Al-Sirah Al-Nabawaiyyah* (Al-Mansurah: Maktabat Al-Iman, 1995) vol. 2, 133.

especially at the hands of state actors. The Qur'an recognizes dialogue among the best methods to repel animosity: "And not alike are the good and the evil. Repel [evil] with what is best, when lo! He between whom and you was enmity would be as if he were a warm friend."[55]

Dialogue with Humility and Freedom of Religion as Divine Commandment

Using grammatically imperative language, the Qur'an commands dialogue with non-Muslims using the best possible way: "Call to the way of your Lord with wisdom and goodly exhortation, and have disputations with them in the best manner; surely your Lord best knows those who go astray from His path, and He knows best those who follow the right way."[56] A Muslim responding to this verse ought to continuously reform her methodology in an attempt to reach excellence, and the best way to improve dialogue is by practicing dialogue, learning from experience. Aiming at excellence should never translate into arrogance, a trait that the Qur'an admonishes against. Belonging to a religion does entail believing that one's religion reflects the truth, so a humble approach reflecting the spirit of the following verse is a polite form that puts both parties on equal footing without compromising or relativizing the truth: "Say: Who gives you the sustenance from the heavens and the earth? Say: Allah. And most surely we or you are on a right way or in manifest error."[57] The relationship between any two religions is like a Venn diagram with an overlapping area; they must have commonalities. One can start with the common platform and build on that gradually. One example of a shared heritage that seems to be exhausted is that of the Prophet Abraham whose image was reconstructed in interfaith dialogue and inflated to the degree it obscured his original story and the theological and political conflicts among his "children"! Participants in interfaith dialogue should not be tempted to create comfort zones in order to deliberately avoid difficult

55. Qur'an 41:34.
56. Qur'an 16:125.
57. Qur'an 34:24.

issues and challenges. In Hans Küng's words, one should aim at avoiding "inter-religious cosiness" while opposing "artificial confrontations."[58]

Either dialogue aims at reaching theological goals, such as explaining the oneness of God, or it aims at social justice. The latter might necessitate changing laws or reforming policies. Religion should not be used to sanction discrimination against the religious other. To end injustice, some aggressive measures, such as boycotting the institution that perpetuates the injustices, even if it is a state, might be necessary. It is acceptable from an Islamic point of view to say that God is on the side of the just state, even if it is non-Muslim. According to a tradition of the Prophet: "The highest form of Jihad is a word of justice addressed to an unjust ruler."[59] One could extend this particular concept of struggle for justice before international political bodies and the powers that dictate the order of the day. This should include reforming the United Nations organization to become truly democratic in order to have one set of international laws for all countries, with no room for veto rights. Working together for a better world, regardless of theological differences, could be described as engaging in 'ecumenical Jihad', to borrow from Peter Kreeft, the Catholic philosopher.[60]

Healthy interfaith relations should promote peaceful coexistence through peaceful methodologies, guaranteeing freedom of religion. Regardless of the desired theological goals, it is prohibited to be aggressive. The continued presence of Jews and Christians in the Muslim world today, after more than fourteen centuries of coexistence shows that they were not forced to convert. This argument deconstructs the stereotyped image that connects the spread of Islam with the use of force. People are granted the freedom of religion in numerous chapters:

> There is no compulsion in religion. The right direction is, henceforth, distinct from error. And he who rejects false deities and believes in Allah has grasped a firm handhold which will never break. Allah is Hearer, Knower.[61]

58. Hans Küng, *Islam: Past, Present and Future*, trans. John Bowden (Oxford: Oneworld, 2009) xxviii.

59. Al-Tirmidhi, *Sunan*, Hadith #2174; online: http://hadith.al-islam.com.

60. Peter Kreeft, *Ecumenical Jihad: Ecumenism and the Culture War* (San Francisco: Ignatius, 1996) 11–42.

61. Qur'an 2:256.

> Say: [It is] the truth from the Lord of you [all]. Then whosoever will, let him believe, and whosoever will, let him disbelieve . . .[62]

> And if your Lord had pleased, surely all those who are in the earth would have believed, all of them; will you then force men till they become believers?[63]

> Say: O disbelievers! I worship not that which you worship; nor do you worship that which I worship. And I shall not worship that which you worship. Nor will you worship that which I worship. Unto you your religion, and unto me my religion.[64]

Moreover, the Jewish and Christian places of worship are also protected: "And had there not been Allah's repelling some people by others, certainly there would have been pulled down cloisters and churches and synagogues and mosques in which Allah's name is much remembered; and surely Allah will help him who helps His cause; most surely Allah is Strong, Mighty."[65] Protection is extended to these places of worship during times of conflict in the traditions of the Prophet, which specifically prohibit harming the monks and inhabitants of the monasteries.[66] This despite the fact that the Qur'an does state that celibacy is a postrevelational human construct:

> Then We caused Our messengers to follow in their footsteps; and We caused Jesus, son of Mary, to follow, and gave him the Gospel, and placed compassion and mercy in the hearts of those who followed him. But monasticism they invented—We ordained it not for them—only seeking Allah's pleasure, and they observed it not with right observance. So We give those of them who believe their reward, but many of them are evil-livers.[67]

62. Qur'an 18:29.
63. Qur'an 10:99.
64. Qur'an 109:1–6.
65. Qur'an 22:40.
66. Ahmad Ibn Hanbal, *Musnad*, Hadith #2592; online: http://hadith.al-islam.com.
67. Qur'an 57:27.

A Common Word between Us and You

In the aftermath of Pope Benedict XVI's Regensburg lecture of September 13, 2006, Muslim scholars responded within a month to the lecture in the spirit of open intellectual exchange, only to be endorsed one year later by 138 Muslim scholars and officials who belong to many Islamic backgrounds. The Regensburg lecture was reductionist; it reduced Muslim scholarship to Ibn Hazm (994–1064 CE), a Muslim scholar from Andalucía, accusing the world of Islam of being irrational. Ibn Hazm's literalist methodology never developed into a popular school similar to the other four major schools of jurisprudence (the Hanafi school is predominant in the Turkish world and the subcontinent, the Maliki school in north and sub-Saharan Africa, the Shafi`i school in the Malay Archipelago, and the Hanbali school in the Arabian Peninsula).[68] Ibn Hazm, nevertheless, is more interesting for interfaith dialogue; because he was a literalist, he considered Mary a prophetess since God revealed to her that she would become pregnant with Jesus Christ. Had the Regensburg lecture instead quoted Ibn Rushd (Averroes) or Al-Mutakallimun (i.e., the rationalist theologians) on the role of reason in Islam, the outcome of the lecture would have been totally different. Islam promotes reason and scientific inquiry for knowledge of this world, without being positivist. It also recognizes that knowledge of the metaphysical world could only be known though revelation, which could be verified by reason: "Will they not then ponder on the Qur'an? If it had been from other than Allah they would have found therein much incongruity."[69] The official website of the Common Word has the following explanation as to what the document aspires to achieve:

> Never before have [had] Muslims delivered this kind of definitive consensus statement on Christianity. Rather than engage in polemic, the signatories have adopted the traditional and mainstream Islamic position of respecting the Christian scripture and calling Christians to be more, not less, faithful to it.
>
> It is hoped that this document will provide a common constitution for the many worthy organizations and individuals who are carrying out interfaith dialogue all over the world. Often these

68. The Shi`ite Ja`fari school is predominant in Iran and southern Iraq.
69. Qur'an 4:82.

groups are unaware of each other, and duplicate each other's efforts. Not only can *A Common Word Between Us* give them a starting point for cooperation and worldwide co-ordination, but it does
so on the *most solid theological ground possible*: the teachings of
the Qu'ran and the Prophet, and the commandments described by
Jesus Christ in the Bible. Thus despite their differences, Islam and
Christianity not only share the same Divine Origin and the same
Abrahamic heritage, but the same two *greatest commandments*.[70]

Though the document emphasizes important points of convergence between Islam and Christianity, I think that one of the things that the document fails to acknowledge is the fact that Muslims and Christians (and
Jews, but they are not mentioned here) have serious differences. And, I
believe, emphasis should be focused on accepting the right of the other to
be different, without this translating into any kind of phobia or unequal
rights, locally or globally.

It is a peculiar position that the prophets of the children of Israel are
never considered the *other*, while their contemporary followers' otherness
is accentuated. Their original revealed books are not representations of
otherness but constructs such as that of the Nicene Council of 325 CE do
contribute to otherness from an Islamic perspective. While it is difficult
to deconstruct all the postrevelational theological additions, it is worthwhile having the following questions as reminders of original position
that could be regained: Was the Prophet Muhammad Sunnite or Shi`ite?
Was the Prophet Jesus Christ Orthodox, Catholic, or Protestant? Was the
Prophet Moses Ultra-Orthodox, Orthodox, Conservative, or Reform?

When Muslim scholars deal with the other, they can detect commonalities but also they have to judge certain theological concepts as
false. Once commonalities and differences are known, Muslim scholars
assume the position of advancing specific theological positions. As an
example of the latter, Murad Hofmann states that "[a] theological reconciliation [between Islam and Christianity] could only be conceivable
if Christianity authoritatively adopted [Hans] Küng's understanding of
Jesus, and accepted the Qur'an as a [revealed] Holy Book."[71]

A true reconciliation between Islam and Judaism, in addition to
theological considerations, could only be achieved upon deconstructing

70. Online: http://www.acommonword.com/.
71. Murad Hofmann, *Islam: The Alternative* (Reading, UK: Garnet, 1993) 28.

the relationship between Zionism and Judaism, freeing Jews from the burden of colonialism in Palestine. Rethinking the relationship with the Holy Land in a way that embraces its indigenous people and apologizing to them are morally imperative steps in the right direction. It is from Judaism that I have learned the organic relation between truth, justice, and peace. Not wanting to be oppressed (any more), nor condoning oppressing others, the golden rule is a prerequisite for a multicultural, multireligious, pluralistic paradigm that could replace imperial and colonial/neocolonial structures.

8

Discernment, Dialogue, and the Word of God

Joseph E. B. Lumbard

The last few years have borne witness to the most far-reaching dialogue in the long and complicated relationship between Christianity and Islam. This was initiated by "A Common Word between Us and You," a letter sent by leading Muslim clerics and scholars of all schools to the leaders of all Christian denominations.[1] Christian leaders and organizations such as the archbishop of Canterbury, the Vatican, the World Council of Churches, and many others responded to the letter enthusiastically, and the ensuing exchange gave rise to a series of conferences that have extended the dialogue between Christianity and Islam in the hopes of advancing their understanding of each other. These encounters at Yale University, Cambridge University (in conjunction with Lambeth Palace and the Vatican), with more conferences being planned in the near future, have provided unprecedented opportunities for Muslims and Christians to engage one another and discuss the many misunderstandings that have plagued Muslim-Christian relations for over 1400 years. But although the first phases of this encounter have been extremely promising, many of the complex theological differences between Islam and Christianity have not been addressed.

1. For the text of "A Common Word between Us and You" and the responses from around the globe, see online: www.acommonword.com. For an analysis of the "Common Word" initiative, see Joseph Lumbard, "The Uncommonality of 'A Common Word'" (forthcoming).

Criteria of Discernment in Interreligious Dialogue

While the dialogue begun by "A Common Word" is encouraging, one hopes that it will lead to a deeper examination of the differences between Islam and Christianity that can in turn lead to greater discernment. For dialogue between Islam and Christianity is all too often conducted under false assumptions regarding the nature of the other religious tradition. Rather than seeking to understand the internal logic of another faith and understand the tenets of that faith in relation to the theological system of which they are a part, Muslims and Christians more often than not evaluate the tenets of each other's theologies in relation to their own theological systems. For Christians this is most evident in their attitudes towards Muhammad, whom they often evaluate through the application of christological categories. For Muslims this is most evident when approaching the Christian understanding of Jesus, whom they too revere as a Messenger of God and the Messiah. But rather than asking what metaphysical principles may be conveyed by the Christian understanding of Jesus, particular doctrines such as the incarnation and the Trinity are usually evaluated by Muslim scholars as if they were components of an Islamic theology. Viewed extrinsically rather than intrinsically, they are then seen as mistaken at best or heretical innovations at worst. Muslim theologians need not agree with tenets of traditional Christian theology, but in refuting them they would do better to encounter them on their own terms.

It has often been observed that 'the least understood aspect of Islam for most westerners is the place of the Prophet Muhammad.'[2] Muslims have thus spent much effort in explaining this aspect of the Islamic tradition, the subtleties of the Prophet's relationship to the Qur'an , and his role in the lives of Muslims today. Yet in seeking to convey to others the place of Muhammad within Islam, Muslims rarely seek to fully understand the place of Jesus within Christianity. Many factors have contributed to this shortcoming: foremost among them is the failure to challenge accepted readings of the Qur'anic proclamations regarding Jesus,[3] the diversity of Christian understandings of Jesus among the many denominations of Christianity, and the subtleties of Christology and Trinitarian theology. Yet if Muslims truly wish to have a dialogue wherein the intricacies of

2. Seyyed Hossein Nasr, *Ideals and Realities of Islam*, rev. ed. (Chicago: Kazi, 2000).

3. For an examination of the understanding of Jesus in the Qur'an in the classical Islamic tradition, see Jane Dammen MacCauliffe, *Qur'anic Christians: An Analysis of Classical and Modern Exegesis* (Cambridge: Cambridge University Press, 2007).

their own faith are appreciated, they too must endeavor to comprehend the intricacies of the other. If Muslims wish for Muhammad to receive the respect they believe he merits within Western civilization, they must endeavor to show that respect to Jesus, not only as a Prophet of their own tradition, but as he is understood within Christianity itself. Otherwise the observation that Muslims, too, believe in Jesus may appear more as a patronizing platitude than as a true source of commonality.

Only by seeking to understand the internal logic of another theological system before evaluating its tenets can one establish a real theological dialogue between Christianity and Islam. But this requires that we recognize limited nature of our theologies, which can imperfectly signify God, as in and of themselves they cannot but be relative. With humility and the awareness that our theologies are but mere approximations, we can then have the courage to embrace new theological potential augured by theological and philosophical exchanges between faiths. In this way we may better bear witness to the revelations at the heart of our traditions, even if it causes us to question particular dimensions of those traditions. For Muslim and Christians can all agree that it is not religious traditions, creeds, or theologies that are absolute but God alone.

The Uncreated Word

One aspect of Islamic theology that can help Muslims to better understand the Christian doctrine of Jesus is the belief in the uncreated nature of the Qur'an to which the vast majority of Muslim theologians adhere.[4] Muslim theologians have at times been uncomfortable with their own doctrine of the uncreated Qur'an, because they understand that admitting to an uncreated Word of God lends more credence to the understanding of Jesus as the Word who is coeternal with the Father. This is especially true if one emphasizes the expression of "Word" found in the Gospel of John, rather

4. Although the vast majority of Shi'a and Sunni Muslims maintain that the Qur'an is uncreated, there are slight variations in how this is understood. See Wilfred Madelung, "The Origins of the Controversy Regarding the Creation of the Quran," in *Religious Schools and Sects in Medieval Islam* (London: Variorum, 1985); and Henry Wolfson, *The Philosophy of the Kalam* (Cambridge: Harvard University Press, 1976). An examination of the different perspectives among those who maintain that the Qur'an is uncreated is available at http://www.masud.co.uk/ISLAM/ust_abd/speech_word.htm/.

than the emphasis upon "Son" found in the Synoptic Gospels. While Muslim theologians would never openly admit that Christ is the Word of God incarnate, their denunciations are not so absolute as they may seem. For in maintaining that the Qur'an is itself eternal and uncreated, the Word 'inlibrate,' as some have expressed it, they fail to provide arguments against the dual nature of Christ—fully divine and fully human—that could not in some way rebound upon certain aspects of the traditional Islamic understanding of the Qur'an as an uncreated pretemporal Book. This was even foreseen by the 'Abbasid Caliph al-Ma'mun (786–833), an opponent of the belief that the Qur'an is uncreated, who wrote that those who believe in the uncreatedness of the Qur'an are "like Christians when they claim that Jesus the son of Mary was not created because he was the word of God."[5]

The Islamic belief in the uncreatedness of the Qur'an derives from three verses: "Truly it is a noble Qur'an , in a Hidden Book" (56:7–78); "Indeed, it is a glorious Qur'an , upon a Preserved Tablet" (85:21–22); and "Truly We have made it an Arabic Qur'an , that you may know. Truly it is in the Mother of the Book, sublime, wise" (43:3–4). The "Hidden Book," the "Preserved Tablet," and the "Mother of the Book" are all understood to refer to an uncreated pretemporal Book; some say this is the Qur'an itself, while others maintain that it is the eternal source of all Scripture of which the Qur'an is one particular manifestation. In either interpretation, it is the Word of God that is believed to be an attribute of the Divine Essence. This is the Divine Logos that, according to some Muslim theologians, partakes of divinity in that it is eternal and uncreated, but that Muslim theologians will always maintain is subordinate to the Ultimate Divine Principle. The Logos or Word is thus said to be absolute in relation to creation, but subordinate to the pure Absolute in both principle and function.

Although the Qur'an is believed to be uncreated, some theologians maintain that the utterance of the Qur'an that one hears, the physically written Qur'an that one reads, and the Qur'an that one has memorized, are all subject to the vicissitudes of time and are therefore created. Nonetheless, others maintain that they are still the Word of God, not mere allusions to it. They call upon Qur'an 9:6 to support this claim: "And if anyone among those who ascribe partners unto God (al-mushrikan)

5. W. M. Patton, *Ahmed b. Hanbal and the Mihna* (Leiden: Brill, 1897) 67.

seek asylum from you, grant it to him, *that he may hear the Word of God*" (emphasis added). To the majority of Muslim theologians, this last phrase indicates that what one hears of the Qur'an, although conveyed by created sound waves, is indeed the actual Word of God. While those theologians who maintain that the Qur'an is uncreated have debated its exact meaning, the consensus of majority is that presented in the words of Abū ʿāmid al-Ghazālī (d. 505/1111):

> He speaks, commanding, forbidding, promising, and threatening, with a speech from eternity, ancient, and self-existing. Unlike the speech of the creation, it is not a sound which is caused through the passage of air or the friction of bodies; nor is it a letter which is enunciated through the opening and closing of lips and the movement of the tongue. And that the Qur'an, the original Torah, the original Gospel of Jesus, and the original Psalms are His Books sent down upon His Messengers. The Qur'an is read by tongues, written in books, and remembered in the heart, yet it is, nevertheless, ancient, subsisting in the Essence of God, not subject to division and or separation through its transmission to the heart and paper. Moses heard the Speech of God without sound and without letter, just as the righteous see the Essence of God in the Hereafter, without substance or its quality.[6]

As the uncreatedness of the Qur'an derives from the very nature of God's speech as an attribute of God's divine essence, Muslims also maintain that uncreatedness of previous revelations. As the Qur'an says of the Jews, "and there was a party among them who *heard the Word of God . . .*" (2:75, emphasis added). It could thus be argued that the notion of the dual nature of God's Word, the divine Logos as both an uncreated, eternal Word that is an attribute of God's very essence, and a created book that conveys that Word to humankind, is something that the Qur'an attributes in some way, shape, or form to all revelations. From one perspective, in the Torah and the Qur'an this Word is made book or 'inlibrated,' but in Christianity the Word is made flesh or 'incarnated.' The Christian understanding of Jesus as both divine and human could thus be understood within an Islamic context as something that derives from the nature of revelation itself. Hence Jesus, though referred to as "a messenger from God" in the Qur'an, is unlike all other messengers in that he is "His [God's] Word that

6. Abū ʿāmid al-Ghazzā l ī, *Qawā'id al- ʿaq ā'id fī l-tawhīd* in *Rasā'il al-Ghazālī* (Beirut: Dār al-Fikr, 1996) 162.

He cast into Mary" (4:171) and thus directly embodies the message with which he was sent, or is the message itself.

Some Muslims would argue that 4:171 simply refers to a word like every other element of creation, of which the Qur'an says: "When He decrees a matter, He simply says to it be, and it is" (2:118; 3:47; 19:35; 40:68), and "His command is simply that when He wants something, He says to it, 'Be!' And it is" (36:82). But all of the other existent things are here referred to as things created through the Word of God. Jesus, however, is referred to as "His Word, which He cast into Mary". So unlike all created things that come about through God's command "Be!" Jesus, by virtue of being God's very Word, in some way participates directly in this divine command. Furthermore, Muslim theologians such as Abu Bakr Ibn al-Baqillani (d. 403/1013) have employed similar verses, such as 16:40: "And Our word unto a thing, when We want it, is only to say unto it, 'Be!' And it is," to emphasize that God's speech is an attribute of His Essence and that the Qur'an is therefore uncreated. To argue that such verses mitigate against the reference to Jesus as "His word" being interpreted as a reference to revelation and to use them as proof texts for the uncreatedness of God's Word would seem disingenuous at best.

In addition, other Qur'anic passages bear witness to a creative, healing, life-giving power in Jesus that was not granted to any other prophet, as in chapter 3 when Jesus says: "Truly, I have come to you with a sign from your Lord; truly, I create for you from clay the figure of a bird, and I breath into it so that it is a bird by the will of God. And I heal the blind and the leper, and I give life to the dead by the will of God" (3:49). And in chapter 5,

> Then God said, "O Jesus son of Mary, remember My blessing upon you and upon your mother, when I supported you through the Holy Spirit. You speak to the people in the cradle and in maturity. And when I taught you the Book and Wisdom, and the Torah and the Gospel. And when you create the figure of a bird from clay and you breath into it, then it is a bird, by My will; and you heal the blind and the lepers by My will; and you raise the dead by My will." (5:110)

Many Muslim theologians will argue that the phrases "by the will of God" and "by My will," employed in 3:49 and 5:110 respectively, confirm that this power ultimately lies with God alone, and thus distinguishes the

Qur'anic account from the biblical one. But the Qur'anic account is not so far from the biblical understanding. For the distinction between Jesus and God the Father is made clear throughout the Gospels, as in John 20:17, "I am returning to my Father and your Father, to my God and your God." In several passages, Jesus states that he is subordinate to the Father: "I can of myself do nothing. As I hear I judge; and my judgment is righteous, because I do not seek my own will but the will of the Father, who sent me." (John 5:30); "For I have not spoken of my own authority; but the Father who sent me gave me a command, what I should say and what I should speak." (John 12:49); and "I am going to the Father, for My Father is greater than I." (John 14:28) Yet despite this duality between Jesus and the Father expressed in these and other verses, Christian theologians insist upon the divinity of Christ and maintain that the Word can never be separate from God. While the manner in which Christian theologians understand "the Word" differs slightly from that of Muslim theologians, it is nonetheless a principle that, as we have seen above, is intrinsic to the Muslim understanding of the divine Word and hence of all revelation.

One may argue that if God's Word gives rise to several different revelations, it is somehow multiple and fragmented and would therefore introduce multiplicity into the divine essence if it were part of the divine essence. But according to Muslim belief, God's Word is on a "Preserved Tablet" as an attribute of the divine essence that is one with his knowledge with which he *encompasses all things* (6:80; 7:89; 20:98) and is therefore infinite. In this sense, the multiplicity of revelation does not contradict the immutability of God's eternal Word but actually manifests another of its intrinsic qualities—infinitude.

The following verses are interpreted as allusion to the inexhaustible infinitude by which words of revelation emanate from the single Word of God: "Were the sea to be ink for the words of my Lord, the sea would be exhausted before the words of my Lord were exhausted, even if We expanded it by another sea" (18:109). "And were all the trees of the earth pens, and God were to extend the sea into seven seas [of ink], His words would not be exhausted" (31:27). Based upon such verses, each word of God in the revelation of the Torah, the Psalms, the Qur'an and even the person of Jesus is understood as an extension of the eternal, uncreated Word of God. Though the words of each revelation are multiple in order to convey the fullness of God's Word to human beings, each word nonetheless partakes of the uncreated essence of the Word. Hence the Qur'an states: "There is no alteration for the words of God" (10:64); "and there is nothing that alters the words of God" (6:34); "and there is nothing that alters His words" (6:115); and "Recite what has been revealed to you from the Book of your Lord; there is nothing that alters His words, and you will find no refuge other than God" (18:27). All the individual words, letters, and even sounds thus partake, as regards their inmost substance, of the inimitable immutability that is ultimately due to God alone.

For Muslims it is difficult to understand the Christian belief that Jesus is "seated at the right hand of the Father." But when this is seen as a reference to the uncreated Word, it can be understood within a Qur'anic context. For, like the Second Person of the Trinity, the Word of God is co-eternal with God, partaking of divinity, but subordinate in principle and in function, as it emanates from God. In its own way, the Qur'an testifies to such an understanding of the Christian position when it confirms the ascension of Jesus into heaven in two passages: "Then God said, "O Jesus, I am taking you, and raising you unto Me, and purifying you of those who disbelieve and placing those who follow you above those who disbelieve until the Day of Resurrection" (3:55). And "and they certainly did not kill him. Rather, God raised him unto Himself; and God is Mighty, Wise" (4:157–58).

Seeing Jesus as the eternal, uncreated Word of God, or one of the faces of that Word, also helps explain certain dimensions of Islamic eschatology. For, like Christians, Muslims believe that Jesus will return at the end of time to make justice reign on earth. As the Prophet Muhammad says: "By Him in whose hand is my soul, the son of Mary will soon descend among you as a just judge."[7] If Jesus has indeed been preserved from death, has dwelled in heaven for over two thousand years, and will be sent again, then Islamic theology must admit that he has a nature that is different not only from other human beings but from other prophets as well. This need not lead to full acceptance of the traditional Christian *logos* theology, but can lead to a better understanding of what is meant by incarnation, Trinity and Sonship, and thus to better dialogue between Muslims and Christians.

The remarkable similarity between the Christian doctrine of the two natures and Islamic doctrine of the uncreated Qur'an also helps to mol-

---

7. *Sahīh Bukhārī, Kitāb Ahādīth al-anbiyā'*, 50.

lify the offense Christians may take when hearing that the Qur'an says of Jesus, "The Messiah does not disdain to be a servant to God" (4:172), and "the Messiah, the son of Mary is but a messenger; messengers before him have passed away. His mother was voracious and both of them ate food" (5:75). When read in the spirit of coming "to a word common between us and between you" (3:64), these can be seen as a reference to Jesus's human nature, and an extension of the many verses in the Gospel of John in which Jesus states that he was sent by the Father (John 5:23, 30, 36–37; 6:39, 44, 57; 8:16, 18, 29, 42; 10:36; 12:49; 14:24; 17:21, 25; 20:21; et passim); for what is a messenger but one who is sent?

Conclusion

Seen in this light, many other aspects of the Qur'anic account of Jesus and Christianity bear further investigation. For example, does the Qur'an criticize traditional Christian Trinitarian theology? Or could it actually be read as opposing the very misunderstandings of Christian theology that Christians themselves have opposed? Does the Qur'an repudiate the idea that Jesus is the Son of God, or does it repudiate the same crude misunderstandings of this doctrine that Christians have repudiated for centuries? Does the Qur'an deny the Crucifixion of Jesus, or is there a more subtle understanding of the text? It may be that when subjected to close reading that is not shaped by centuries of polemic, the Qur'anic verses regarding Jesus can lead to more common ground than is often assumed. But we must first recognize that our interpretations will always reflect the premises we bring to the text and the spirit in we choose to read them.

This paper only provides a glimpse of one of the ways in which the Muslim understanding of the Qur'an can bring Muslims to a more perspicacious understanding of the principles that underlie traditional Christology. Perhaps these reflections can in some small way serve to illustrate David Burrell's observation that "comparative inquiry will inevitably highlight dimensions of our own theological task, by accentuating items in our own traditions which need clarification and development."[8]

8. See David Burrell's contribution to this volume, "Dialogue between Muslims and Christians as Mutually Transformative Speech."

Only when our texts are read in relation to one another in a spirit of faith seeking understanding, rather than a spirit of polemic seeking division that has so often plagues us, can we establish a dialogue that is based upon the central teachings that lie at the core of our religious traditions.

From one perspective, seeking such understanding is a central calling of both the Qur'an and the Bible. For as one famous Qur'anic verse states: "O mankind! Truly We created you from a male and a female, and We have made you peoples and tribes that you may know one another" (49:13). And as another declares: "For each [people] We have made a law and a way. And if God willed He would have made you a single people, but [He made you as you are] in order to try you regarding what has come to you—so compete in good deeds. To God is your return, all of you. Then He will inform you of that wherein you differed" (5:48).

Similarly, Saint Paul writes: "Now there are diversities of gifts, but there is only one spirit. And there are diversities of ministries, but there is only one Lord. And there are diversities of powers, but it is the one God Who works in all things in all men" (1 Cor 12:4–6).

In light of such verses, perhaps we can find elements of our traditions that help us to view the divine Word in a manner that transcends the bounds of one particular tradition, understanding that it is infinite and therefore cannot be limited to a single revelation, or that divine mercy will not be confined to one religious tradition, for as God says in the book of Hosea: "I desire mercy not [ritual] sacrifice, and the knowledge of God rather than burnt offerings" (Hos 6:6). Approaching our Scriptures in a spirit of open inquiry will not resolve all of the disputes between Christians and Muslims. But it can help the faithful to come to a deeper understanding of the treasures that lie buried within each tradition and to a deeper appreciation of divine mercy and infinitude. For as the Gospel of John says: "The wind bloweth where it listeth, and thou hearest the sound thereof but canst not tell whence it cometh, and wither it goeth " (3:8). This in turn may help Christians and Muslims move from discourse and tolerance toward understanding and acceptance, seeing that in God's house there are many mansions (John 14:2), and that "those who believe and who do virtuous deeds and humble themselves before their Lord, they are the companions of the Garden, abiding therein forever" (Qur'an 11:23).

Part IV
Hindu Perspectives

9

One Goal, Many Paths? The Significance of Advaita Apologetic Norms for Interreligious Dialogue

Anantanand Rambachan

Introduction: One Goal, Many Paths?

A recent survey by the Pew Forum on Religion and Public Life revealed that 89 percent of Hindus in the United States believed that many religions could lead to eternal life. Eighty-six percent of Buddhists shared the same view. Only 5 percent of Hindus professed Hinduism to be the one truth faith.[1] The view that all religions are different paths to the identical goal of eternal life is a elaboration of the idea that the multiplicity of ways within the Hindu tradition and, in particular, the disciplines of *karmayoga, bhaktiyoga, jnanayoga*, and *rajayoga* can be direct and independent ways to the attainment of liberation (*moksha*). This argument that there are multiple paths to the attainment of liberation was championed vigorously by Swami Vivekenanda (1863–1902), the renowned disciple of Sri Ramakrishna (1836–1886) and the first to present the Hindu tradition systematically to the Western world. The impact of Vivekananda's interpretation of the Hindu tradition and its relationship to other religions is profound and enduring. As the late Ninian Smart has pointed out, "Not only did he interpret Hinduism to the West so eloquently, but he also

1. See http://religions.pewforum.org/.

155

interpreted it to India itself."[2] Agehananda Bharati rightly noted that "modern Hindus derive their knowledge of Hinduism from Vivekananda, directly or indirectly."[3]

Vivekananda's representation of Hinduism as advocating a theology of religions grounded in the view of many paths and one goal continues to be widely and uncritically presented, by both Hindus and others, as being true of the Hindu tradition, past and present. Although there is a lot to applaud in Vivekananda's attitude to other religions, there are serious contradictions, however; and these become evident when we try to understand what he means by his doctrine of a common goal for all religions. The world of religions is, according to Vivekananda, "only a traveling, a coming up of different men and women, through various conditions and circumstances, to the same goal."[4] Movement in religion is not a growth from error to truth, but from a lower to a higher truth, and the highest truth is non-duality (*advaita*) or the knowledge of the undifferentiated reality underlying and uniting all reality. Religions are at various stages of evolution towards this ultimate goal of nonduality. In popular classifications of theologies of religion, Vivekananda would be a Hindu inclusivist for his proposal of a hierarchical scheme in which all others are included, assigned a theological location, and where Advaita occupies the apex.[5] For him, all partial and incomplete truths find their fulfillment in Advaita. Recently Swami Bhaktivedanta, founder of the International Society for Krishna Consciousness, articulated a similar position. While he also acknowledged truth in other religions, he understood these to be incomplete. The sure way to liberation is the path of *bhakti* (devotion) to Krishna. The Hindu tradition has also generated its own brand of exclusivism (though this is rare), characterized by the denunciation of other traditions. The Arya Samaj founder, Swami Dayananda Saraswati (1824–1883), took his stand on the Vedas, which he understood to be the

2. Ninian Smart, "Swami Vivekananda as a Philosopher," in *Swami Vivekananda in East and West*, ed. Swami Ghanananda and Geoffrey Parrinderr (London: Ramakrishna Vedanta Center, 1968) 82–83.

3. Agehananda Bharati, "The Hindu Renaissance and its Apologetic Patterns," *Journal of Asian Studies* 29 (1970) 278.

4. *The Complete Works of Swami Vivekananda*, 8 vols. (Calcutta: Advaita Ashrama 1964–1971) 1:18.

5. See, for example, Paul Knitter, *Introducing Theologies of Religion* (Maryknoll, NY: Orbis, 2002).

infallible repository of all knowledge, secular and sacred. On the basis of his interpretations of the Vedas, he launched a vigorous attack on Jainism, Buddhism, Islam, and Christianity. His methods were very similar to what Christian missionaries at that time were doing with the Bible as a basis. He was selective in his reading of the texts of other traditions, and his method was apologetic and polemic. While he demythologized the Vedas, he did not treat other texts in this manner.[6]

The thesis that there are different paths leading to the same goal was employed by Vivekananda to demonstrate the superiority of Hinduism in relation to Christianity, in its ability to cater to people of different religious needs and temperaments. When Vivekananda's arguments are subjected to close scrutiny in relation to fundamental Advaita propositions, they are not convincing. There is no effort to relate the nature of each path to the Advaita worldview, and Vivekananda's discussion becomes obscure and vague.[7]

If we turn from the neo-Vedanta tradition as systematized by Vivekananda to the classical Advaita tradition as interpreted by Sankara (ca. eighth century CE), we do not find a similar articulation of the one-goal, many-paths theology. Unlike neo-Vedanta exponents, Sankara does not overlook or treat doctrinal differences, orthodox or heterodox, lightly. In his worldview, there *are* false claims and paths that do not lead to the end of liberation, as he understands this ultimate goal. Such divergent teachings and paths that are contrary to Advaita contentions must be engaged and refuted in order to maintain the truth of the Advaita position. Unlike neo-Vedantins, Sankara is not concerned with underplaying differences in the interest of highlighting a fundamental unity among India's philosophical traditions. He is not motivated by the political considerations that informed Vivekananda's interpretations.

Sankara's approach to rival theologies, internal and external, is identified accurately in Paul J. Griffiths's description of the NOIA (the Necessity of Interreligious Apologetic) principle. In Griffiths words, "If representative intellectuals belonging to some specific community come to judge at a particular time that some or all of their doctrine-expressing sentences are incompatible with some alien religious claim(s), then they should feel

6. See Howard G. Coward, "The Response of the Arya Samaj," in H. G. Coward ed., *Modern Indian Responses to Religious Pluralism* (Albany: SUNY Press, 1987) 49–50.

7. See Anantanand Rambachan, *The Limits of Scripture: Vivekananda's Reinterpretation of the Vedas* (Honolulu: University of Hawaii Press, 1994).

obliged to engage in both positive and negative apologetics vis-à-vis these alien religious claim(s) and their promulgators."[8] Sankara is a "representative intellectual" in Griffiths's definition since he proffers interpretations that are regarded at authoritative by members of the Advaita religious community. Sankara also holds that Vedic sentences are truth-expressing sentences that make "claims about the nature of things, or claims about the value of a certain course of action."[9] This is point to which we will return later. He also attests to the fact that there are doctrine expressing sentences of other traditions that are incompatible with Advaita propositions, either in their truth claims or in the modes of action that these prescribe. His response to rival theological claims is apologetically negative and positive in Griffiths's terminology.[10] Negatively, Sankara defends Advaita claims against the critiques of other systems and seeks to demonstrate the coherence and consistency of the tradition. Positively, Sankara labors to establish the truth and superiority of Advaita over rival claims.

Vedas as the Source of Norms of Discernment

What then are the norms of discernment that Sankara employs, explicitly or implicitly, in his engagement with rival traditions? Since these norms are inseparable from their source, it is necessary to begin by identifying this source and its necessity. Valid knowledge (*prama*), according to Sankara, the equivalent of norms of discernment, can only be generated by a valid source of knowledge (*pramana*): "A means of knowledge is or is not such according as it leads or does not lead to valid knowledge. Otherwise even a post, for instance, would be considered a means of knowledge in perceiving sound etc."[11] The purpose of knowledge is to

---

8. Paul J. Griffiths, *An Apology for Apologetic* (1991; reprint, Eugene OR: Wipf & Stock, 2007) 3.

9. Ibid., 9.

10. Ibid., 14–17.

11. Bfhadaranyaka Upanishad Bhasya of Shankara 2.1.20, 214. Page references to Sankara's commentaries are from these translations: Gambhirananda, Swami, trans., *Eight Upanishads with the Commentary of Sankaracarya* (Isa, Kena, Katha, and Taittiiriya in vol. 1; Aitareya, Mundaka, Mandukya and Karika and Prasna in vol. 2) 2nd ed. (Calcutta: Advaita Ashrama, 1965–1966); Gambhirananda, Swami, trans., *Brahmasutrabhasya of Sankaracarya*, 3rd ed. (Calcutta: Advaita Ashrama, 1977); Jha, Ganganatha, trans., *The*

reveal the nature of things, and valid knowledge conforms to the nature of the object it seeks to reveal. Since an object must be known at it is, knowledge is not governed by human choice but by the character of the object to be known. But a thing cannot be judged to be of such a kind and not to be of such a kind, to be existent and nonexistent (simultaneously). Options depend on human notions, whereas valid knowledge of the true nature of a thing is not dependent on human notions. On what does it depend then? It is dependent on the thing itself.[12]

A valid source of knowledge establishes its credibility by revealing something that cannot be known through any other valid source and that stands uncontradicted by what may be known through other valid sources.[13] Noncontradictedness, as far as Advaita is concerned, is the crucial test of truth. All other tests are seen as conforming to this. It implies that a cognition, the purpose of which is to reveal reality, is held to be valid until contradicted by the revelations of a superior source of knowledge.

The Advaita understanding of the nature of valid knowledge (*prama*) and the necessity for a valid source of knowledge (*pramana*) apply to knowledge of every kind, religious and secular. The valid sources of knowledge accepted by Advaita are perception, inference, comparison, presumption, verbal testimony, and nonapprehension.[14] Sankara does not express any doubts or reservations about the ability of the *pramanas* to generate knowledge in their respective spheres. He claims that the everyday affairs of the world will become impossible if the *pramanas* are considered to be unreliable.[15] The consequence of establishing a *pramana* for religious knowledge is that it cannot claim exemption from being subject to the same criteria used to establish the validity of all knowledge.

Chandogyopanishad with the Commentary of Sankara. (Pune: Oriental Book Agency, 1942); Jha, Ganganatha, trans., *The Puvrva Mimamsā Sutras of Jaimini with an Original Commentary in English* (Varanasi: Bharatiya, 1979); Swami Madhavananda, trans., *The Brhadaranyaka Upanishad with the Commentary of Sankaracarya*, 5th ed. (Calcutta: Advaita Ashrama, 1975); A. Mahadeva Sastry, trans., *The Bhagavadgita with the Commentary of Sankaracarya.* (Madras: Samata, 1977; reprinted 1979).

12. *Brahmasutrabhasya of Shankaracarya* 1.1.2, 16–17.

13. *The Bhagavadgita with the Commentary of Sankaracarya.* 18:66, 294.

14. See Anantanand Rambachan, *Accomplishing the Accomplished: The Vedas as a Source of Valid Knowledge in Sankara* (Honlulu: University of Hawaii Press, 1991) chapter 1.

15. *The Brhadaranyaka Upanishad with the Commentary of Sankaracarya*, 4.3.6, 425.

Advaita puts religious knowledge in the wider stream of discourse about the nature of reality and stands opposed to any compartmentalization of human knowledge. This is another reason for Sankara's apologetic obligation to defend Advaita claims against rival schools.

The authoritative *pramana*, according to Sankara, for religious knowledge is the Vedas. Sankara classifies religious knowledge as being of two types: *dharma* and *brahman*. *Dharma* is concerned with right ethical and ritual action and their respective results. From the Vedas alone, argues Sankara, can we know which acts are virtuous and which are not. The reason is that these are supersensuous realities, beyond the capacity of human perception and inference. In addition, *dharma* and *adharma* vary with time and place. An act that may be sanctioned at a certain time and place may not be approved with a change of these factors. It is impossible to learn of *dharma* from any other source.[16] One must, for example, accept the existence of the self in a future life in order to be motivated to avoid pain and attain happiness in that life. The knowledge of the existence of the self in a future body is revealed in the Vedas.[17]

The entire Veda aims at revealing the means to gain what is beneficial and to avoid what is harmful when such means are not known through perception and inference . . . In matters coming within the scope of what is visible, there is no need for an investigation by means of scripture, since the knowledge of the means to gain what is beneficial and to avoid what is harmful is available just through perception and inference.[18]

Arguing about the Nature of the Source

In arguing that the authoritative sphere of the Vedas is both *dharma* and *brahman*, Sankara has to part company with the most important orthodox tradition of his time: Purva Mimamsa. The Mimamsa contends that the Vedas have their authority only in the inculcation of *dharma*, defined by Jaimini as "that which being desirable is indicated by Vedic injunction."[19]

16. *Brahmasutrabhasya* 3.1.25, 585–86.

17. *The Brhadaranyaka Upanishad with the Commentary of Sankaracarya*, intro., 2–3.

18. Ibid.

19. See *Mimamsa Sutras of Jaimini* 1.1.2, 3.

On the basis of this view, Purva Mimamsa argues that only injunctions (*vidhi*) inculcating the performance of acceptable acts, and prohibitions (*nisedha*) instituting restraint from acts opposed to *dharma*, are direct and independent in authority. The authority of all other texts is indirect and dependent for its meaningfulness on a connection with the injunctions. They are not viewed as having any independent end in themselves. Those Vedic texts, for example, that speak about the self (*atman*) or *brahman* are understood as having their purposefulness only in praising what has been enjoined in the injunctions. If such sentences are taken by themselves, they are absolutely meaningless because they neither impel us to activity nor restrain us from a prohibited action. These texts are merely an appendage to the main body of injunctive texts. Their value is in praising the prescribed action or in providing some useful information such as knowledge of the deity or agent for the performance of a particular rite. If they are statements about already-accomplished entities, then they are without fruit, for they prompt neither the performance of *dharma* nor the avoidance of *adharma*.

In his characterization of the authoritative source of religious teaching, Sankara rejects the Mimamsa argument that the Vedas are only a valid source of knowledge for *dharma*. Although agreeing that *dharma*, inculcated through injunctions, is a principal focus of Vedic teaching, he understands the Upanishad portion of the Vedas to have an independent purpose and authority in revealing *brahman*. For Sankara, the path of action (*karma*), centered on the performance of *dharma,* and the path of knowledge, centered on knowing *brahman* by inquiring into the sentences of the Upanishads, are not mutually exclusive. Although he is adamant that action cannot eliminate ignorance or engender knowledge, the performance of *dharma* without attachment to the results remove obstacles to the gain of knowledge and render the mind receptive.[20] He rejects the Mimamsa argument that sentences cannot have a factual referent. Even though a sentence might have its ultimate purport in initiating some activity, it does not cease to communicate valid information. Even as a person traveling to some destination perceives the existence of leaves and grass at the side of the road, a statement might have its purport in activity, but its factual content is not thereby invalidated.[21] Injunctions

20. *Brahmasutrabhasya* 4.1.18.

21 *Brahmasutrabhasya* 1.3.33, 225.

are valid, not merely because they are injunctions, but because they are revealed in an authoritative *pramana*.[22] In response to the Mimamsa argument that mere factual statements which neither persuade us into activity nor dissuade from inactivity are fruitless and thus without authority, Sankara asserts that "the test of the authority or otherwise of a passage is not whether it states a fact or an action but its capacity to generate certain and fruitful knowledge."[23] He never tires in reminding us of the independent fruitfulness of the Upanishad sentences. These sentences, by helping us to distinguish the self from the nonself, release us from the sorrow of taking ourselves to be incomplete and finite beings. The fruit of *dharma* is worldly or heavenly prosperity. The Upanishads, on the other hand, address the person who knows the limits of these, and the fruit of Upanishad instruction is liberation (*moksha*).

Another proposition of the Mimamsa is that if the sentences of the Vedas are understood to independently signify already-existent things, they become redundant. Existent things are knowable through ordinary ways of knowing. While agreeing that most existent things can be so known, Sankara contends that *brahman* is unique. Possessing no characteristics apprehensible through any other *pramanas*, it can be cognized only though the sentences of the Upanishads.

> As for the view that there must be other means of knowledge about Brahman since Brahman is an already existing entity, that is mere fanciful thinking. The thing (Brahman) is not an object of perception, because it is without form etc. Nor is it an object of inference etc., since it has not a mark (*linga*) from which an inference can be made. But like religious duty, it is to be known solely from the scriptures.[24]

Although *brahman* is an existent entity, it cannot be known though the senses, because it possesses none of the qualities (form, sound, taste, scent, and sensation) known through the senses.[25] Perceptual knowledge involves a process of objectification or knowing by making things the objects of our knowledge. *Brahman*, however, is awareness, the illuminator

22. *The Brhadaran yaka Upanishad with the Commentary of Sankaracarya* 1.3.1, 33.

23. Ibid., 1.4.47, 92.

24. *Brahmasutrabhasya* 2.1.6, 313.

25. *Kena Upanishad* 3:15.

of the body, senses, and mind. It is the constant subject, and its objectification would require the existence of another self that does not exist.

As far as the origin of the Vedas is concerned, Sankara occupies a position that is between Mimamsa and Nyaya. Mimamsa rejects the view that the Vedas were ever composed by anyone. Nyaya, on the other hand, ascribes authorship to God, whose existence it seeks to establish inferentially. Like Mimamsa, but unlike Nyaya, Sankara admits the Vedas to be authorless (*apauruseya*). He seems, however, to understand this concept quite differently. Commenting on *Brahmasutra* 1.1.3, Sankara explains why *brahman* alone can be the source of the Vedas. It is a well-known fact, he asserts, that the author of a text on any subject is more informed than the text itself. The grammar of Panini, for example, represents only part of the subject known to him. It is obvious, therefore, that the source of texts such as the Vedas, divided into many branches and illuminating lamp-like a variety of subjects, must be omniscient and omnipotent. This is even more apparent from the effortlessness with which these emerge from God. The Vedas compare their own emergence with the ease of breathing.[26] Sankara states clearly that it is the eternally composed and already existent Vedas that are manifest like a person's breath. God does not produce the Vedas, but reveals them as they were in a previous creation.

It is important to note, however, that Sankara does not attempt to establish the authority of the Vedas from the fact of God's omniscience. The reason is that he finds it impossible to demonstrate the existence of God by any kind of independent reasoning. In the absence of such a proof, all arguments become helplessly circular, "omniscience being proved from the authority of the scriptures and the (authority of the) scriptures being proved from the knowledge of the omniscience of the author."[27] Ultimately, for Sankara, the Vedas are normative because they satisfy the criteria of being a valid source of knowledge. They reveal something that cannot be ascertained through any other source, and their revelations are not contradicted by what is known through other valid sources.

26. *Brhadaranyaka* 2.4.10.
27. *Brahmasutrabhasya* 2.2.38, 436.

Brahman—The Source of the Universe

Having identified and clarified the source of norms in Advaita, as well as Sankara's defense of this source, we are now in a position to identify specific criteria of truth emerging from Sankara's interpretation of the revelations of this source.

The first such criterion is that the infinite *brahman* is the omnipotent and omniscient source of the birth, continuance, and dissolution of the universe. This criterion of truth had to be asserted, in particular, against the Sankhyans who proposed the origin of the universe in a nonsentient and nonintelligent material cause (*pradhana*). Sankara was well aware of the prestige and influence of Sankhya and Yoga and of shared teachings with Advaita. This made it all the more important to refute their doctrines about the cause of the universe.

> Though there is an agreement in respect of a portion of the subject-matter, still since disagreement is in evidence in respect of others, as shown above, an effort is being made against the Samkhya and Yoga Smritis, though many Smritis dealing with spiritual matters are extant. For the Samkhya and Yoga are well recognized in the world as means for the achievement of the highest human goal (liberation), and they are accepted by the good people and are supported by Vedic indicatory marks, as in, "One becomes freed from all the bondages after realizing the Deity that is the source of these desires and is attained thorough Samkhya and Yoga." Their refutation centers round only this false claim that liberation can be attained through Samkhya knowledge or the path of Yoga independently of the Vedas. For the Upaniṣads reject the claim that there can be anything apart from the Vedic knowledge of the unity of the self that can bring about liberation, as is denied in, "By knowing Him alone, one goes beyond death. There is no other path to proceed by" (SU. III.8). But the followers of Samkhya and Yoga are dualists, and they do not perceive the unity of the Self. [28]

Although the authoritative source for the knowledge of the world's cause is the Vedas, Sankara does advance rational argument to counter Sankhyan cosmology. In addition to the numerous Vedic texts citing a sentient and intelligent cause of the universe, Sankara adds that perception never provides examples of a nonintelligent cause producing objects

28. Ibid., 2.1.3, 306.

that serve the purposes of human beings, without the aid of an intelligent being. In other words, the teleological ordering of worldly objects points to an intelligent cause.

> what is noticed in the world is that houses, palaces, beds, seats, recreation grounds, etc., are made by the intelligent engineers and others at the proper time and in a way suitable for ensuring or avoiding comfort or discomfort. So how can the insentient Pradhana create this universe, which cannot even be mentally conceived of by the intelligent (i.e. skilful) and most far-famed architects, which is seen in the external context to consist of the earth etc. that are fit places for experiencing the results of various works, and in the context of the individual person, of the body and other things having different castes etc., in which the limbs are arranged according to regular design, and which are seen as the seats for experiencing various fruits of action? For this is not noticed in the case of a lump of earth or stone.[29]

In addition, Sankara argues, the supposed motion of *pradhana* requires an intelligent agent. In response to the Sankhya argument (BSB 2.2.3) that insentient milk has a natural tendency to act for the nourishment of calves, Sankara contends that milk is induced to flow under the affectionate desire of the cow. Sankara advances similar arguments against the Vaisesika doctrine of a nonintelligent *adrista* becoming the cause for the conjoining of bodies and selves and in the shaping of objects.[30] The origin of existence from nonexistence, a viewpoint associated by Sankara with certain strands of Buddhism, is summarily rejected on the grounds that " it becomes useless to refer to special kinds of causes, since non-existence as such is indistinguishable everywhere."[31] In addition, the argument for the emergence of existence from nonexistence leads to the attribution of nonexistence to all effects. Such an argument contradicts the experience of effects as positive entities with unique distinguishing features.

29. Ibid., 2.2.1, 369.
30. Ibid., 2.2.12.
31. Ibid., 2.2.25, 414.

Brahman as Intelligent and Material Cause

The fact of *brahman*'s being the intelligent, omniscient, and omnipotent source of the universe leads to the second criterion of truth advanced by Sankara. This is the teaching that for the universe, *brahman* is both intelligent and material cause. Sankara describes the doctrine of God's being only the intelligent or efficient cause as un-Vedic and having various forms. One expression is found in Sankhya-Yoga argument that "God, who is ruler of *prakriti* and *purusa* (Nature and soul), is merely an efficient cause, and that God, Nature, and soul are totally different from one another."[32] The Vaisesikas and Saivas advance other forms of this dualism, according to Sankara.

The argument that *brahman* is both operative (*nimittakarana*) and material cause (*upadanakarana*) is advanced throughout Sankara's commentaries. In his commentary on BSBh 1.4.27, Sankara cites various passages where *brahman* is described as the *yoni* (source) of the universe: "The word *yoni* is understood in the world as signifying the material cause as in, 'The earth is the *yoni* (source) of the herbs and trees.' The female organ too (called *yoni*) is a material cause of the foetus by virtue of its constituent (materials)."[33] Sankara's response to the argument that creation after deliberation is seen only in the case of operative causes, as in potters and others, but not in the case of material is revealing. He refutes arguments derived from common sense, affirming that this is a truth not to be arrived at through inference. "Rather, it being known from the Vedas (alone), its meaning should conform to Vedic statements. And we said that the Vedas affirm that the deliberating God is the material cause as well."[34] Sankara also finds support for his understanding of the unity of operative and material cause in those Upanishad passages that speak of an instruction through which "the unheard becomes heard, the unthought becomes thought, and the unknown becomes known" (CU 6.1.2). Such texts point to the possibility of gaining the knowledge of all things through knowing one thing, and this is possible "only from the knowledge of their material cause, since the effect is non-different from its material, whereas the effect is not non-different from its efficient cause,

32. Ibid., 2.2.37, 433–34.

33. Ibid., 1.4.27, 296.

34. Ibid.

as is evident from the difference noticed in the world between the architect and his architecture."[35]

In BSBh 2.1.13, the opponent argues that if *brahman* is both operative and material cause, *brahman* becomes both subject and object, and the well-known and experienced distinction between experiencer and object of experience will break down. The proposition of *brahman* as the material cause "leads to a denial of the well-known division between the experiencer and the thing experienced." Sankara responds with the help of the analogy of ocean, foam, ripples, waves etc. According to Sankara, the essential nondifference between the ocean and ripples does not diminish the differences between foam, ripples, and waves. "The experiencer and the thing experienced never get identified with each other, nor do they differ from the supreme Brahman . . . Thus it is said that that though all things are non-different from the supreme cause, Brahman, still there can be such a distinction as the experiencer and the things experienced on the analogy of the sea and its waves etc."[36]

Brahman-World Non-Difference

Sankara's affirmation of *brahman* as both intelligent and material cause leads him to propose logically the essential nondifference between cause and effect and the truth of nonduality. This is the third criterion of discernment. In his remarks on BSBh 2.1.14, he grants the distinction between experiencer and things experienced in ordinary experience. In reality, however, such a distinction does not exist, because "a non-difference between those cause and effect is recognized. The effect is the universe, diversified as space etc. and the cause is the supreme Brahman. In reality it is known that the effect has non-difference from, i.e., non-existence in isolation from, that cause."[37] To clarify and ground his argument in the teaching of the Upanishads, Sankara turns to the famous *vacarambhhana* text in Chandogya Upanishad (6.1.4). "My boy, just as through a clod of clay all that is made of clay would become known;—all products being due to words, a mere name; the clay alone is real." In his exegesis

35. Ibid., 1.4.23, 292.
36. Ibid., 2.1.13, 325–26.
37. Ibid., 2.1.14, 326.

of this text, Sankara argues that when a lump of clay is known as nothing but clay, all things made out of clay become known since they are non-different as clay. The modification has its origin in speech alone and derives its existence ("it is") from this fact alone. It has its existence only in name while, from the standpoint of the clay, no such separate reality exists. In other words, a difference of name and consequent form does not constitute a difference in the essential nature of the object. Name and form multiplication do not bring into existence separate ontological entities. There can be any number of name-created objects with functional or pragmatic (*vyavahara*) value, but these do not have separate ontological reality or existence apart from their material cause. In reality only *brahman* has reality and existence.

Sankara anticipates several possible problems with the use of the analogy of clay and clay objects for the *brahman*-world relationship. Although the multiplication of clay into various clay objects does not bring new ontological realities into existence, clay, as a finite object, does undergo a modification of form. In BSBh 2.1.26, the objector contends that if *brahman* consists of parts, it is possible to see how one part could change while the other remains intact.[38] The Upanishads, however, describe *brahman* to be without parts and without distinctions of any kind. Are we to understand that *brahman* changes wholly? If so, do we have to accept that *brahman*, having become the visible world, no longer exists? If there is a transformation of the entirety of *brahman* into the world, "the instruction about seeing (i.e. the realization) of Brahman becomes useless since the created things can be seen without any special effort, and there remains no other Brahman outside these products."[39]

Sankara's response is to assert, first of all, that the nature of *brahman* is ascertained only from the Upanishads (*sabdamulatvat*). These texts assert *brahman* to be changeless while asserting also that *brahman* is the material cause of the universe. Are we constrained then, retorts the objector, to accept even self-contradictory statements because these originate from the Vedas? Sankara takes recourse in his earlier argument that any argument about change has to be understood as name and form variation, which do not bring about change in *brahman*.

38. Of course, this will present its own problems since a composite *brahman* will be subject to change and disintegration.

39. *Brahmasutrabhasya* 2.1.26, 353.

> Brahman becomes subject to all kinds of (phenomenal) actions
> like transformation, on account of the differences of aspects, con-
> stituted by name and form, which remain either differentiated
> or non-differentiated, which cannot be determined either as real
> or unreal, and which are imagined through ignorance. In Its real
> aspect, Brahman remains unchanged and beyond all phenomenal
> actions. And since the differences of name and form, brought
> about by ignorance, are ushered into being through mere speech,
> the partlessness of Brahman is not violated.[40]

In the case of *brahman* and the world, we have a cause-effect relationship in which the cause, without any loss of nature, produces an effect
from which it is essentially nondiffferent. Sankara, however, does not go
to the extreme of fully equating the world with *brahman*. The fact that
brahman is described as cause and the world as effect implies some difference. If there were no difference, the distinction would be meaningless.
"As between cause and effect, some distinction has got to be admitted as
existing, as in the case of clay and pot, for unless some peculiarity exists,
it is not possible to distinguish them as cause and effect."[41]

The relationship between *brahman* and the world as effect is an
asymmetrical one. The world as an effect shares in the nature of *Brahman*,
but the characteristics of the world do not constitute the essential nature
of *brahman*. "The effect," as Sankara puts it, "has the nature of the cause
and not vice-versa."[42] We may illustrate this point with the help of the
analogies used above. Clay, in the form of a jar, still retains its essential
nature as clay and even in this sense, the jar may be said to be nondiffer-
ent from clay. The jar, however, possesses some characteristics that do no
belong to the essential nature of clay. The shape of the jar, for example,
does not belong to clay as clay. Sankara illustrates the argument that effects possess characteristics that do not belong to their causes by arguing
that when the effects are destroyed, they do not become part of the nature
of their causes. They belong only to the effects.

> For instance, such products as plates etc., fashioned out of the ma-
> terial earth have peculiarities of being high, medium, and flat dur-
> ing their separate existence; but when they become re-absorbed

40. Ibid., 2.1.27, 356.
41. Ibid., 2.2.44, 442.
42. Ibid., 2.19, 318.

into their original substance, they do not transfer their individual features to it. Nor do products such as necklaces etc., fashioned out of gold transfer their individual peculiarities to gold during their merger into it.[43]

Tat Tvam Asi (That Thou Art)

Sankara's understanding of the Upanishads as teaching the essential non-difference between *brahman* and the world leads to the fourth, and perhaps most important norm of truth discernment in Advaita. This is the proposition of the identity between *brahman* and the self (*atman*). The revelation of this identity is the central purpose of the scripture and the means to human liberation. This norm is articulated in what Advaita regards as the four great Upanishadic sentences taken from each of the four Vedas. These are as follows: "That Thou Art (*tat tvam asi*)" is taken from Chandogya Upanishad (6.8.7) of the Sama Veda; "This *atman* is *brahman* (*ayam atma brahman*)" is taken from the Mandukya Upanishad (2) of the Atharva Veda; "Consciousness is *brahman* (*prajnanam brahma*)" is taken from the Aitaryea Upanishad (5.3) of the Rg Veda; and "I am *brahman* (*aham brahmasmi*)" is taken from the Brhadaranyaka Upanishad (1.4.10) of the Yajur Veda. In his commentary on Brahmasutra 1.1.1, Sankara admits and offers a detailed summary of different views about the nature of the *atman*.

Ordinary people as well as the materialists of the Lokayata school recognize the body alone to be the Self possessed of sentience. Others hold that the mind is the Self. Some say that it is merely momentary consciousness. Others say that it is a void. Still others believe that there is a soul separate from the body, which transmigrates and is the agent (of work) and the experiencer (of results). Some say that the soul is a mere experiencer and not an agent. Some say that there is a God who is different from this soul and is all knowing and all powerful, others say that he is the Self of the experiencing individual. Thus there are many who follow opposite views by depending on logic, texts and their semblances. If one accepts any of these views without examination, one is liable to be deflected from emancipation and come to grief.

43. Ibid.

The teaching about the unity of the *atman* and its identity with *brahman* was advanced by Sankara against many rival traditions, orthodox and heterodox. This was one of his principal contentions with Sankhya. In the Sankhyan worldview, there is a plurality of *atmans*, but a single *pradhana* (matter) in association with which the *atmans* experience both bondage and release. The Sankhyan argument for the plurality of *atmans* is the fact of diversity of experiences. If many *atmans* did not exist, all experiences will be common ones. Although conceding variety in experiences, Sankara attributes such variety to differences in the mind and not in the *atman*.[44] Sankara similarly questions arguments for the plurality of the self in Vaisesika and Jainism.

Sankara's arguments against the Bhagavatas, an early Vaisnavite school, have a different flavor.[45] Although approving of their theism and devotion to God, Sankara takes issue with their essential dualism. The doctrine of the Bhagavatas, as presented by Sankara, describes God as *Vasudeva*, and understands God to be both efficient and material cause of creation. God divides Godself fourfold as *Vasudeva, Sankarshana, Pradyumna,* and *Aniruddha. Vasudeva* denotes the highest Self from which proceeds *Sankarshana* (the individual soul), *Pradyumna* (the mind) and *Aniruddha* (the ego). Sankara agrees with the Bhagavatas that "Narayana who is superior to Nature and is well known to be the supreme Self and the Self of all has divided Himself by Himself into many forms; for from such Vedic texts as, "He assumes one form, He assumes three forms (*Chandogya Upanishad* 7.26.2) etc., it is known that the supreme Self does become multifarious."[46] Sankara's problem is with the claim that the individual self (*Sankarshana*) is a creation of the supreme self. Such an argument results in a doctrine of impermanence of the self and the impossibility of liberation. "If the individual soul has any origin, it will be subject to such defects as being impermanent and so on. Owing to this drawback liberation, consisting in attaining God, will not be possible for the soul for an effect gets completely destroyed on reaching back to its source."[47]

44. Ibid., 1.4.10, 263.
45. See ibid., 2.2.42–45.
46. Ibid., 2.2.42, 440.
47. Ibid., 2.2.42, 440–41.

In his exegesis of the *mahavakya, tat tvam asi,* Sankara explicitly tries to refute any interpretation other than the identity of *atman* and *brahman.*[48] The sentence is not comparable in meaning to the attribution of the idea of Visnu on an icon and the contemplation of the latter as if it were Vishnu. The *mahavakya* does not ask us to contemplate *atman as if* it were *brahman* but asserts a definite identity. It is not to be conceived figuratively (*gauna*) also as in the sentence, "You are a lion." If identity were a mere figure of speech, knowledge alone could not lead to the identity with *brahman* and the attainment of liberation. *Tat tvam asi* is not a eulogy (*stuti*). Svetaketu is not an object of worship in the discussion, and it is no praise to *brahman* to be identified with Svetaketu. Being identified with his servant does not complement a king. Apart from these interpretations, Sankara concludes, there is no other way of understanding the *mahavakyas.*

Moksa as Already Accomplished

Sankara's understanding of the identity of *atman* and *brahman* as articulated in the *Upanishad mahavakyas* brings us to our the fifth and final norm of discernment. There are three dimensions of this norm that I wish to highlight. *Moksa* (liberation), in Advaita, is identical with the nature of the *atman,* and since the self does not have to be accomplished, *moksa* is already and always accomplished. "The cessation of ignorance alone," alone says Sankara, is commonly called liberation.[49] Bondage is essentially an erroneous idea (*bhranti*) in the mind and liberation is its removal. Liberation is not a change in the state or nature of the *atman.* The conditions of ignorance or knowledge in the mind do not suggest any change in the self. "Really there is no such distinction as liberation and bondage in the self, for it is eternally the same; but the ignorance regarding it is removed by the knowledge arising from the teaching of the scriptures, and prior to the receiving of these teachings, the effort to attain liberation is perfectly reasonable."[50]

---

48. *Chandogya Upanishad Bhasya of Shankara* 6.16.3, 363–64.

49. *The Brhadaranyaka Upanishad with the Commentary of Sankaracarya* 4.4.6, 502.

50. Ibid.

Sankara's arguments for the eternally accomplished nature of liberation have at least three important dimensions. First is his emphasis, supported by numerous scriptural citations, that release is simultaneous with the gain of knowledge. He is emphatic in his denial of the necessity for any intervening action between the two. In fact, from the standpoint of Sankara, it is not even accurate to say that liberation is the effect of knowledge. The function of knowledge is the removal of obstacles that stand in the way of knowing the liberated nature of the self. Knowledge does not create anything new or alter the nature of an existent reality. Its role as a *pramana* is entirely revelatory and informative.

The second dimension of Sankara's argument is his refutation of action as a direct means to liberation. His arguments, in this context, are directed most specifically against the Mimamsakas, who equated liberation with the attainment of a heavenly world and understood proper ritual action to be the means. Action, according to Sankara, becomes a direct means where the attainment involved is one of accomplishing something not yet accomplished. If one admits that liberation is effected through action, then the action necessary, whether physical, mental, or vocal, should be one of four kinds.[51] These are creation, modification, attainment, and purification. If liberation is regarded as the product of an act of creation or modification, it becomes finite and noneternal. *Brahman*'s being the very nature of the *atman*, there is no question of its accomplishment through an act of reaching or any movement. Sankara adds that even "if *brahman* be different from oneself, there can be no acquisition, for *brahman* being all-pervasive like space, it remains ever attained by everybody."[52] As far as action as purification is concerned, Sankara refutes the possibility of adding or removing anything to or from *brahman*. It is very important to take note of the fact that Sankara includes mental actions in the category of actions and distinguishes such actions from knowledge (*jnana*). This is a point that I have labored in detailed elsewhere.[53] Mental actions (*dhyana* or *upasana*) are not concerned with gaining correct knowledge of an object. In such contemplation, an object may be conceived to be different from its real nature. In addition, the aim of meditation is the production of a nonexistent result. Where knowledge (*jnana*) is concerned,

---

51. See *Brahmasutrabhasya* 1.1.4, 32–34.

52. Ibid., 32.

53. See Rambachan, *Accomplishing the Accomplished*, chap. 4.

there is no question of conceiving an object differently from what it is, and the aim of knowledge is to inform us of an already-existing entity. Meditation, in any of its forms, is nowhere presented by Sankara as a valid source of knowledge (*pramana*).

The third dimension of Sankara's argument for the accomplished nature of liberation is the view that it is possible here and now. It is not an end that must await the death of the body since ignorance is not synonymous with the association of the self with a body but with their erroneous identification. This state of embodied liberation is called *jivanmukti*, and the liberated person is a *jivanmukta*. Though still associated with a mortal body, the liberated, through wisdom, is bodiless and immortal.[54] Liberated in life with a body (*jivanmukti*), such a person is liberated in death without a body (*videhamukti*). There is no postmortem travel to a spatial destination. *Brhadaranyaka Upanishad* (4.4.6–7) describes this condition of this person.

> Of him, who is without desires, who is free from desires, the objects of whose desires have been attained, and to whom all objects of desire are but the Self—the organs do not depart. Being but Brahman, he is merged in Brahman.
>
> Regarding this there is this verse: "When all desires that dwell in his heart are gone, then he, having been mortal, becomes immortal, and attains Brahman in this very body." Just as the lifeless slough of a snake is cast off and lies in the ant-hill, so does this body lie. Then the self becomes disembodied and immortal, becomes the Supreme Self, Brahman, the Light.

Commenting on the above text, Sankara adds that a liberated person, after death, "has no change of condition—something different from what he was in life, but he is only not connected with another body . . . if liberation was a change of condition, it would contradict the unity of Self that all the Upanishads seek to teach. And liberation would be the effect of work, not of knowledge-which nobody would desire. Further, it would become transitory, for nothing that has been produced by an action is seen to be eternal, but liberation is admitted to be eternal . . ."[55]

---

54. *The Brhadaran yaka Upanishad with the Commentary of Sankaracarya* 4.4.7, 506.

55. Ibid., 4.4.6, 501.

The Accessibility of Advaita Norms

It is clear that the norms of discernment in Advaita, as articulated by Sankara, are informed deeply by his understanding of the Vedas as a *pramana* or valid source of knowledge. If the significance of this is not grasped, the norms of discernment in Advaita will not be properly contextualized. How accessible are Sankara's arguments for the Vedas as a *pramana* and the norms that he derives from their exegesis? Do the arguments for these norms exist in a privileged and private cultural universe where they are exempt from wider critical questioning? This question arises from the fact that the nature of the Vedas as a *pramana* is not as obvious as other sources of knowledge such as perception or inference, the universal character, operation and applicability of which are more easily demonstrable.

There are important arguments that can be advanced in favor of the universal accessibility of Advaita contentions for source and norms. Advaita understands the human problem it describes to be universal. I have characterized this problem elsewhere as the experience of the limits of the finite.[56] A tradition making such a universal claim cannot circumscribe access on the basis of religious or other boundaries. More important, however, is the classification of the Vedas as a *pramana*. This classification means that the authority of the text cannot be justified on the basis of antiquity or cultural value. As noted earlier, although Sankara understands the Vedas to have its source in *brahman*, he does not establish the authority of the text on this basis. Such an argument will undermine the rational basis of his claim for the validity of the Vedas, The Advaita tradition finds it impossible to demonstrate the existence of God by rational arguments independent of the scriptures. In the absence of such proofs, all arguments become hopelessly circular, "omniscience being proved from the knowledge of the authority of the scriptures and the (authority of the) scriptures being proved from the knowledge of the omniscience of the author."

Ultimately, for the Advaita tradition, the Vedas are authoritative because they fulfill the criteria for being a *pramana*. They provide knowledge (of *dharma* and *brahman*) not available through any other source, and their revelations are not contradicted by the revelations of any other

56. See Rambachan, *The Advaita Worldview*, chap. 1.

valid source. Novelty and freedom from contradiction are considered to be the crucial characteristics of valid knowledge. Since this argument is an essentially epistemological one, it lends accessibility to Advaita claims that may not be possible with other kinds of arguments for the legitimacy of scripture.

Treating the Vedas as a *pramana* grants an accessibility to the text and its teachings while at the same time limiting its sphere of authority. It is not the function of the Vedas to disclose matters ascertainable through other means of knowledge. It is not the purpose of the Vedas, for example, to inform us of the details and order of the creation since we neither observe nor are told by the texts that the welfare of human beings depends on this kind of knowledge. It is not also the concern of the scripture to describe the nature of the human being with regard to such characteristics that are available for observation.

> *Sruti* is an authority only in matters not perceived by means of ordinary instruments of knowledge, such as *pratyaksa* or immediate perception;—i.e., it is an authority as to the mutual relation of things as means to ends, but not in matters lying within the range of *pratyaksa*; indeed, *sruti* is intended as an authority only for knowing what lies beyond the range of human knowledge.[57]

The limiting of the authority of the Vedas to matters that cannot be known through other means of knowledge does not imply that norms are exempt from critical examination or that manifestly absurd propositions are protected from refutation. If a Vedic revelation contradicts a well-established fact, it cannot be considered authoritative. "A hundred *srutis*," declares Sankara, "may declare that fire is cold or that it is dark; still they possess no authority in the matter. If *sruti* should at all declare that fire is cold or that it is dark, we would still suppose that it intends quite a different meaning from the apparent one; for its authority cannot be otherwise maintained; we should in no way attach to *sruti* a meaning which is opposed to other authorities or to is own declaration."[58] It is an implicit assumption of Sankara that the revelations of one *pramana* do not contradict another. Each reveals knowledge that cannot be obtained by another. He labors throughout his commentary, therefore, to clarify

---

57. *Bhagavadgita bhasya* 18:66 (p. 513).
58. Ibid.

seeming contradictions between the Veda *pramana* and other *pramanas*. In his commentary on BRUBh 1.4.7, for example, he denies that there is any conflict between the Vedas and perception with regard to the nature of the *atman*. The teaching of the Vedas about the limitlessness of the *atman* is not refuted by perception about a limited *atman* since perception is describing the *atman* as wrongly identified with various adjuncts (*upadhis*), and the Vedas is describing the *atman* as free from all such identifications. The Vedas do not contradict what is known about human beings and the world through perception; what it does is to negate the erroneous assumptions that are made on the basis of perceptual experiences. He reminds us that reality does not always conform to the impressions of perception: "For instance, the ignorant think of fire-fly as fire, or of the sky as a blue surface. These are perceptions no doubt, but when the evidence of the other means of knowledge about them has been definitely known to be true, the perceptions of the ignorant, though they are definite experiences, prove to be fallacious."[59] In fact, Sankara makes a special argument in his commentary on *Brahmasutra* 1.1.2 for the use of other *pramanas* in inquiring about *brahman*. Although not compromising the position that the knowledge of *brahman* arises from deliberation on the texts of the Vedas and not from any other source, he finds support for other *pramanas* in the Upanishads themselves.

> When, however, there are Upaniṣadic texts speaking of the origin etc., of the world then even inference, not running counter to the Upaniṣadic texts, is not ruled out in so far as it is adopted as a valid means of knowledge reinforcing these texts; for the Upaniṣads themselves accept reasoning as a help. For instance, there is the text, "The Self is to be heard of, to be reflected upon" (BRU.2.4.5). And the text, "A man well-informed and intelligent, can reach the country of the Gandharas; similarly in this word, a man who has a teacher attains knowledge" (CHU 6.14.2) shows that the Vedic texts rely on the intelligence of man.

Sankara argues further by distinguishing the inquiry into *dharma* from the inquiry into *brahman*. In the case of *dharma*, the Vedas alone can be employed, for the result is yet to be produced and is dependent on human effort. The result cannot be experienced prior to its production.

59. *The Brhadaranyaka Upanishad with the Commentary of Sankaracarya* 3.3.1, 318–19.

The inquiry into *brahman*, however, Sankara says, relates to an already-existing entity and admits, therefore, of the use of other *pramanas*. Unlike *dharma*, *brahman* is not outside the range of human experience and knowledge. These *pramanas*, however, are not independent or alternative means for knowing *brahman* but only supplementary and supportive in their roles.

At the same time, although confident that the revelations of one *pramana* will not contradict another *pramana*, and dealing only with what are apparent contradictions, the revelations of the Vedas must be accorded primacy where the nature of *brahman* is concerned and where reconciliation with other *pramanas* may not be possible. In his commentary on BSBh 1.4.27, Sankara deals with the difficulty of finding an analogy in everyday experience for the unity of intelligent and material causes. The absence of an example from everyday experience does not, however, falsify the Vedic teaching. "As for the argument that creation after deliberation is seen in the world only in the cases of such efficient causes as the potter and others, but not in the case of materials, that is being answered. Any argument from common sense is not applicable; for this is not a truth to be arrived through inference. Rather, it being known from the Vedas (alone), its meaning should conform to Vedic statements." Without the help of the Vedas, one cannot even guess about the nature of *brahman*.[60] The self, "which is the witness of the idea of the 'I,' which exists in all creatures, which is without any difference of degrees, and which is one, unchanging, eternal and all-pervasive consciousness—(such a Self is not known as the Self of all by anyone in the section of the Vedas dealing with virtuous deeds, or in the scriptures of the logicians."[61]

It is clear therefore, that the norms of discernment in Advaita are not to be treated as the products of rational speculation. This is entirely opposed to the nature of these norms and their source in the Veda *pramana*. At the same time, as we nave noted throughout, these norms are not exempt from rational scrutiny and the evidence of other *pramanas*, once the limits of these sources are appreciated.

---

60. *Brahmasutrabhasya* 2.1.11, 322.
61. Ibid., 1.1.4, 36–37.

Conclusion: Whither Dialogue?

Having outlined certain central Advaita norms for the discernment of truth, I wish to conclude by offering a few brief comments on the participation of Advaita in interreligious dialogue. What is the necessity or value for the tradition to engage in interreligious dialogue? With such clearly defined norms of discernment, what will an Advaitin gain from dialogue with another tradition? My contention is that there is value, necessity, and even an obligation for dialogue on the part of the Advaitin.

Contemporary Advaitins, following the example of Sankara, have an obligation to engage in positive and negative apologetics defending the tradition against rival claims and establishing the validity of Advaita teachings. Dialogue is an appropriate context in which this activity may be conducted. Advaita needs to engage the sophisticated dualistic theologies of traditions like Judaism, Christianity, and Islam that offer alternative ways of understanding the nature of God, the self, and the God-world relationship. Differences with these traditions need to be highlighted and their arguments against the nondual worldview contested. Advaita scholars will have to take these traditions more seriously through proper inquiry into textual sources, commentaries, and learning from scholar-practitioners. In ways similar to Sankara's engagement with traditions like Lokayata, Sankhya, and Yoga, that propose the origin of the universe in the a nonsentient and nonintelligent material cause, Advaita must become a vigorous participant in the dialogue with the "new atheism" and make anew its case for the origin of the universe in an omniscient, eternal, and intelligent cause. It must similarly establish why arguments proposing the origin of existence from nonexistence are untenable. In this context, Advaita has unique contributions to make to our understanding of consciousness, an exciting subject of study and reflection across many disciplines. Advaita, of course, identifies consciousness as *brahman*, the source, ground, and essential nature of all reality. Interreligious dialogue is an appropriate forum also for Advaita to fulfill its obligation to share those insights about the nature of human beings that it considers necessary for human well-being.

Although Advaita makes truth claims that speak of the ultimate nature of reality and are in this sense transhistorical, these claims were articulated in specific historical and cultural contexts and in dialogue with a variety of conversation partners, orthodox and heterodox. There is a finitude and historical character therefore to both the language and content of these formulations. The awareness of this fact, not always prominent in discussions of the tradition, necessitates a sustained effort on the part of Advaitins to articulate the claims of the tradition in the new historical, cultural, social, and intellectual contexts. Interreligious dialogue is a fertile source of the new questions that need to be addressed, calling our attention to formulations that are problematic and inadequate and suggesting new and enriching possibilities for understanding and articulating the meaning of the Advaita worldview. My own work as an Advaitin testifies to this fact. Interreligious dialogue is one of the significant catalysts for my concern, for example, with caste and gender injustice in Advaita and for my own effort to establish such oppression as fundamentally inconsistent with the Advaita understanding of the unity of self and the equal and identical presence of *brahman* in all beings. Interreligious dialogue has also contributed to my examination and effort to reformulate popular Advaita constructions of the status of the world in relation to *brahman*, *brahman* as God, and the meaning of liberation (*moksa*). One of the necessary and potentially most enriching dialogues for Advaita, I believe, is the conversation with other nondual traditions and, more particularly, with Buddhist expressions of nondualism. This will be very helpful in presenting Advaita with alternative possibilities for understanding and expressing the meaning of nonduality. Advaita will benefit significantly from dialogue with nondual Buddhists who are leaders and thinkers within contemporary Engaged Buddhism movements.

Perhaps more than any other Hindu religious tradition, Advaita exemplifies an awareness of the limits of human language and symbols in relation to the infinite and absolute *brahman*. Although clearly proposing that the teaching of the Upanishad about the identity of *atman* and *brahman* is liberating in its outcome, Advaita consistently affirms that no words can describe or reveal the intrinsic nature of *brahman*. Word formulations about truth are necessary, but we should always be attentive to the finitude of such assertions. As the Taittiriya Upanishad (2.9.1) reminds us, *brahman* is "that from which words turn back with the mind." The constitutive nature of *brahman* eludes all direct definition. Its intrinsic nature can only be alluded to by denying the validity of all descriptions, as in the famous Brhadaranyaka Upanishad text (2.3.6) *neti neti* (not this, not this). The consequence of such a radical sense of our human limits ought to be deep attentiveness and openness to considering and learning from multiple ways of speaking about the ultimate that occur in different traditions. It is the wise, after all, as Rg Veda (I.164.46) reminds us, who speak differently.[62] By attributing differences of speech to the wise, this text invites a respectful and inquiring response to theological differences. We must not associate wisdom only with our way of speaking, as precious as this must be to us. The possibility for mutual enrichment and learning is a significant justification for engagement in interreligious dialogue, and Advaitins must not think arrogantly that they are excluded from this possibility. The Bhagavadgita (6:18), after all, correlates wisdom (*vidya*) with humility (*vinaya*).

62. "The One Being the wise call by many names."

10

Madhva Dialogue and Discernment

Deepak Sarma

Madhva Vedanta is found within a commentarial framework, which serves as the basis for discerning the truth and value of other religions. This framework is shared by all of the schools of Vedanta and centers on a body of text known as the *Vedas*. According to the Madhva perspective, reflection that occurs outside of this framework is valuable only insofar as it sharpens the debate skills of Madhvas and concurrently increases the epistemic confidence that Madhvas have in the truth of their own religion.[1]

In this essay I will first characterize "commentarial frameworks" and "exclusive commentarial frameworks." I will then place Madhva Vedanta within these frameworks. My intention is to show that for Madhvas, religions outside of the Vedanta commentarial fold have no truth whatsoever and are valued only as living examples of proverbial "straw men" for Madhva students.

---

1. For more on "epistemic confidence," see Paul J. Griffiths's *Problems of Religious Diversity* (Oxford: Blackwell, 2001). I am grateful to Peter Haas for helpful conversations at the preliminary stages of my reflections on this topic and to Paul Griffiths for reading earlier versions of this paper.

Commentarial Frameworks

Religions that operate within a commentarial framework (commentarial religions) must have a body of texts that are the objects of commentary, and that serve as their epistemic foundation. I will refer to these as the "root texts." Root texts may be preserved and disseminated orally or textually. These religions have virtuoso readers of the root texts, whose commentaries are deemed epistemologically authoritative.[2] Their authority derives from criteria that are likely to be found in the root texts. The doctrines, teachings, and practices, of religions outside the framework of a commentarial religion (I will refer to these as alien religions)[3] will be relevant only insofar at they assist (or detract from) the commentaries offered by virtuoso readers. Similarly dialogue with members of alien religions is valuable if it assists with readings of the root texts, if it is prescribed by the root texts themselves, if it confirms the beliefs of those of the home religion,[4] or if its content is merely descriptive of or informative about the home religion. It is possible that there are intrareligious disputes about the accuracy of readings. In such cases, intrareligious dialogues are between disputing virtuoso readers, who are operating within the same framework despite their disagreement. Typically methods for adjudicating disputes are found in the root texts of commentarial religions.

Insider-Epistemologies and Commentary

Among religions that operate within a commentarial framework, there are religions whose root texts and commentaries are not made available to outsiders. These religions operate within an exclusive commentarial framework. They may limit access to books if the root texts are in written format, or they may restrict attendance to oral recitations of root

2. For more on "virtuoso readers," see Paul J. Griffiths's *Religious Reading* (Oxford: Oxford University Press, 1999); and Deepak Sarma's *Epistemology and the Limitations of Philosophical Inquiry: Doctrine in Madhva Vedanta* (Oxford: Routledge/Curzon, 2005).

3. I am reliant upon Griffiths's formulation of "alien" religions as found in his *Problem of Religious Diversity*.

4. I am reliant upon Griffiths's formulation of "home" religions as found in his *Problem of Religious Diversity*.

texts and subsequent oral commentaries offered by virtuosos if the root texts are preserved and disseminated orally. Some may allow outsiders to convert and, therefore, to obtain access to these root texts and commentaries. These are open, exclusive commentarial religions. The ensuing dialogue that might occur between the new convert and a virtuoso would, of course, be an intrareligious dialogue and not an interreligious one.

There are religions that do not permit conversion and thus severely limit access to their root texts and commentaries. These are closed exclusive commentarial religions. An informed interreligious dialogue with the virtuosos of such religions becomes impossible or, if it does occur, it must be only on a superficial level. These religions are founded on highly restrictive insider epistemologies. It is possible that members of these religions have conversations with outsiders, in which they offer simple accounts of their doctrines or merely correct misunderstandings. It is also possible that members may learn about alien religions for the purpose of finding flaws in them and, consequently, in confirming the truth of their own. This learning could occur in the context of dialogues or via texts. The value of the doctrines of alien religions, then, is merely to verify the truth of the doctrines, teachings, and practices put forth by the home religion.

The Madhva School of Vedanta is a closed exclusive commentarial religion that does not permit outsiders to access root texts and also does not permit conversion. It also places little importance on the value of alien religions, other than the pedagogical importance for students of finding their internal flaws. I will first offer a brief characterization of the school of Vedanta. I will then turn to Madhva Vedanta. After contextualizing historically, I will examine the rules that it enforces to maintain the secrecy of its root texts and to create a closed exclusive commentarial framework.

Vedanta

Madhva Vedanta identifies itself as a school of Vedanta. Its predecessors include the Advaita (non-dualism) school, founded by Sankaracarya in the eighth century CE, and the Visistadvaita (qualified nondualism) school founded by Ramanujacarya in the eleventh century CE.

Leaving aside their widely differing epistemologies and ontologies, the schools share similar core root texts. In fact, the term *vedanta*, a determinative compound (*tatpurusa*) composed of the two terms *veda* and *anta*, means "the culminating sections of the *Vedas*." That Vedanta is named after this body of texts marks the importance and centrality they give to commentary. These texts are the *Vedas*, of which there are four, namely the *Rg*, *Yajur*, *Sama*, and *Atharva Vedas*. Each *Veda* can be further subdivided into the *Samhitas*, the *Brahmanas*, the *Aranyakas*, and the *Upanishads*. The *Vedas* are believed to be revealed root texts (*sruti*), without human origin (*apauruseya*) and are self-valid (*svatah-pramana*). For this reason, they are held to be eternal (*nitya*) and free from defects (*nirdosa*). The schools of Vedanta were not the only ones to hold the *Vedas* in such high esteem and grant them unquestioned epistemic authority. Their most important predecessor was the Mimamsa school (Jaimini composed the *Mimamsa Sutras* in c. 25 CE), which devoted the entirety of its intellectual efforts to interpreting the ritual injunctions prescribed in the *Vedas*. Much of the hermeneutic foundations of Vedanta, in fact, can be found in Mimamsa texts. The insider epistemology shared by all the schools of Vedanta also relied heavily on the writings of Mimamsa thinkers like Sabara (400 CE) and his commentators. For these reasons, Vedanta is sometimes known as *Uttara Mimamsa* (Later Investigation).

Though the schools of Vedanta include the *Vedas* in their canon, each expanded its boundaries to include additional texts. Leaving aside these supplements to the canon, the *Vedas* are the primary root texts for the schools of Vedanta and are the critical objects of commentary. Above and beyond the *Vedas*, all the schools also include the *Brahma Sutras* as a root text. The *Brahma Sutras*, composed by Badarayana (also known as Vyasa) in the fifth century CE, is regarded as a summary of the teachings of the *Vedas*, specifically the *Upanishads*, and, indirectly, an explanation of how to obtain liberation (*moksha*). In the introduction to his commentary (*bhasya*) on it, Madhvacarya explains, "He, namely Vyasa, composed the *Brahma Sutras* for the sake of the ascertaining the meaning of the *Vedas*."[5] The text is four chapters long and is comprised of 564 pithy aphorisms (*sutras*). Its brevity makes it difficult to read without the com-

---

5. Madhvacarya, *Brahma Sutra Bhasya*, 1.1.1. Madhvacarya, *Brahma Sutra Bhasya*. R. Raghavendracharya ed. (Mysore: Government Branch Press, 1911). All translations are mine.

mentaries produced by the founders of each of the schools of Vedanta and the multiple subcommentaries produced by subsequent thinkers. It is likely that the aphorisms were merely mnemonic devices used for pedagogical purposes. Whatever the reasons, the elusive nature of the *Brahma Sutras* lends itself to concealment, limits the extent to which aliens can speak with Madhvas, and is an important component in their exclusive commentarial framework.

The *Vedas* and *Brahma Sutras* were interpreted in conflicting ways by each school, and each has different theories about the nature of the liberated state and how it can be achieved. Training in Vedanta centered on close studies of these root texts, the production of new commentaries, and the careful study of old ones, where all these activities were conducted in the confines of monasteries (*mathas*) and in other traditional teaching environments such as the residences of teachers (*gurukulas*). The importance that the schools of Vedanta gave (and give) to commentary and commentarial activities are reminiscent of their counterparts among the Scholastics in medieval Christianity.

Madhva Vedanta: Historical Context

Madhvacarya (1238–1317 CE) was born of Śivalli Brahmin parents in the village of Pajakaksetra near modern-day Udupi in the Tulunadu area of southern Karnataka. Southern Karnataka was filled with a diversity of theologies and people, making it an exciting place within which to develop a new religious tradition. The majority of traditions in the area were far outside the exclusive commentarial framework within which is found Madhva Vedanta. This pluralistic environment had a significant effect on Madhvacarya. His innovations included strategies for maintaining religious identity as well as ways to maintain the existing social system that he felt was being threatened. Madhvacarya's school of Vedanta is in part a reaction against the multiplicity of theologies and social structures in thirteenth- and fourteenth-century Karnataka.

There is very little information about Madhvacarya's education, and much of it must be surmised from rather limited data. Madhvacarya was, of course, familiar with the literature of the schools of Vedanta; this is proven by the 292 texts that he mentions by name in his works. According to Panditacarya's *Madhva Vijaya*, a hagiography of Madhvcarya, Madhvacarya studied the *Vedas* and other relevant texts with a teacher who was of the Pugavana family. He then studied aspects of the Advaita School of Vedanta. Madhvacarya, an inquisitive student, was still not satisfied with what he had learned, so he next sought a new teacher in order to be granted ascetic (*samnyasa*) status. Madhvacarya met Acyutapreksa, an ascetic who was also dissatisfied with the tenets of Advaita Vedanta, and underwent the prescribed ascetic rites.[6] According to Panditacarya's hagiography, Acyutapreksa then changed Madhvacarya's name to Purnaprajna, 'The One Whose Knowledge Is Fully Developed.' According to the hagiographic evidence, Madhvacarya did not have much luck with his new teacher due to their vehement disagreements. Even the name given to Madhvacarya did not last, as Madhvacarya refers to himself as Anandatirtha, 'The Teacher of Bliss,' in colophons. Madhvacarya studied with several teachers and his experiences with them may be why he advises students in his *Brahma Sutra Bhasya* that they can opt to change teachers if the new one is superior![7]

After becoming an ascetic, he studied Vimuktatman's *Istasiddhi* (ninth century CE), an Advaita text. This is the only mention of an Advaita text in the *Madhva Vijaya*, which is somewhat surprising since he devoted much of his life to refuting their doctrines.[8] After again disagreeing with his teacher, Acyutapreksa installed Madhvacarya as the head of the monastery in deference to his student's superior abilities.[9] Madhvacarya's education ended when he rose from the rank of student to become the head of an educational institution and was able to teach his own methods for obtaining *moksha* (release from the cycle of birth and rebirth).

Madhvacarya's travels took him to Mahabadarikasrama, the home of Vyasa, and author of the *Brahma Sutras*, to meet the founder of the Vedanta tradition himself. Vyasa is believed to be an incarnation (*avatara*) of Lord Vishnu, the deity on which the Madhva Vedanta is centered.[10]

---

6. Panditacarya, *Madhva Vijaya*, 4.4–30; 4.49–54. Narayana Panditacarya, *Sumadhvavijayah, Bhavaprakasikasa*, ed. Prabhanjanacarya (Bangalore: Sri Man Madhwa Siddantonnahini Sabha, 1989).

7. Madhvacarya, *Brahma Sutra Bhasya*, 3.3.46–47.

8. Panditacarya, *Madhva Vijaya*, 4.45.

9. Ibid., 5.1.

10. Madhvacarya, *Brahma Sutra Bhasya*, 0.

Above all, Madhva Vedanta is a Vaisnava, Vishnu oriented, tradition. Under the guidance of Vyasa, Madhvacarya is said to have composed his *Brahma Sutra Bhasya*, a commentary on Vyasa's *Brahma Sutras*.

Madhvacarya himself has an unusual background, as he proclaims himself to be the third incarnation of Vayu, the wind God, who is also the son of Vishnu.[11] He is preceded by the first and second incarnations, who are found in the two epics of Hinduism, namely, Hanuman, the monkey deity in the *Ramayana*, and Bhima, one of the Pandavas in the *Mahabharata*. Vayu, namely Madhvacarya, is a guide for devotees (*bhaktas*) on their journey towards Vishnu and has a dynamic position as a mediator between devotees and Vishnu. This self-identification is unusual in the history of South Asian hagiographies.

Data taken from colophons, along with genealogical and chronological data found in the monastaries, lead non-Madhva scholars to conclude that Madhvacarya died in 1317 CE.[12] Panditacarya records that Madhvacarya disappeared and was immediately honored with a shower of flowers from the deities.[13] According to the Madhva tradition, then, he did not die and is considered to be alive and residing in Mahabadarikasrama in the Himalayas with Vyasa-Visnu, his teacher and father.

Religious Context

The thirteenth and early fourteenth centuries CE were periods of religious excitement in southern Karnataka, given the presence of both philosophical traditions based on the *Vedas* and in the Madhva commentarial framework (*astika*), philosophical traditions not based on the *Vedas* (*nastika*), and indigenous traditions. Adherents to Vedanta, both Advaita and Visistadvaita, along with Jains and Virasaivites, populated Tulunadu and propagated vastly differing solutions to end the cycle of birth and rebirth. These literati and commentarial traditions were juxtaposed with indigenously based traditions, including Śaivism, worship of apparitions

11. Madhvacarya, *Chandogyopanisadbhasyam*, 3.15.1. In *Sarvamulagranthah*, ed. Govindacarya (Bangalore: Akhila Bharata Madhwa Mahamandala, 1969–1974).

12. B. N. K. Sharma, *History of the Dvaita School of Vedânta and its Literature* (Delhi: Motilal Banarsidass, 1981) 77–78.

13. Panditacarya, *Madhva Vijaya*, 16.58.

(*bhutaradhana*), worship of female power (*sakti*), and worship of snakes (*nagas*), among others, each with less systematized solutions to the problem of birth and rebirth.

The Hoysala kings, who considered themselves supporters and protectors of the various traditions that existed in Tulunadu, permitted this religious pluralism. The rulers may not have had much of a choice but to allow pluralism, given that coastal Karnataka was a center for trade with both south Asian and non–south Asian communities. It may be that the diversity encouraged the rise of a cosmopolitan society wherein religious heterogeneity prevailed. Economic conditions may have also indirectly affected prevailing religious attitudes. It is thus likely that this variegated setting had a dramatic effect upon the development of Madhvacarya's school of Vedanta.

Astika Traditions: Vedanta

As already mentioned, the philosophical and religious realm, Madhva Vedanta competed with Advaita and Visistadvaita, among other schools. Both the Advaita and Visistadvaita schools of Vedanta had many followers in the area, making medieval southern Karnataka a ferment of philosophical dispute. In fact, Ramanujacarya, the founder of the Visistadvaita school of Vedanta who lived in the twelfth century CE, is known for converting Visnuvardhana (1110–1152 CE), a Hoysala king, from Jainism to Vaisnavism in 1093 CE.[14] This conversion may have helped to hinder the growth of Jainism and other non-Vaisnava traditions. The heart of Visistadvaita activity, moreover, lay in nearby Melkote. Temples, which were officiated by priests who followed ritual and other worship texts found in the Advaita and Visistadvaita canons, were built in the area, as were affiliated monasteries (*mathas*). According to the *Sankaradigvijaya*, a hagiography of the founder of Advaita Vedanta, Sankaracarya visited southern Karnataka in the ninth century and disputed with scholars of local traditions. One of the four *mathas* established by Sankaracarya himself was located in Srngeri, only about fifty kilometers from Udupi.

14. Diwakar, R.R. ed. *Karnataka Through the Ages* (Bangalore: Govt. of Mysore, 1968), 420.

These two cites, Melkote and Srngeri, were (and continue to be) centers for Vedanta studies in Karnataka.

The *astika* Vedanta traditions were well established in southern Karnataka and may have competed with one another for political support and for adherents. Aside from disputes about philosophical themes, there are no accounts of disagreements about land, patronage, or other political issues between the Madhva School and these two Vedanta traditions.

Two Non-Vedanta Traditions: Virasaivism and Jainism

Virasaivism and Jainism, two non-Vedic, non-Brahmanical traditions, were prevalent in the Tulunadu. Buddhism also had some historical significance in Tulunadu but by medieval times, Jainism and the Advaita and Visistadvaita Schools displaced it. There were still vestiges of Buddhism in medieval Tulunadu in the form of images and monuments even though there was no longer a community of adherents. Buddhism, Jainism, and Virasaivism conflicted with the orthodox Vedanta traditions and were oriented toward making their doctrines accessible to the masses. These traditions operate within open, inclusive, commentarial frameworks. In contrast, maintaining the integrity of class (*varna*) and caste (*jati*) was and is essential to Madhva Vedanta and its closed, exclusive commentarial framework. Use of the vernacular, Kannada, for example, instead of Sanskrit, in conjunction with appeals to the teachings of contemporary mystic saints, helped to spread interest in Virasaivism among non-Brahmins. Virasaivas, in fact, not only granted equal status to women but loosened the rigidity of the class system in their tradition. *Sudras*, who occupied the lowest position in the class system, for example, were given status in both worship and religious practices.[15] The methods for obtaining *moksha* were not restricted according to class as they were in the schools of Vedanta. None of these non-Vedanta traditions, moreover, was interested in the kinds of debates about texts that concerned Vedanta. Although Virasaivism and Jainism were open, inclusive commentarial traditions, their canon was completely different from those of the schools of Vedanta. Their social program, as well as their interest in philosophical

15. P. Gururaja Bhatt, *Studies in Tuluva History and Culture* (Manipal: Manipal Power, 1975) 448.

speculation outside the Vedanta canon, made them considerable adversaries to the *astika* traditions and social system.

Some of these non-orthodox traditions even enjoyed the patronage of local rulers. Local rulers such as Narasimha III supported the Jain institutions as is evidenced by the large numbers of inscriptions and documents that pertain to the funding of Jain institutions.[16] The most important Jain monastary in south India was also located in southern Karnataka at Sravana Belgola. In fact, the majority of feudal states in Tulunadu were Jain.[17] For these reasons, Jain activities in Tulunadu far outweighed those of the Vedanta traditions.

Non-Vedic *nastika* traditions, which were opposed to Vedanta, were prevalent in Tulunadu in the thirteenth and fourteenth centuries CE and competed with other one another and especially with Vedanta. Their rejection of class and caste opposes the social systems expounded by the Vedanta traditions. Their open inclusivism conflicts significantly with the closed, exclusivism of Vedanta. Such egalitarian tenets undoubtedly helped to foster religious and theological excitement at the time. The cosmopolitan nature of the area surrounding medieval Udupi sparked interest among both literati and laypeople in these egalitarian traditions, in addition to inciting interest in the schools of Vedanta and propelling their scholars into action.

Indigenous Traditions

These commentarial and exegetical traditions, Vedanta, Virasaivism, and Jainism, were juxtaposed with traditions that did not place any value on commentarial activity and did not systematize their theological positions. These traditions were often localized and more popular among the lower two classes such as the *vaisyas* and *sudras*. Many fostered methods to *moksha* via devotion (*bhakti*) and did not encourage the study of esoteric texts or rituals.

Worship of Śiva stands foremost among these traditions and was the prevalent religion in Tulunadu. Most temples in pre-Madhva Tulunadu are Śaiva. Interestingly, the Udupi Sri Krishna temple, founded by

16. Bhatt, 453; for further reading, see ibid., 426–51.

17. Ibid., 441.

Madhvacarya in the thirteenth century CE, and the *astamathas* form a circle, within which is enclosed the Sri Anantesvara temple. The Sri Anantesvara temple, built in the eighth or ninth century CE, has an aniconic form of Śiva (*linga*) as its centerpiece.[18] Madhvacarya's Vaisnava tradition was thus developed in a Śaiva-dominated context.

Śiva temples were often found in the vicinity of those devoted to Sakti (female power).[19] The Sakti traditions were also dominant in Tulunadu. Worshiped as Devi, Durga, and, more often, as a local female deity, they were sometimes linked to male counterparts who were worshiped by the *astika* traditions.[20] For example, Mukambika, a fifteenth-century–CE form of the Goddess, was absorbed into the Madhva tradition. Vadiraja, the fifteenth-century–CE religious leader (*svami*) of the Sode monastary in Udupi, invoked Mukambika in his *Tirthaprabhanda*.[21] More recently, the Mahakali temple in Ambalpadi Udupi, a temple devoted to the worship of the goddess Kali, was made a part of the Janardhana temple, a Madhva temple devoted to an incarnation of Vishnu. These local and indigenous traditions cannot be discounted. The Śaiva and Sakti traditions may have been the most dominant traditions in Tulunadu. Madhvacarya's Vishnu-based theology was in stark contrast to the prevailing and principal traditions.

The Sakti traditions were also affiliated with *tantric* rituals and worship regimens. These *tantric* texts and practices were very different from those of the prevailing Vedic tradition. Further, though *tantric* worship often entailed initiation rites, these rites were not restricted to literati or other elite groups. They thus allowed all devotees to engage in and lead worship practices. Such traditions were widespread among the lower social classes. It is likely that such *tantric* traditions were intellectual and social challenges for the *astika* literati, who attempted to defend and uphold Vedic orthodoxy and class restrictions.

Perhaps the most well-known indigenous religious tradition of Tulunadu is the worship of apparitions (*bhutaradhana*). Considered to be an indigenous Dravidian form, it is directly opposed to the *astika* and

---

18. Ibid., 282.

19. Ibid., 283.

20. Ibid., 302.

21. Vadiraja, *Tirthaprabandhah*, ed. V. Prabhanjanncnrya (Udupi: Bhandarkere Math, 1990) 56, 58; Bhatt, 301–2.

nastika traditions.[22] The practice of apparition (*bhuta*) worship was fully accepted by the majority of the population and outweighed the importance of Śiva and Vishnu for most.[23] The worship of apparitions often centered on Sakti and was integrated into both later Vaisnavism and Śaivism. *Bhutaradhana*, for example, is central to the worship at the Mahakali temple, which, as mentioned above, is part of the Janardhana temple. The tradition may not have had a noticeable effect on the doctrines of the Madhva school of Vedanta or the other schools. Nevertheless it indicates the presence of traditions that predated many of the *astika*, *nastika*, and related traditions and were in total variance with them.

The religious world at the time when Madhvacarya first developed his school of Vedanta was challenging given the diverse and disparate traditions that existed. There were many competing theologies and methods for obtaining *moksha*. It is likely that this atmosphere of plurality too affected Madhvacarya and made him aware of the boundaries between religious worlds and the ways to maintain those boundaries.

The Madhva Tradition (*sampradaya*), Community, and Institutions

In addition to composing treatises on Vedanta matters, Madhvacarya founded the Madhva tradition (*sampradaya*) in Udupi. According to traditional accounts, Madhvacarya discovered an idol of the god Krishna, an incarnation of Vishnu, encased in mud in the ocean and installed it at a temple in Udupi. The idol is still worshipped in Udupi today.

After ordaining eight monks, Hrsikesa, Narasimha, Janardana, Upendra, Vamana, Vishnu, Srirama, and Adhoksaja, Madhvacarya established each of them as religious leader (*svami*) of a monastery (*matha*) thereby establishing the eight monasteries (*astamathas*) as an institutional tradition.[24] These are the Palimar, Adamar, Krsnapur, Putige, Sirur, Sode, Kanuur, and Pejavar monastaries. Visnutirtha, Madhvacarya's younger brother, who is included among the eight *svamis*, was ordained as head of the Sode monastary. Madhvacarya placed the monasteries of his disciples

22. Bhatt, 360.

23. Ibid., 359.

24. Panditacarya, *Madhva Vijaya*, 15.128–29.

under his tutelage. The *astamathas* still exist today and are loci for studying both doctrines and rituals and for the training of virtuosos. Madhvacarya may have developed a rotating system of leadership (*paryaya*) that would begin after his disappearance.

Although the community established by Madhvacarya has spread to different parts of India, it is still centered in Karnataka state and, most importantly, in Udupi. The Uttaradi, Vyasaraya, Rayara, Sripadaraya, Raghavendra, and Kukke-Subramanya *mathas* among others, are also central to the contemporary Madhva tradition.

The Contemporary Madhva Community

The community and institutions that Madhvacarya founded in the thirteenth and fourteenth centuries has grown far outside the boundaries of the southern Karnataka. As in many other communities in south Asia, British colonization and later diasporic migration has led Madhvas to move within India as well as to leave the subcontinent. The end result has been a wide dissemination of members of the Madhva community. In recent times, Madhvas have maintained their community by establishing a directory of Madhvas in the United States and developing burgeoning Web sites and list serves. Though such globalization is likely to conflict with traditional modes of instruction and transmission, it has been embraced by the religious leaders of the *astamathas*, some of whom are now even journeying outside India. Only time will tell just how much the tradition will change given these new transformation and incarnations.

Basic Madhva Theology

The Madhva School posits that the relationship between the impersonal absolute (*brahman*) and the individual self (*atman*) is dual (*dvaita*). Furthermore, Madhvacarya claims that the universe is governed by five types of differences (*pancabheda*) that are real and not illusory:

> The universe has five [intrinsic] differences: There is a difference between [each] enduring self (*jiva*), and Lord [Vishnu]. There is a difference between Lord [Vishnu] and nonsentient material

entities (*jada*). There is difference between the individual *jivas.*
There is a difference between *jivas* and *jadas.* There is a difference
between one *jada* and another. The [difference between these five]
is real.[25]

Knowing this, and exhibiting the proper devotion towards Vishnu, adherents can eventually obtain liberation (*moksha*) from the cycle of birth
and rebirth (*samsara*).

Madhvacarya separates all reality into independent (*svatantra*) and
dependent (*asvatantra*) entities. The only independent entity is Vishnu.
All other entities are dependent. Among the independent existent entities, there are those that are sentient (*cetana*) and not sentient (*acetana*).
The nonsentient entities comprise the *Vedas*, the *Puranas*, time (*kala*), and
materiality (*prakrti*). According to Madhvacarya, *prakrti* has twenty-four
emanations. The intellect (*buddhi*, also known as *mahat*) is the first to
emerge from *prakrti*. It is followed by ego (*ahamkara*); the mind (*manas*);
the ten capacities that enable sensing, motor functioning, and thinking
(*indriyas*); the five subtle elements (*panca-tanmatras*); and the five gross
elements (*panca-bhutas*).

All creatures are located in a hierarchy or gradation (*taratamya*)
where Vishnu holds the highest position. He should be worshipped always. In fact, one achieves release (*moksha*) from the seemingly never-
ending cycle of birth and rebirth only by means of his grace obtained
via enlightened devotion. The emphasis that Madhvacarya places on
devotion (*bhakti*) distinguishes his system from Advaita Vedanta, which
upholds knowledge (*jnana*) as the primary means to *moksha*. According
to Madhvacarya, Vishnu is to be worshipped, is the object of meditation,
and can be known in part after in-depth study. Proper knowledge of the
nature of God and of one's dependence upon him eventually leads to
unmediated knowledge (*aparoksa-jnana*) of Vishnu granted by Vishnu
himself.

Liberation (*moksha*), the goal of the Madhva school, is the realization that the individual self (*atman*) is dependent upon the impersonal
absolute (*brahman*). Madhvacarya holds that the path via devotion
(*bhakti-yoga*) is the only way to achieve unmediated knowledge of *brahman*, and, subsequently, *moksha*. According to Madhvacarya, this vision

25. Madhvacarya, *Visnutattva(vi)nirnaya* in *Dasaprakaranani*, 4 vols., ed. P. P.
Laksminarayanopadhyaya (Bangalore: Purnaprajna Vidyapitha, 1971).

is the climax of intellectual life of all devotees (*bhaktas*) in worldly experience (*samsara*).

The Madhva Closed, Exclusive, Commentarial Framework

As already mentioned, the significant difference between the Vedanta commentarial tradition and those of medieval Christian Scholastics, is that the schools of Vedanta gave access to the root texts and commentaries only to male Brahmins. The schools of Vedanta thus operate within a closed, exclusive commentarial framework. According to Madhvacarya, "Not everyone possess the eligibility (*adhikara*)" for acquiring knowledge of the Supreme Being (*brahman*) and for obtaining release (*moksha*) from the cycle of birth and rebirth.[26] Not every enduring self (*jiva*) has full access to Madhva root texts, the source of the knowledge that is efficacious for learning about the nature of the Supreme Being, for obtaining release, and for learning the intricacies of Madhva dialectics. The Madhva insider epistemology hinged on this restriction of access to the root texts and made possible their exclusive commentarial framework.

Madhvacarya directly addresses eligibility requirements in his gloss of the first complete word (*pada*), of the first decree (*sutra*), of the *Brahma Sutras* of Badarayana: "Then, therefore, the inquiry into *brahman*." (*athato brahmajijñasa*). The term "then" (*atha*) glosses the sequence of eligibility. The expanded passage reads as follows: "Therefore, after having met the requirements for eligibility, the inquiry into *brahman* is to be undertaken."[27] In his *Brahma Sutra Bhasya*, a commentary on the *Brahma Sutras*, Madhvacarya explicates the requirements for eligibility. He thereby establishes rules and regulations as to who can and cannot become a virtuoso reader of Madhva root texts.[28]

Given the rich and complex ontology envisioned by Madhvacarya, he must determine the eligibility for a wide variety of sentient beings,

---

26. Madhvacarya, *Brahma Sutra Bhasya*, 3.4.10.

27. Ibid., 1.1.1. The word "then" is used as an auspicious expression and for sequence of eligibility. The word "therefore" refers to the reason.

28. For more on these virtuoso readers in Madhva Vedanta, known in the tradition as *apta-gurus*, see Deepak Sarma, "Exclusivist Strategies in Madhva Vedanta," PhD dissertation (Chicago: University of Chicago, 1998).

both human and nonhuman. Not surprisingly, he restricts eligibility and, therefore, training as a virtuoso reader to a select group of sentient beings based on gender and class (*varna*) In the human realm, initiated males of the highest three classes, the *brahmins, ksatriyas,* and *vaiśyas,* also known as the twice-born (*dvijas*) have eligibility to access some texts and doctrines. Among them *brahmins* have the highest access. Only they can become virtuoso readers. Male members of lower classes and women from all classes only have limited access to summaries of Madhva doctrine conveyed orally by virtuoso readers. Their limited access does not allow them to join monasteries (*mathas*), to examine Madhva doctrine, and to obtain training as virtuoso religious readers. Only male *dvijas* who undergo the prescribed training in Madhva monasteries can become virtuosos. Thus, Madhva Vedanta as operating within a closed, exclusive commentarial framework.

Madhva Vedanta also is founded upon a position of predestination. There are those qualified for release who can be liberated from suffering (*mukti-yogyas*), and those who cannot be liberated from suffering (*mukty-ayogyas*).[29] Neither can these sentient beings be released from suffering, nor can they achieve liberaration (*moksha*). They are further subdivided into those who are fit only for darkness (*tamo-yogyas*), and those who are eternally caught in the cycle of birth and rebirth (*nitya-samsarins,* literally, "those who remain in the journey").[30]

Whom do the Madhva virtuosos speak to? Typically they speak and have spoken to others in the Vedanta commentarial fold and to other lay Hindus, though not exclusively. Throughout history, there are numerous cases of virtuosos from the Madhva tradition engaging the textual depiction and refutation of representations of doctrines of (thanks to Paul J. Griffiths for this language) Buddhist and Jain scholars, as well as debating with their members, though neither Buddhists nor Jains are included in the Vedanta commentarial framework.[31] So why does a tradition that operates within an exclusive commentarial framework appear to debate with religious aliens or depict and refute representations of their doctrines?

---

29. Madhvacarya, *Tattvasamkhyana,* 5, in *Sarvamulagranthah,* ed. B. Govindacarya (Bangalore: Akhila Bharata Madhwa Mahamandala, 1969–74).

30. Madhvacarya, *Tattvasamkhyana,* 5.

31. See Sarma, "Exclusivist Strategies."

Debate with Heretical Religions

If a religion prepares its adherents to debate with members of alien religions, then it would seem that conversion of outsiders is a possibility. Depending on the topics of the debate, access to relevant doctrines may also be permitted to the debaters, regardless of class, caste, gender, or other factors. There are several places in Madhvacarya's corpus where he addresses issues of debate and argues against doctrines of alien religions that are outside their commentarial framework, the so-called *nastika* religions. This interest in debate with religions outside of the commentarial framework must be explained, given that they are within an exclusive commentarial framework. Why is there an interest in debating with outsiders? Why, for example, did Madhvacarya examine Buddhism, and why did he summarize debates with Buddhists in his texts? What was the purpose of critically examining the doctrines of religions outside of the commentarial framework of Vedanta?

To approach these questions I examine two locations in the Madhva corpus where such matters are discussed. First I examine Madhvacarya's *Vadalaksana*, a text devoted to the rules and regulations surrounding debate. Then I examine several passages in Madhvacarya's *Anuvyakhyana* in connection with *Brahma Sutra* 2.1, known as *Samayavirodha*, "the contradictions [in other] doctrines." Finally, I speculate as to why there are accounts in Madhvacarya's hagiography, the *Madhvavijaya*, of debate with Buddhists and other outsiders. Though this hagiographic text is not composed by Madhvacarya, it nonetheless may contain important information about the actual, rather than the ideal, community that must be addressed.

The *Vadalaksana*

The *Vadalaksana*, also known as the *Kathalaksana*, is a brief text in which Madhvacarya sets out the proper types of debate in which devotees can engage. Madhvacarya lists three types of appropriate debating methods. These are *vada*, *jalpa*, and *vitanda*.[32] Although this treatise on polemics

---

32. Madhvacarya, *Vadalaksana*, 2, in *Dasaprakaranani*, 4 vols., ed. P. P Laksminarayanopadhyaya (Bangalore: Purnaprajna Vidyapitha, 1971). The threefold [debating

is useful as a dialectical handbook for adherents who wish to debate, it does not contain any explicit summaries of restrictions regarding debate with outsiders, with those who do not have eligibility (*adhikari*) to read the root texts of Vedanta and, therefore, who may not be able to become virtuoso readers. That is, Madhvacarya states the rules and regulations regarding the practice of debate but does not address any restrictions in connection with the eligibility and qualifications of each of the participants of the debate.

Several conclusions may be drawn from this. First, it may be that there are no restrictions regarding who can and who cannot participate in debate. Second, it may be that Madhvacarya has assumed that all participants have eligibility and are legitimate (and virtuoso) religious readers. In this case, there would be no need to address the eligibility and literacy of the participants. Though the first conclusion is possible, the second clearly is more likely; one must have familiarity with the Vedas and similarly restricted texts to argue with the Madhva about his own doctrines. Arguing with a Madhva about his doctrine presumes knowledge of the root texts. These root texts, as I have shown above, are restricted. If a debate were to take place between a Madhva and an outsider (*mleccha*), it would have to be one sided as the outsider/ religious alien would not be able to partake in arguments about the proper interpretation of passages. It is thus reasonable to conclude that debate with Madhvas about Madhva doctrine can only be undertaken by those who are (or can become) skilled readers of Madhva doctrine. That is, only intrareligious dialogue is possible.

Third, it also is reasonable to conclude that these debating rules could be employed by Madhvas when they argued via *reductio* against the doctrines of other schools. This way Madhvas can refute rival positions and, at the same time, need not reveal their own doctrine. To this end, Madhvacarya characterizes the *vitanda* style of argument: "The *vitanda* argument is [characterized] for the sake of truth [when the argument is] with another [wicked opponent]. The Real is hidden in this [argument style]."[33] This style is not unusual in the history of debate among south

---

methods] are *vada, jalpa,* and *vitanda. Vada* is a debate whose purpose is the pursuit of truth. *Jalpa* is a debate whose purpose is to bring fame and glory to the competitive victor. More on *vitanda* below.

33. Madhvacarya, *Vadalaksana,* 3, Jayatirtha, Vadalaksanatika, 3 in *Dasaprakaranani,*

Asian religions. Nevertheless, this passage indicates that it was part and parcel of Madhva debate. It moreover provides a reasonable explanation for the occurrence of Madhva debates with debaters who are not skilled readers of Madhva texts.

Brahma Sutra 2.1, *Samayavirodha*: "The Contradictions [in Other] Doctrines"

The relevance of debate with other traditions is exemplified in the introduction to *Brahma Sutra* 2.1, known as *Samayavirodha* (the contradictions [in other] doctrines). The passages in Madhvacarya's *Anuvyakhyana*, a commentary on the *Brahma Sutras*, are introductions to this series of refutations of rival positions. They are the textual depictions and refutations of representations of the doctrines of rival schools. These rival schools are the Nyaya, Vaisesika, Samkhya, Yoga, Carvaka, Buddhism, Jainism, Saiva, and, finally, the Sakta school. Madhvacarya first states reasons as to why these doctrines exist: "The adherence to the knowledge regarding the falseness of the world is because of ignorance, because of the scarcity of correct understanding, because of the abundance of those who have little knowledge, [and] because of the ceaseless hatred for the highest Reality and for the knowledge of the Real."[34] He next locates the upholders of these rival doctrines in his threefold distinction of sentients (*jivatraividhya*), and in his threefold doctrine of predestination (*svarupa-traividhya*): "The doctrines are maintained because of the fitness of the endless impressions of many demons (*asuras*) due to their being caught by foolishness."[35] The doctrines are kept alive by those who are predestined to do so. The phrase "endless impressions" refers to their predestined status. Having thus accounted for the existence of rival traditions in his cosmology, Madhvacarya states the importance of studying and refuting these traditions: "Therefore, those who are suitable for that which is connected with the understanding of the Lord, [who are suitable] for correct

---

ed. P. P. Laksminarayanopadhyaya (Bangalore: Purnaprajna Vidyapitha, 1971). [The word] "with another" [means] along with wicked [opponents].

34. Madhvacarya, *Anuvyakhyana*, 551–52. Madhvacarya, *Anuvyakhyana*, ed. K. T. Pandurangi (Bangalore: Prabha Printing House, 1991).

35. Ibid., 553.

understanding, who observe the [doctrines of the] sacred texts (*agamas*), they would always destroy the darkness [that is, the ignorant]."[36] He further addresses the reason why these refutations are important: "Therefore [Vyasa] the lord of knowledge composed the refutations of each of the [rival] doctrines for [his] own devotees for the purpose of establishing a sharpened intellect."[37] Given these portions of the introductory passages, it appears that examination and refutation of the doctrines of religious aliens is primarily for the sake of having a correct understanding of one's own position and for increasing one's mental dexterity. Neither a correct understanding nor mental dexterity is an end in and of itself. Both contribute to obtaining proper knowledge of the Lord, increasing one's skill as a religious reader, and eventually obtaining liberation (*moksha*).

If this is the case, then there is no need to reveal one's own position even if one debates with a religious alien. One can argue *vitanda* style and employ *reductio ad absurdum* methods, find fault with the doctrines of others, yet reveal nothing about one's own position. The intent then, is not to convert those who are most opposed to the Madhva position. Instead, the intent is to reaffirm the truth of one's own position for oneself through argument with outsiders. Conversion due to loss in a debate may indeed be possible if the interlocutor is a twice-born (*dvija*) (or former *dvija*), eligible, and, therefore, can become a skilled religious reader of Madhva Vedanta.

Research has not uncovered any instances in Madhva works of responses to critiques of Madhva doctrine by those outside the Vedanta commentarial framework. The responses that I have discovered refer to criticisms made by Advaita and Viśistadvaita opponents. If there were responses to external critiques, then this may indicate that Madhva thinkers permit the possibility of outsiders, twice-borns and otherwise, to understand Madhva doctrines. However, I found no cases of this type of response.

36. Ibid., 554. Jayatirtha, *Nyaya Sudha* 3162. Jayatirtha, *Nyaya Sudha*, ed. Uttaradi *matha* (Bangalore: Uttaradi *matha*, 1982).

37. Madhvacarya, *Anuvyakhyana*, 555.

Accounts in the *Madhva Vijaya*

Although Narayana Panditacarya's *Madhva Vijaya* is a hagiographic text and often contains hyperbolical anecdotes, the descriptions of successful debates against outsiders nevertheless need to be explained. The instances when Panditacarya states that Madhvacarya debated with Buddhists, among others, are too numerous to be documented here. How are they to be understood, given the doctrines that restrict access to the root texts that Madhvacarya has set down? It is not clear whether Madhvacarya argued via the *vitanna* style, or whether his interlocutors were only twice-borns (*dvijas*). This, however, is unlikely since, according to the hagiography, he won a debate against a Buddhist. Buddhisagara, a Buddhist, is mentioned as a disputant encountered by Madhvacarya in Panditacarya's *Madhva Vijaya*.[38] Panditacarya may be signaling the legitimacy of the debater, and consequently of the debate, when he states that his interlocutor was a twice-born. In his *Bhavaprakasika* Panditacarya states: "He whose name is Vadisimha, the twice-born, is a knower of the essence of the Vaisesika [system]."[39] It is also not clear if the debates were conducted in Sanskrit, or if they occurred in vernacular languages. These debates, though in a hagiographical text, may indicate that the actual Madhva community was less restrictive than the one envisioned by Madhvacarya.

Conclusion

I first offered a stipulative characterization of "commentarial frameworks" and "exclusive commentarial frameworks." I then placed Madhva Vedanta within these frameworks. I showed that for Madhvas, religions outside of the Vedanta commentarial fold have no truth whatsoever and are valued only as living examples of proverbial "straw men" for Madhva students. I showed that there is very little of value in the doctrines, teachings, and practices of alien religions when placed in the particular religious framework within which Madhva Vedanta functions.

38. Panditacarya, *Madhva Vijaya*, 5.8.

39. Panditacarya, *Bhavaprakasika*, 5.8, ed. Prabhanjanacarya (Bangalore: Sri Man Madhwa Siddantonnahini Sabha, 1989).

Part V

Buddhist Perspectives

11

Buddhist Perspectives on Truth in Other Religions: Past and Present*

John Makransky

Since the time that Gotama the Buddha passed away (ca. fifth century BCE), Buddhism has had no single institutional hierarchy with a leader at the top.[1] Most of the Buddha's teaching was situation specific, unsystematized, open to further interpretation over time in contexts of evolving individual and communal practice. Adaptations of language, cultural expression, and practice followed upon the recurrent influx of new cultures into the Buddhist fold, especially from the time of King Ashoka in the third century BCE, mentioned later in my article.

Thus, Buddhist traditions vary much across history and cultures. But their views on salvific truth in religions are all related to Buddha Gotama's fundamental teaching of the Four Holy Truths: the Holy Truths of suffering, of the conditioned arising of suffering, of ultimate freedom from suffering, and of the path to ultimate freedom.

According to these Four Holy Truths, the core problem of persons is their subconscious tendency to absolutize their own representations of

* This article was first published in *Theological Studies* 62.2 (2003).

1. I give thanks to Francis Clooney, SJ, and Michael Fahey, SJ, for their incisive feedback, and to my Buddhist Studies colleagues who kindly offered bibliographic suggestions for my topic: Roger Jackson, Donald Swearer, Nobumi Iyanaga, Rupert Gethin, John Lobreglio, James Egge, Mahinda Deegalle, Paul Griffiths, Ken O'Neill, Bob Zeuschner, and Charles B. Jones.

self, other, and religious objects, mistaking the representations for the realities and thus misreacting to them painfully through entrenched habits of clinging and aversion.

The Buddha, in his recorded responses to individuals from other religious and philosophical traditions, established for his followers two basic paradigms of response to non-Buddhists. On the one hand, non-Buddhist traditions came under the Buddha's critique insofar as they might contribute to the very problem he had diagnosed, by absolutizing their religious objects and concepts of self as objects of clinging or aversion. This paradigm was developed by the Buddha's scholastic followers into critiques of non-Buddhist religious systems.

On the other hand, the Buddha was skilled at speaking his truths in remarkably accessible ways, often communicating them to others through their own (non-Buddhist) modes of thought. This second, inclusive paradigm for relating to non-Buddhists inspired a tendency within Buddhism to explore how others' symbol systems and modes of thought might serve to communicate, in their own ways, the very truths the Buddha had taught. This tendency became formalized in the special doctrine of "skillful means," which informed the successful missionary activity of Buddhism in the first millennium CE as it spread to the cultures of East Asia and Tibet. The doctrine of skillful means also supported mystical, universally inclusive views of ongoing Buddhist revelation that stand in tension with the paradigm of scholastic criticism of non-Buddhists.

Contemporary Buddhist scholars who relate Buddhist truth to other religions, such as Gunapala Dharmasiri, Buddhadasa, and His Holiness the Dalai Lama, still draw upon those two basic Buddhist paradigms: scholastic critique of the other or inclusion of the other through skillful means.

The Buddha's Four Holy Truths

The First Two Holy Truths: Suffering, and Its Conditioned Arising[2]

The Buddha taught that all experience of ordinary beings is laced with suffering, dissatisfaction, and anxiety whether obvious or subconscious.

---

2. Buddhist technical terms in parentheses throughout this essay are in Sanskrit.

Ordinary persons are existentially imprisoned in dissatisfying patterns of thought and reaction that center upon a false sense of self misconceived as substantial, unchanging, isolate, and autonomous.

Each person, it is said, feels as if an autonomous self somewhere within the person, thinks, feels, and reacts—a "self" within or behind one's mind who controls or creates one's thoughts. But the Buddha taught, in meditation, when rigorous attention is directed toward that very sense of self, no such substantial, autonomous self can be found. What is found are simply patterns of thought, including thoughts of "self," causally conditioned by prior habits of thought. There is no self-existent, substantial me autonomously thinking thoughts of oneself and others. Rather, patterns of thought each moment create the impression of a substantial, self-existent "me" and "other" to which our minds and bodies grasp and react. This confusion (*avidya*) mistaking inaccurate thoughts of self and other for the actualities supports a subconscious habit of clinging to self, of seeking to prop up or protect self in every situation. And that pattern of self-clinging, in diverse and changing circumstances, transforms into a host of suffering emotions through which each person continually struggles to prop up and protect his or her false sense of self.

The stream of self-clinging thought and emotion—anxiety, hostility, jealousy, pride, fear, etc.—is suffering. And because it projects narrow representations of others as "friend," "enemy," or "stranger" that hide their fullness and mystery, we continually misreact to others, causing ourselves and others further misery. The Buddha taught that those patterns of thought and emotion are one aspect of the conditioned arising of suffering. The other aspect is nonvirtuous *karma*, i.e., nonvirtuous actions of body, speech, and mind propelled by those patterns.

Useful introductions to Buddhism include Peter Harvey's *An Introduction to Buddhism* (New York: Cambridge University Press, 1990); Jean Smith, ed., *Radiant Mind* (New York: Riverhead, 1999); and Joseph Kitagawa and Mark Cummings, ed., *Buddhism and Asian History* (New York: Macmillan, 1989). Connections between fundamental Buddhist concepts and meditation practices are accessibly explained for Theravada insight meditation in Joseph Goldstein and Jack Kornfield, *Seeking the Heart of Wisdom* (Boston: Shambhala, 1987); for Tibetan Buddhist meditation in Reginald Ray, *Secret of the VajraWorld* (Boston: Shambhala, 2001); Lama Surya Das, *Awakening the Buddha Within* (New York: Broadway, 1997); and Ken McLeod, *Wake Up to Your Life* (New York: HarperCollins, 2001); and for Zen meditation, in Thich Thien-An, *Zen Philosophy, Zen Practice* (Berkeley: Dharma, 1975); and T. P. Kasulis, *Zen Action, Zen Person* (Honolulu: University of Hawaii, 1987).

For example, in a moment of intense anger at someone, very quickly a narrow, inaccurate image of self and other is projected (e.g., oneself as simply righteous wronged one, the other as simply demonic being). That mental projection is accompanied by a painful mental feeling. From that projection and feeling, the emotive energy of rage takes shape in the wish to hurt the other by word or physical action. That intention, and any actions following from it, is an example of nonvirtuous karma. Karma is activity of mind and body reacting to one's own thought-made projections of self and other, unaware that the projections have been mistaken for the actualities. As we react in that way, it is taught, we make new karma; i.e., we further imprint the habit of experiencing the world through our own mental projections and reacting to them unawares.

A person's inner capacity for happiness or misery is explained as the fruition of karma, i.e., the outflow of past habits of thought, feeling, and reaction. Nonvirtue (self-clinging, hostility, intolerance, and the like) patterns the subconscious mind for unhappiness, misery, even in seemingly pleasant circumstances. Virtue (generosity, kindness, patience) patterns the subconscious mind for happiness and well-being, often even in seemingly difficult circumstances.

In classical Buddhist writing, the flow of uncontrolled thought that projects a confused, distressing human world is extrapolated through ancient Indian cosmology into diverse realms of repeated rebirth. Buddhist cosmologies serve to describe both the moment-by-moment existential "worlds" of human emotive projection ("hell" in the moment of anger, "heaven" in the moment of kindness) and worlds of embodiment over different lifetimes, conceived as realms of existence distinct from the human realm (hellish, ghostly, godly realms, or the like).[3]

Thus, having seen deeply into the various dimensions of suffering (the First Holy Truth), Gotama Buddha's enlightened mind is said to have discerned the Second Holy Truth: the conditioned causes of suffering within the minds and bodies of beings, the self-clinging patterns of thought, projection, and reaction that further imprint the habit of experiencing the world through projection and reaction. If these root causes

3. See Harvey, *Introduction to Buddhism* 32–46, 53–59; and Herbert Guenther, *Philosophy and Psychology in the Abhidharma* (Berkeley: Shambhala, 1976) chap. 4. For a classical Buddhist source, see *Abhidharma-kosa-bhasyam* by Vasubandhu, vol. 2, trans. Louis de La Valllee Poussin; English trans. Leo Pruden (Berkeley: Asian Humanities, 1988) chaps. 3 and 4.

and their subconscious tendencies are not fully cut, there can be no final freedom from cycling through lifetimes of confused projection and reaction, the flow of suffering experience called *samsara*.[4] If those root causes and tendencies are fully cut, then freedom from bondage to self-clinging and uncontrolled rebirth is attained. Such is understood to be the attainment of the Buddha, his accomplished disciples, and their accomplished disciples to the present time.

When human beings are so little conscious of the extent to which they mistake inaccurate representations of self and other each moment for the actualities, it is questionable whether they are conscious of the subtle ways in which specifically religious representations (of God, good, evil, and so forth) function to further obscure rather than express reality, further contributing to individual and social mechanisms of self-clinging and aversion instead of ameliorating them.

For this reason, Buddhist scholars, when they have encountered any religion that emphasizes prayer or ritual directed to a seemingly external divine power without explaining clearly how the subtlest subconscious tendencies of self-clinging are thereby cut, have been skeptical that the actual causes of suffering are thereby addressed. The proof is in behavior: does the other religion provide means through which committed followers actually learn, in the very moment of intense anger or self-grasping, to see through the mental projections of those emotions, to come to rest in equanimity, empathy, and compassion for all similarly trapped in projections of anger and grasping? If so, that religion would have some real knowledge of salvific truth as it is understood by Buddhists: the truth that frees. Otherwise not.

The Holy Truth of the Cessation of Suffering (Nirvana)

The Buddha likened the sufferings of mind and body to a fire that burns as long as its causes are present.[5] When those causes are removed, the fire ceases, and infinite, clear, empty space appears, unobstructed by fire,

---

4. On the conditioned arising of suffering described here, see Joseph Goldstein's essay "Dependent Origination," in *Radiant Mind*, ed. Jean Smith, 80–85; and Harvey, *Introduction to Buddhism*, 54–60.

5. *Adittapariyaya sutta*, Walpola Rahula, *What the Buddha Taught* (New York: Grove Weidenfeld, 1974) 95.

smoke, or ashes. Likewise, suffering does not cease until its root causes are cut: the confusion that mistakes one's thought-made representations of self and other for absolute realities, and the habit of clinging to those representations. When such confusion, clinging, and their subtlest propensities are completely cut, the karmic process of suffering ceases, revealing an infinite, open, unconditioned dimension utterly beyond the causes of suffering: nirvana. Direct, embodied knowledge of that is called *bodhi*, which can be translated "transcendent knowing," "enlightenment," or "awakening." The fullest such realization is that of a Buddha, referred to as *samyak-sam-bodhi*, "complete, perfected enlightenment."

Buddhist texts often point to nirvana by negating what obstructs the vision of it. Nirvana is the cessation of causes of suffering; it is the unconditioned (*asamskrta*), the uncreated. Sometimes positive metaphors are used, connoting absolute safety, refuge, and release: nirvana is freedom (*vimukti*), supreme bliss, the eternal (*amrta*), the infinite (*ananta*), in which awareness is signless, boundless, all luminous; it is utter peace, the island amid the flood, the cool cave of shelter. It is not an eternal thing, soul, or entity. Rather it is eternal like unconditioned, boundless space, whose essential nature is never changed by wind, cloud, or storm.[6]

But nirvana's most striking qualities are those embodied by holy beings far on the path to its realization, described in stories or met in person. Such qualities include deep inner peace, stability of attention, profound receptivity to others, equanimity viewing all persons as equal in their causes of suffering and potential for freedom, unconditional love and compassion, joy, humor, humility, penetrating insight that sees through others' projections, and remarkable ability to communicate such wisdom to others as they become receptive. Such qualities of enlightenment are undivided from the qualities cultivated on the path to its realization.[7]

6. Rahula, *What Buddha Taught* 35–44; Harvey, *Introduction to Buddhism* 60–68; Stephen Beyer, *The Buddhist Experience: Sources and Interpretations* (Encino, CA: Dickenson, 1974) 199–206; John Makransky, *Buddhahood Embodied: Sources of Controversy in India and Tibet* (Albany: SUNY Press, 1997) 27–28, 320–22; *The Long Discourses of the Buddha* (*Digha Nikaya*), trans. by Maurice Walshe (Boston: Wisdom, 1995), 179–80. On nirvana as an unconditioned reality (not merely an extinction of conditioned existence), see Buddhagosa, *The Path of Purification* (Visuddhimagga), trans. Bhikku Nyanamoli (Colombo: Semage, 1964) 578–82, 819–20.

7. On qualities of enlightenment, see Goldstein and Kornfield, *Heart of Wisdom* 61–77, 127–37; Harvey, *Introduction to Buddhism*, 25–31; A. K. Warder, *Indian Buddhism* (Delhi: Motilal Banarsidass, 1980) 81–106; His Holiness Tenzin Gyatso (14th Dalai

Holy Truth of the Path

Summing up the Buddha's teaching thus far, there are conditioned and unconditioned aspects of being. In ego-centered life, the conditioned processes of mind and body, dominated by confusion and self-clinging, obscure the unconditioned aspect, nirvana. But the Buddha taught practices to repattern mind and body to permit the unconditioned, nirvanic aspect to be realized. All such practices as taught by the Buddha and generations of his followers are referred to as the "Dharma," the holy pattern, the path to enlightenment. Put another way, the Dharma is the revelation of the unconditioned through a Buddha's mind and body, imparting practices through which others' minds and bodies may be similarly opened to the unconditioned, so as to reveal the way to freedom afresh, again and again, from the Buddha's time to the present.

Only a Buddha, someone who entirely transcends the causes of suffering and abides in such freedom, can fully demonstrate the way to it for others. And only devoted reliance upon that way in practice (the Dharma), supported by a community of such practitioners (called "Sangha"), can open oneself to the same transcendent freedom. Thus the path to such freedom begins by taking refuge in those three "jewels": Buddha, Dharma, Sangha. Buddhist perspectives on other religions follow from that understanding. Do other religions know and impart to their followers precise practices to realize freedom from the subtlest, moment-by-moment habits of confusion, clinging, and aversion?

The Buddhist path following upon such refuge is summarized as a threefold cultivation: of virtue (*shila*), of meditative concentration (*samadhi*), and of penetrating insight that sees through the ego's illusory projections (*prajna*).[8] Cultivation of virtue includes cultivation of generosity, kindness, care for others, truthfulness, patience, and ethical precepts for monks, nuns, and laity. Such practice is said to generate the spiritual power of mind and body (*punya*) that may be harnessed to support meditative stability and insight. To realize ultimate freedom, all layers of confusion

---

Lama), *Opening the Eye of New Awareness*, trans. Donald Lopez (Boston: Wisdom, 1999) 89–99. For stories communicating such qualities, see, e.g., Paul Reps, *Zen Flesh, Zen Bones* (New York: Anchor, 1968); Surya Das, *Snow Lion's Turquoise Mane* (San Francisco: Harper, 1992); Nelson Foster, ed., *The Roaring Stream*, (Hopewell, NJ: Ecco, 1996).

8. Walshe, trans., *Long Discourses of Buddha*, 171–74; Buddhaghosa, *Path of Purification*; His Holiness Tenzin Gyatso, *Opening the Eye*, 43–74.

and clinging must be penetrated by insight. Since most of those layers are subconscious, insight must penetrate deep into the psyche. This requires great stability of attention, unmoved by habits of thought, and a laserlike power of attention, that sees through distorted representations of self and other in the instant they arise.

The cultivation of such capacities is supported by cultivation of love, compassion, joy, equanimity, and vivid attention to the impermanent processes of thought, feeling, and perception. Repatterned by such practices, one learns to experience the momentary arising and dissolving of all such processes, to see through projections of unchanging self and other even as they arise, allowing the unconditioned dimension of being—nirvana—to dawn. As the path unfolds over the course of lifetimes, the qualities of enlightenment, of nirvana realized and embodied, are said to manifest more and more fully and spontaneously: empathy, joy, tranquility, generosity, patience, equanimity, unconditional love, compassion, penetrating wisdom.[9]

How the Buddha Engaged Others' Worldviews: Critique or Inclusion by Skillful Means

The Four Holy Truths are the doctrinal expression of the salvific truth that Buddha Gotama and his followers proclaimed to the world. During the Buddha's forty-year career as itinerant teacher in fifth-century-BCE India, he met people adhering to a wide variety of religious philosophies who brought their questions and problems to him. In numerous such dialogues recorded in Buddhist scriptures, Gotama inquires into the beliefs of his interlocutors before responding to their questions. Does the other's belief system reinforce the inmost causes of suffering, the confusion that mistakes inaccurate thoughts of self and other for realities, that clings and reacts to them? Or could the other's belief system support practices that undercut or ameliorate those inmost causes of suffering? In the first situation, the Buddha leads his interlocutor into a critical inquiry of his erroneous beliefs, causing him to give them up. In the second situation,

9. Harvey, *Introduction to Buddhism* 68–72, 121–28, 196–216, 244–79; Goldstein and Kornfield, *Heart of Wisdom*, parts 2 and 3. Chagdud Tulku, *Gates to Buddhist Practice* (Junction City, CA: Padma, 2001).

the Buddha challenges some of his interlocutor's beliefs while reinterpreting others so as to guide him in the direction of the Buddha's freedom.

Often early Buddhist scriptures end when the Buddha's interlocutors are so overwhelmed by the power and clarity of his teaching that they have a sudden deep glimpse of freedom (*dharma-caksu*), and enter into the threefold refuge of his religious community. Occasionally, however, the Buddha's interlocutor is profoundly affected by the Buddha's teaching yet continues to be a participant or leader within a different religious system.[10]

The Buddha's Critique of Others' Views

A famous example of the first kind of situation occurs in the *Brahmajala sutta* ("scripture concerning the net of Brahmanic opinions") where the Buddha rejects sixty-two types of "speculative opinion" (*drshti*) prevalent in the India of his time. Here are some examples of such opinions: those who extrapolate from their memories of a few past lives that they will be reborn eternally, those who believe that one of the ancient Vedic gods of India, Brahma, is the creator of all other gods, those who believe some of the Brahmanic gods are eternal and others not, those who believe in an unchanging self-substance surviving death, those who believe that there is a substantial self which is totally destroyed at death.

In the Buddha's view, such speculative thought processes are intrinsically confused because they occur within a mode of attention that only looks outwardly, away from their own mechanisms of concept making, reification, and clinging. Religious figures that cling to such representations of reality as absolutes are trapped unawares in the "net" of their own subconscious habits of thought, which hide the unconditioned reality that transcends them. "Thus, monks, when those ascetics and Brahmins . . . proclaim [such views], it is merely the opinion of those who do not know and see directly; the worry and vacillation of those immersed in clinging attachment . . . When a monk understands as they really are the arising and passing away of the six bases of [sense perception], their

---

10. For example, on Sonadanda, the Brahmin leader, see Walshe, *Long Discourses of Buddha*, 125–32; on Upali, the supporter of the Jains, see David Chappell, "Buddhist Responses to Religious Pluralism," in *Buddhist Ethics and Modern Society*, ed. Charles Fu (New York: Greenwood, 1991) 357.

attraction and peril [as bases of distorted emotion and suffering], and deliverance from them [nirvana], he knows that which goes beyond all these views."[11]

As the scholar K. N. Jayatilleke notes, the Buddha also severely criticized a religious figure of his time, Makkhali Gosala, whose system he characterized as a theistic form of fatalism. In Makkhali's system, all is said to be predetermined by divine will. No way of life, virtuous or nonvirtuous, is better than another since salvation is eventually granted to all by God anyway. The Buddha is reported to say he knows "no other person than Makkhali born to the detriment of so many people." The reason is that by denying the causal processes behind suffering (Second Holy Truth), Makkhali negated the means to cut through them, discouraging people from entering into specific practices of the path, the way to realize the unconditioned reality beyond suffering.[12]

The Buddha's Inclusion of Others through Skillful Means

Yet the Buddha did not simply reject theism carte blanche in his encounters with theists. It is reported that the Brahmin priest Vasettha, a devotee of the supreme God Brahma, asked the Buddha which of the Indian traditions that claim to teach the way to union with the God Brahma is correct (Brahma was asserted by such traditions to be the creator of the universe and lord of all lesser gods). First, the Buddha inquires whether any of the sages in those traditions has seen God face to face (comparable to the direct realization of the unconditioned in the Buddha's system). Vasettha replies no. "Well, Vasettha, when these Brahmins [priests] learned in the Vedas [the ancient Indian scriptures] teach a path that they do not know or see, saying: 'This is the only straight path . . . leading to union with God,' this cannot possibly be right." Yet the Buddha does not simply reject here Vasettha's belief in Brahma, God. Rather, he sows doubt about whether others who claim to know the path to union with such a God actually do.

11. Walshe, *Long Discourses of Buddha*, 87–90.

12. K. N. Jayatilleke, "Extracts from 'The Buddhist Attitude to Other Religions,'" in *Christianity through Non-Christian Eyes*, ed. Paul Griffiths (New York: Orbis, 1990) 147–48 (Anguttara Nikaya 1:33). See also Walshe, *Long Discourses of Buddha*, 181–86, on the Buddha's decisive rejection of the Brahmin Lohicca's belief that there is no point in teaching virtue.

He asks Vasettha whether authoritative Vedic traditions teach that the God Brahma is encumbered by attachment, hate, ill will, an impure heart, and lack of discipline. Vasettha replies no. Then the Buddha asks whether the Brahmins who trained in the Vedas *are* encumbered in those ways. Vasettha admits that they are.

"So, Vasettha," says the Buddha, "the Brahmins learned in the Vedas are thus encumbered . . . and God is unencumbered. Is there any communion, anything in common between these encumbered Brahmins and the unencumbered God?"

"No, Reverend Gotama."

"That is right, Vasettha. That these undisciplined Brahmins should, after death, attain union with God is just not possible."

Vasettha says he has heard that the Buddha knows the way to union with God. The Buddha confirms that he does. Vasettha implores the Buddha to teach him that way. The Buddha then details four special meditations that methodically suffuse all living beings with boundless love, compassion, equanimity, and sympathetic joy. A monk who practices in this way, says the Buddha, "is unencumbered [by attachment, hate, ill will, an impure heart, and lack of discipline]" He then asks Vasettha, "Has that unencumbered monk anything in common with the unencumbered God?" Vasettha replies, "Yes indeed, Reverend Gotama."

"That is right, Vasettha," the Buddha concludes, " that such an unencumbered monk, after death . . . should attain to union with the unencumbered God—that *is* possible."

Vasettha rejoices.[13] The leading commentary on the text says that Vasettha later received higher ordination as a Buddhist monk and eventually attained nirvana.[14] Thus the entry point of Vasettha's particular path as follower of the Buddha was imitation of God in love and compassion, a practice which made him receptive to higher stages of the Buddhist path, i.e. more receptive to the unconditioned reality (nirvana) beyond all self-clinging patterns of thought about God.

Similarly in other scriptures, the Buddha guides various Brahmins through inquiries into their Vedic beliefs, because of which they abandon some beliefs while accepting the Buddha's reinterpretation of others. In the Kutadanta scripture, the Brahmin Kutadanta plans a great Vedic

13. Walshe *Long Discourses of Buddha*, 188–95.

14. Ibid., 559 n. 258. "DA" is Buddhaghosa's commentary on the sutta.

sacrifice that consists of vast material offerings to the gods. He asks the Buddha for advice. The Buddha explains, step by step, that more fruitful offering would consist more simply of sincere generosity, threefold refuge, upholding the moral precepts, virtue, stability of attention, penetrating insight, cessation of distorted patterns of emotion.[15] In the Sigalaka scripture, the Buddha comes upon a householder named Sigalaka paying traditional Vedic homage to the six directions. The Buddha explains that a more fitting way to make homage to the six directions is to practice virtue in six types of relationship: with respect to one's mother and father (east), teachers (south), wife and children (west), friends (north), servants (nadir), ascetics and priests (zenith).[16] In each such case, the Buddha's interlocutors are moved to adopt practices taught by the Buddha as the very way to fulfill their own traditions' deepest intent for virtue, salvific truth, and freedom.

The Buddha, as portrayed in such scriptures, displayed two central concerns in his critical treatment of others' religious views. First, he rejected speculative approaches to reality, which pay insufficient attention to the conditioned mental processes through which concepts of "self," "other," "God," or "world" are constructed and projected as absolutes (as if not thought constructed), giving rise to conditioned reactions to one's own projections in the form of clinging attachment, aversion, and nonvirtuous action, all of which further obscure rather than disclose the unconditioned reality: nirvana. Second, he vehemently rejected any theory theistic or nontheistic that denies the causal genesis of suffering (Second Holy Truth), thereby denying the possibility that the conditioned arising of suffering may cease through proper practice of the path (Fourth Holy Truth) to reveal the unconditioned reality beyond suffering (Third Holy Truth).

As I have already shown, the Buddha employed two key pedagogical methods: (1) By reinterpreting inherited Indic terms, he established a new philosophical-religious discourse engaging enough to attract traditional Brahmins and rigorous enough to guide his followers in the distinctive practices of his path. (2) The Buddha was remarkably skillful at triggering in others, right through *their own* worldviews and modes of thought,

---

15. Ibid., 138–41.

16. Ibid., 466–69; see also ibid., 129–32, where the Buddha inquires of the Brahmin Sonadanda what qualities truly constitute a Brahmin (a priest).

the distinctive insights of his path to freedom. Several of the encounters noted above exemplify that skill, traditionally referred to as the Buddha's "skillful means" for communicating salvific truth (*upaya-kaushalya*).

Later Buddhist traditions elaborated on those concerns and methods of Gotama Buddha. His concern to refute speculative views, and the discourse he developed for such purposes were further developed by scholastic Buddhists into detailed critiques of theism, which went beyond what the Gotama had done. And Gotama's skillfulness at triggering others' insights right through their own worldviews (skillful means) became a central tenet and inspiration for the emergence of the Mahayana movement of Buddhism that became dominant in East Asia and Tibet.

Those two approaches—scholastic critique *of* other worldviews and skillful means to reveal Buddhist truth *through* other worldviews—developed in support of each other and in tension with each other. They are explored in what follows.

Buddhist Scholastic Critiques of Theism

Buddhist scholastic critiques of theism seek to assert the Four Holy Truths over against any concept of God as the single, undivided, unchanging, and perfect cause of the multiple, diverse, continually changing, and imperfect content of beings' experience and of their universe. Vasubandhu, an eminent Indian Buddhist scholar (fifth century CE), posed three lines of inquiry leading to refutation of such a God: (1) how can a single, undivided, and unchanging God be the sufficient cause of the diverse content of beings' minds, bodies, and worlds in their particular changes over time? (2) Why would a perfect being have any need to create? What sense would it make for beings to worship a God who is the ultimate creator and sustainer of so much suffering (problem of evil)? (3) Or, if such a God is not sufficient cause but just one of many causes of creating and sustaining the universe, what need is there to posit such a God at all?

These inquiries, leading to refutation of such a God, were further developed by the renowned scholastic Buddhist philosophers Dharmakirti (seventh century CE), Shantarakshita, and Kamalasila (eighth century CE).[17]

17. Richard Hayes details these arguments in his "Principled Atheism in the Buddhist

It is important to note that such refutations of "God" are not intended to refute the unconditioned dimension of being that is the Buddhist promise of salvific freedom (nirvana, Third Holy Truth), or to refute qualities of limitless love, compassion, liberating power, and wisdom in those who embody the unconditioned or are on the path to its realization (Fourth Holy Truth). Rather, such refutations are intended to clear away constructs of "creator God" that both serve as reified objects of self-clinging and turn attention away from the ongoing causal processes of confusion and clinging that must be seen through to permit the unconditioned to actually reveal itself. In the very moment one thinks about God as the seemingly external cause of all being and experience, one is not looking directly in that moment into the causal genesis of clinging and aversion in one's own mind, or seeing through them to the unconditioned dimension that transcends them.

In this regard, as Richard Hayes has pointed out, Buddhist arguments against God's unity, simplicity, and permanence are just one expression of a much broader Buddhist concern to critically deconstruct all concepts of unity, identity, and selfhood that are routinely mistaken for absolute realities (as if not conceptual constructs), that are reified as such, and that thereby give rise to clinging, aversion, and reaction—the conditioned genesis of suffering that obscures the unconditioned. So the Lankavatara scripture states: "It is just mental process that is erroneously discriminated as personal self, continuum, group, condition, atom, primordial matter, and God the creator."[18]

Skillful Means of Conversion and Inclusion

Another Buddhist development in the centuries following Gotama was the ongoing exploration of skillful means to reveal Buddhist truth to oth-

---

Scholastic Tradition," *Journal of Indian Philosophy* 16 (1988) 5–28. Roger Jackson summarizes Dharmakirti's arguments against permanent self and creator God in his article: "Atheology and Buddhalogy in Dharmakirti's Pramanavarttika," *Faith and Philosophy* 16 (1999) 472–505. For Buddhist Madhyamaka critiques of Brahmanic views, see D. Seyfort Ruegg on Aryadeva's *Catuhshataka* and Bhavaviveka's *Tarkajvala*, *Literature of Madhyamaka School* (Wiesbaden: Harrassowitz, 1981) 52, 62–63.

18. See Hayes, "Principled Atheism" 20–24. The quotation is my retranslation of the Sanskrit he quotes in n. 29.

ers through their own symbols, languages, and worldviews. This served both as means for converting others to Buddhism through forms adapted to their own cultures, and as means to see others mystically as coparticipants in the salvific work of the Buddhas, sometimes in tension with the more exclusive posture of the scholastic critiques described in the prior section. The doctrine of skillful means also focused new attention upon the Second Holy Truth, the human problem of mistaking thought-made representations of self, others, and religious objects for the actualities and clinging to them as such. According to the doctrine of skillful means, the wisdom that sees through such representations as empty, thought-made constructs can creatively use diverse representations (of language, gesture, symbol) as skillful means to cut through the human tendency to reify representations and cling to them as absolutes.

Key developments in the doctrine of skillful means accompanied the emergence of Mahayana Buddhism in India and central Asia, contributing to the development of Zen, Pure Land, and Tibetan Buddhist traditions in east Asia and Tibet. This section focuses on the doctrine of skillful means in Mahayana traditions.

Buddhist thought and practice developed much from the time of the Buddha to the first millennium CE, affected by the entry of many cultures into the Buddhist fold: first within the empire forged by the Indian Buddhist king Ashoka (third century BCE); then through migrations of central-Asian peoples into India; then through the trade routes ("silk routes") within the empire established by the Kushanas in the early centuries CE that extended from China through central Asia to present-day Afghanistan and north India. Trade along the Kushana silk routes of central Asia brought Buddhists, Hindus, Zoroastrians, Chinese religious, and Christians into extensive new contact with one another.

In the early centuries CE, as evidenced by the appearance of many new Buddhist sacred texts, some learned Buddhist monks were increasingly dissatisfied with scholastic conservatives of their own schools regarding their fixation upon old questions no longer asked; regarding their outdated ontologies; their inability to speak afresh, attuned to diverse cultures of the time, the direct experience of enlightenment which the Buddha had embodied. The new movements, which called themselves *Mahayana* ("great, all inclusive vehicle" of enlightenment), gave new voice to prior centuries of Buddhist developments in philosophical analysis, meditation, and ritual praxis. There arose a new Buddhist cosmology, consisting of radiant Buddha divinities arrayed in pure, luminous realms—a development supported by the central-Asian cultural matrix and by continuing practice of ancient Buddhist devotional meditations that commune with the qualities of the Buddhas.[19]

The Four Holy Truths were strictly conserved as the doctrinal foundation of these new Buddhist movements. Yet, especially with regard to the Third and Fourth Holy Truths (nirvana and path), Mahayana texts expressed new shifts in emphasis that had developed over prior centuries.

Mahayana texts articulated the path of *Bodhisattvas*, those resolved to attain the most complete form of enlightenment, Buddhahood, in order to guide all beings to liberation from suffering. The Bodhisattva path centers upon two fundamental practices: cultivation of wisdom that discerns the empty nature of things, and cultivation of universal compassion. Prior Buddhist philosophy had directed attention to the impermanent nature of conditioned things. Mahayana texts went further. Not only are conditioned things impermanent, but each such "thing" is empty of the kind of separate, autonomous existence it appears to have. This may sound abstract until we consider the apprehension of, e.g., an enemy, a person who appears as such autonomously, as if there were no fuller or more mysterious person there. In the moment we falsely apprehend "enemy" as nonempty (not as a thought construct projected upon another person, but as an object inherently deserving of hatred), we feel hatred, act from hatred, and the conditioned arising of suffering goes on. Until we discern the emptiness of our moment-by-moment construction of reality, we reify our representations of it, cling to them unawares, grasp to some, hate others, and suffer.

Compassion for all beings caught in the subtle confusion that reifies and clings to representations, who suffer for it in all realms of rebirth, is called "universal compassion" (*maha-karuna*). Transcendental wisdom (*prajña-paramita*), by seeing through that confusion into its empty,

---

19. On the emergence of Mahayana Buddhism and its basic teachings, see Harvey, *Introduction to Buddhism* 89–138; Hirakawa Akira, *A History of Indian Buddhism* (Honolulu: University of Hawaii Press, 1990) 247–74; Paul Williams, *Mahayana Buddhism* (New York: Routledge, 1989); Gregory Schopen, *Bones, Stones, and Buddhist Monks* (Honolulu: University of Hawaii Press, 1997); John Makransky "Historical Consciousness as an Offering to the Trans-historical Buddha," in *Buddhist Theology*, ed. Roger Jackson and John Makransky (London: Curzon, 2000).

thought-constructed nature, realizes freedom from it, eliciting even more intense compassion for all who are caught in it. Thus transcendental wisdom and compassion, mutually empowering, are cultivated in synergy on the Bodhisattva path to full enlightenment.

Compassion impels the communication of liberating wisdom to others, the wisdom that sees into the emptiness of all one's representations of reality. But ordinary beings are lost in habits of reifying and grasping to their representations of reality. It is the Bodhisattva's wisdom that discerns what form the message of liberating truth must take for others to really catch on to it, to release their grasping. That skillfulness at imparting salvific truth and practice is called "skillful means" (*upaya-kaushalya*), hearkening back to Gotama Buddha's skillful means for triggering liberating insight in his interlocutors.

Other Mahayana themes further inform this doctrine of skillful means. In a Mahayana mode of understanding, nirvana is not far away. It is no longer conceived as an unconditioned reality *separate* from the conditions of ordinary life (*samsara*) to be encountered only after long practice of the path. Rather, nirvana is the empty, radiant nature *of* life, of this very mind, body, world, directly encountered in the very moment one is prepared to recognize it. For example, as soon as one's construction of inherent "enemy" falls apart in the perception of its emptiness, accompanied by compassion for all who are trapped in such constructs, one glimpses the unconditioned freedom and joy that was always already at hand in the radiant, empty nature of one's world.

This implies that any aspect of the experienced world can function as skillful means, sacramentally expressing the nirvanic nature of ordinary things, to whoever is prepared to perceive it. The story is told of the ascetic Tibetan yogi Milarepa (twelfth century CE), whose dedication to practice was so one-pointed that he would not take time to look for food, just eating soup made from nettle bushes near his cave. One day his soup bowl dropped and shattered, leaving a film of nettle residue in the shape of the bowl; a nettle residue "bowl." In that moment, his reifying thought habits suddenly broke apart, and the unconditioned, empty nature of experience dawned.

If a soup bowl can disclose nirvana, even more powerful is its disclosure through persons who embody the enlightened qualities of nirvana. It is for this reason that the accomplished "spiritual friend" or Buddhist teacher plays such a central role in many Mahayana scriptures. Some Mahayana scriptures, extending the principle of discovering nirvana where it had not been expected, also talk of apprehending venerable teachers of *non-Buddhist* religions as if they were Bodhisattvas, embodiments of nirvana, who use non-Buddhist means to prepare their followers for the Buddha's path to liberation. As its says in the Vimalakirti scripture: "[Bodhisattvas], by devoting themselves . . . to all the strange sects of the world, develop all beings who have attached themselves to dogmatic views."[20] Such texts communicate a theological inclusivism, subsuming the truth or virtue of venerable non-Buddhist teachers to a Buddhist worldview.

In many Mahayana scriptures, practices of devotion to Buddhas, Bodhisattvas, and spiritual teachers, which include ritual bowing, offering, and putting oneself in their service develop in synergy with meditations on the wisdom of emptiness. Furthermore, to realize the empty nature of all experience is not merely to negate being per se but to become newly receptive to radiant, visionary dimensions of it previously hidden by the long habit of grasping to things. Thus in many Mahayana scriptures, the dawning wisdom of emptiness reveals luminous pure realms of holy beings, Buddhas and Bodhisattvas, whose radiant power and blessing pervade all persons. Such holy vision is supported by meditations envisioning the radiant qualities and power of such holy beings and their pure realms. The opening of such holy vision further empowers the person's faith and courage to be released into the infinite, unconditioned, empty nature of being, into transcendental wisdom.[21]

Practice synergies of wisdom, devotion, and holy vision described in such texts reveal Buddhahood as an all-pervasive, cosmic power, blessing and drawing all beings to its realization through infinite skillful means: radiating liberating power to beings and manifesting as Bodhisattva saints in diverse ways to persons as soon as they become receptive.[22] "In order to help beings, they voluntarily descend into the hells . . : In order

20. *The Holy Teaching of Vimalakirti*, trans. Robert Thurman (University Park: Pennsylvania State University Press, 1986) 69. Similar statements occur in the *Avatamsaka, Lotus, Prajna-paramita* scriptures.

21. Makransky, *Buddhahood Embodied*, 329–34.

22. Ibid., 90–108, 208, 323–35, 350–53. Luis Gomez, "The Bodhisattva as Wonder Worker," in *Prajnaparamita and Related Systems*, ed. Lewis Lancaster (Berkeley: University of California Press, 1977) 221–62.

to help living beings, they become chieftains, captains, priests, ministers, or even prime ministers . . . They become great holy men . . . thereby inducing beings to the morality of tolerance, gentleness and discipline. Well trained in skillful means, they demonstrate all activities, whatever may be a means to make beings delight in the Dharma."[23]

The wisdom-mind of the Buddhas, which pervades all existence in the nondual awareness of emptiness (*Dharmakaya*), pervasively communicates itself through visionary dimensions of being (*Sambhogakaya*), through nature, and through persons (*Nirmanakaya*).[24] Indeed, as the above quotations make clear, Buddhahood communicates through holy persons of any tradition who impart elements of the path to freedom as understood by Buddhists: virtue, generosity, compassion, and wisdom penetrating self-grasping patterns of thought and action. Here are elements of an all-encompassing mystical pluralism inscribed within a Buddhist inclusivism.

But then why don't ordinary beings usually perceive the unconditioned freedom in the very nature of their being, the potential for any aspect of their experience to disclose the unconditioned (nirvana), or the pervasive activity of Buddhas and Bodhisattvas throughout the cosmos, radiating blessings and communicating freedom in limitless ways? Because although all beings possess the intrinsic capacity to awaken to such realities, it is obscured by their habits of self-clinging thought and reaction (as taught in the Second Holy Truth).[25]

This brings out a further connotation of the doctrine of skillful means. In order to penetrate the self-protective habits of beings, the messages of Buddhist teachers must be adapted to their hearers. Any message is mediated by the receiver's own distinctive thought patterns, cultural and individual. So the teaching of the Buddhas, to be effective, requires skillful means to conform the message to the mentalities of the receivers. This requires deep wisdom, the wisdom that understands how persons

---

23. *Vimalkirti* 68–69.

24. On the all-pervading salvific activity of Buddhahood as active nirvana, see Makransky, *Buddhahood Embodied*, chap. 13; Harvey, *Introduction to Buddhism*, 118–38, 170–90, 258–70; Williams, *Mahayana Buddhism*, chaps. 8–10.

25. On this, see, e.g., *Tathagatagarbha sutra*, trans. William Grosnick, in *Buddhism in Practice*, ed. Donald Lopez (Princeton: Princeton University Press, 1995) 92–106; Harvey, *Introduction to Buddhism*, 114–16.

construct their experienced worlds, reify, and grasp to them through their own particular habits of thought.[26]

The doctrine of skillful means has been key in the construction through history of different systematic self-understandings for Mahayana movements. It enabled Mahayanists to make ahistorical sense for themselves of the historical diversity of Buddhist teachings. For example, early Buddhist expressions of the Four Holy Truths as a dualism between nirvana and the ordinary world were explained as Gotama Buddha's skillful way of imparting truth to disciples at a lower level of readiness, gradually preparing them for his more subtle (Mahayana) teaching that nirvana and the ordinary world are ultimately undivided. By ascribing Buddhist teachings that developed later in history and in specific cultures all to Gotama in his place and time, each Buddhist subtradition sought to legitimate and absolutize its own culturally constructed views as Gotama Buddha's very teaching. All Buddhist teachings through history could then be arranged in a hierarchy, the "lower" teachings preparing people for the "higher" teachings, arranged differently according to different Buddhist traditions, unaware of their own cultural conditioning. In the history of various Mahayana traditions, this was sometimes extended as a hierarchy that could include non-Buddhist teachings, like those of Chinese Confucianism and Taoism, as preparation for the "higher" teachings of particular Chinese Buddhist schools. Elsewhere I have argued that these particular uses of the skillful means doctrine no longer make sense within historical consciousness and do harm to contemporary Buddhist traditions.[27]

26. See Harvey, *Introduction to Buddhism*, 121–22; Williams, *Mahayana Buddhism*, 51.

27. On skillful means as a strategy to make ahistorical sense of the historical diversity of Buddhist teachings, and as a rationale for the construction of doctrinal hierarchies through which each Buddhist subtradition sought to authorize and absolutize its own culturally conditioned views as the Buddha's original and highest view, see Makransky, "Historical Consciousness as an Offering" (*Buddhist Theology*, 111–35). In that essay, I argued for contemporary Buddhist thinkers to reject those particular uses of the doctrine of skillful means as erroneous in light of historical consciousness, as contradicting the central thrust of Buddhist understanding (which identifies the tendency to reify and absolutize views as the very cause of suffering), and as harmful to the continuing power and relevance of Buddhism for the contemporary world.

For examples of such absolutized doctrinal hierarchies established by Japanese Buddhist teachers, through which Buddhist and non-Buddhist teachings were viewed as skillful means leading to their own teaching as the highest way, see sections on Kukai and

The doctrine of skillful means also supported Buddhist adaptation and successful mission within diverse cultures of Asia that differ greatly from one another. The doctrine implies that for liberating truth to be authentically appropriated, persons must receive it through their own forms of thought, culture, and aesthetics, not in just one rigidly standardized way from a culture of origin. The literary forms of Indian sacred texts, whose repetitious elaborations expressed Indian forms of reverence, became marginal to Chinese Buddhist culture in which Zen (Ch'an) and Pure Land (Ching-t'u) emerged as native Buddhist traditions emphasizing Chinese values: economy of expression, immediate relevance and practicality, directness, piety, aesthetics, and nature as revelatory.

The doctrine of skillful means is an implicit theme in many of the stories of Zen masters and tantric adepts that Westerners have found so intriguing. In one such popular story, a Chinese student asked his Zen teacher: "How am I truly to enter the path?" The teacher, pointing to a flowing stream nearby, replied, "Enter here." In that moment the student's habits of mind dissolved providing a sudden glimpse of unconditioned freedom. Such a story expresses the Indian Mahayana teaching that the unconditioned (nirvana) is undivided from the flow of conditioned experience but also weds it to a Chinese Taoist appreciation of the revelatory qualities of nature, immediacy, and brevity of expression. Skillful means becomes a spontaneous expression of inculturated wisdom.

Often, however, Buddhist skillful means reverse traditional Buddhist expectations, challenging or subverting unquestioned cultural and religious forms. The story is told of a revered Tibetan monk lama, Jamyang Kyentse, who shocked onlookers by suddenly throwing stones at one of his most devoted disciples chasing him all the way to the river! The disciple dived into the freezing Tibetan waters and swam for his life! Although Jamyang Kyentse upended all expectations of what gentle, kind monks do, the disciple later reported that his mind had been powerfully blessed by the surprising encounter. To communicate a wisdom that frees, skillful

Nichiren in Ruben Habito's article "Japanese Buddhist Perspectives and Comparative Theology: Supreme Ways in Intersection," *Theological Studies* 64 (2003) 362–87. For a Chinese example, see Tsung-mi's system as reported in David Chappel's "Buddhist Responses to Religious Pluralism," 358. For a Tibetan example, see Tsong-kha-pa's *Great Treatise on the Stages of the Path to Enlightenment*, ed. Joshua Cutler (Ithaca: Snow Lion, 2000) with reference to the "three types of persons" (129–41), which implicitly include people of non-Buddhist religious traditions to the degree they develop nonattachment to this life through their own forms of practice.

means must not only meet the mentalities of persons but sometimes radically challenge their subconscious clinging to religious forms or identities as absolute.[28]

Given, then, that skillful means have sometimes communicated Buddhist salvific truth in ways that have upturned all expectations, is it even possible that the usual nontheistic pattern of Buddhist doctrine and praxis itself could be upturned to employ theistic forms as skillful means for Buddhist liberation? Yes, this has occurred.

For example, tantric forms of Buddhism that developed in medieval India (ca. sixth century CE and following) explicitly appropriated imagery and ritual forms of theistic Indian traditions. Buddhist tantric traditions taught ritual practices that focused upon Buddhist deities, theistic embodiments of enlightenment, some of whose iconic qualities paralleled Hindu deities. Yet Buddhist commentaries interpret the symbolism of such divine forms in explicitly Buddhist ways: each element of the deity expressed qualities of the Four Holy Truths, the Buddhist path, the unity of compassion and wisdom, nirvana undivided from this world. Buddhist tantric practices draw directly upon the power of Buddhahood, the all-pervasive power of the unconditioned within this world, through holy vision and devotional practice. Ritual practices directed to such theistic forms, in praising, reverencing, offering to the deity, and receiving the deity's blessing, elicit the spiritual power that finally releases such dualistic forms into the non-dual wisdom that sees into the emptiness of all constructs of "self" and "deity." That wisdom of emptiness itself then manifests as a luminous divine form, a Buddhist deity, radiating salvific power to beings within an enlightened realm of activity, a *mandala*. Such tantric cultivations utilize theistic forms as skillful means in synergy with the wisdom of the empty (thought-constructed) nature of such forms. Thus, a uniquely Buddhist awareness of the unconditioned reality (nirvana) and its liberating power is given expression through Indic analogues of kataphatic and apophatic theism.[29]

---

28. Das, *Snow Lion's Turquoise Mane*, 161–62.

29. On tantric practice forms, see David Snellgrove, *Indo-Tibetan Buddhism*, vol. 1 (Boston: Shambhala, 1987); Geoffrey Samuel, *Civilized Shamans* (Washington DC: Smithsonian, 1993); Reginald Ray, *Secret of the Vajra World* (Boston: Shambhala, 2001); Chagdud Tulku, *Gates to Buddhist Practice: Essential Teachings of a Tibetan Master* (Junction City, CA: Padma, 2001).

In sum, then, the doctrine of skillful means has profoundly informed the adaptation of Buddhist forms to new places and times, contributing to the successful missionary activity of Buddhism in diverse cultures of Asia (while ironically also providing the means for each subtradition to absolutize and cling to its own teaching as the highest teaching originally taught by Gotama Buddha). As we have seen, the doctrine of skillful means has also informed Buddhist mystical worldviews that have viewed other religions within a cosmic Buddhist inclusivism. According to that doctrine, salvific truth discloses itself in incalculably diverse ways through diverse worldviews, cultures, and religions—non-Buddhist as well as Buddhist. But what counts as salvific truth remains the Buddhist understanding and experience of it: the Four Holy Truths. Those Truths may be expressed in accustomed or unexpected ways. But only when such expressions actually function to liberate beings from the deepest causes of suffering (especially from the tendency to misconstrue one's representations of reality as absolutes) do they authentically communicate the power of the Buddha's salvific truth. As the Mahayana Avatamsaka scripture puts it:

> In this world there are four quadrillion . . . names to express the Four Holy Truths in accord with the mentalities of beings, to cause them all to be harmonized and pacified . . . [And] just as in this world . . . there are four quadrillion names to express the Four Holy Truths, so in all the worlds to the east— . . . immeasurably many worlds, in each there are an equal number of names to express the Four Holy Truths, to cause all the sentient beings there to be harmonized and pacified in accordance with their mentalities. And just as this is so of the worlds to the east, so it is with all the infinite worlds in the ten directions.

Contemporary Expressions of Traditional Paradigms: Gunapala Dharmasiri, The Dalai Lama, Buddhadasa

Contemporary Buddhist scholars who relate Buddhist truth to other religions continue to draw upon the two basic paradigms described above: scholastic critique of others' religious concepts, or inclusion of the other through a Buddhist understanding of skillful means.

Gunapala Dharmasiri exemplifies the former approach. A Sri Lankan Buddhist who studied at the University of Lancaster in England,

Dharmasiri criticizes in his book, *A Buddhist Critique of the Christian Concept of God*, Christian concepts in line with earlier Buddhist critiques of Hindu theism (see my earlier section, "Buddhist Scholastic Critiques of Theism"). Like his Buddhist predecessors, but now also drawing support from philosophers such as Gilbert Ryle and James Strawson to critique Christian philosophy, Dharmasiri rejects Christian concepts of an eternal soul as a substantial, eternal entity by arguing that such a substance is not observable within the impermanent minds and bodies of persons. Then how are persons to be affirmed as individual moral agents who experience the consequences of their own actions? Following his classical Buddhist forbears, Dharmasiri argues that each individual's virtuous or nonvirtuous actions have consequences for his or her own causal continuity of mind and body without having to posit an unchanging substance within him or her. Since, in line with the Second Holy Truth, clinging to false representations of a permanent, substantial self or soul is a primary cause of ego grasping and suffering, and since such representations are not observed to have any referent, they are refuted. Since a Christian concept of soul as eternal substance is correlated with the concept of an eternal, substantial God, Dharmasiri extrapolates his refutation of the former into a rejection of the latter: "Therefore, to a Buddhist, the conception of God either as analogous to or as identical with the soul would not be able to make any sense."[30]

His Holiness Tenzin Gyatso is the fourteenth Dalai Lama of Tibetan Buddhism, a Mahayana tradition in which the doctrine of skillful means has had a central role. He recognizes in all the great religious traditions several broadly common purposes: to open persons to a "higher force" that transforms them toward love, compassion, inner peace, deep respect for others, and lasting happiness.[31] But persons are tremendously diverse in their mentalities, due to both cultural and individual differences. If only one religious system or means were provided for all individuals, it would not be possible for many to really undergo such a profound inner transformation. Given this fact, the differences among religions in doc-

30. Gunapala Dharmasiri, "Extracts from a Buddhist Critique of the Christian Concept of God," in *Christianity through Non-Christian Eyes*, ed. Paul Griffiths (Maryknoll, NY: Orbis, 1990) 153–61.

31. His Holiness Tenzin Gyatso, "'Religious Harmony' and Extracts from the Bodhgaya Interviews," in Griffiths, ed. *Christianity through Non-Christian Eyes*, 163–64, 167.

trine and practice are needed for a diverse humanity. Recall the Buddhist teaching of skillful means: messages of liberating truth must be conformed to the thought forms of the receivers if they are to be deeply realized. The Dalai Lama takes this principle, previously applied mainly to Buddhist teaching methods, and extends it beyond Buddhism: "There is a richness in the fact that there are so many different presentations of the way [to be transformed through love and compassion in different religions]. Given that there are so many different types of people with various predispositions and inclinations, this is helpful."[32]

Because the Dalai Lama draws so heavily upon the Buddhist doctrine of skillful means, and emphasizes shared goals of world religions (peace, compassion, and the like), he may appear to promulgate simply a theological pluralism, as if he assumes that all world religions realize precisely the same salvific goals. But when functioning as a Buddhist systematician, he does acknowledge that different religions certainly seem to posit different salvific goals, which would require different means of practice for their attainment. In that light, he suggests that nirvana, posited as the unique ultimate goal of Buddhism, requires uniquely Buddhist means for its attainment:

> Here . . . it is necessary to examine what is meant by liberation or salvation [in different religions]. Liberation in which 'a mind that understands the [empty] sphere of reality annihilates all defilements in the [empty] sphere of reality' is a state that only Buddhists can accomplish. This kind of *moksha* [liberation] or nirvana is only explained in the Buddhist scriptures, and is only achieved through Buddhist practice. . . According to certain religions, however, salvation is a place, a beautiful paradise, like a peaceful valley. To attain such a state as this, to achieve such a state of *moksha* [liberation], does not require the practice of emptiness, the understanding of [ultimate] reality.[33]

Bhikku Buddhadasa, a leading Thai monk scholar of the twentieth century, pioneered new ways of relating ancient Buddhist teachings to the modern world, including the problem of truth in other religions. Buddhadasa applies three levels of meaning to religious discourse. On the outermost level of meaning, religious traditions appear dissimilar in their

32. Ibid., 165–66.
33. Ibid., 169.

expressions. On an inner level, all the great religions are the same in their essential concern to eliminate selfishness and to foster the inner freedom of love and humility. On the inmost level of meaning, historical religions in themselves are empty of substantial, independent existence. They are merely temporal constructs expressing the unconditioned, empty nature of things that transcends concepts of "my religion" or "your religion."

Buddhadhasa clarifies this analysis with the analogy of water. On the outer level, various kinds of water may be distinguished, since they come from different sources containing different minerals or pollutants. But on the inner level, when all such minerals or pollutants are removed, all the "waters" turn out to be the very same substance, just pure water. Finally, on the inmost level, when water is investigated most deeply, even the concept "water" dissolves: "If you proceed further with your analysis of pure water," he says,

> you will conclude that there is no water—only two parts of hydrogen and one part of oxygen. Hydrogen and oxygen are not water. The substance that we have been calling water has disappeared. It is void, empty . . . In the same way, one who has attained to the ultimate truth sees that there is no such thing as religion! There is only reality . . . Call it what you like—dharma or truth—but you cannot particularize that dharma or truth as Buddhism, Christianity, or Islam . . . The label "Buddhism" was attached only after the fact, as it was with Christianity, Islam and every other religion. None of the great religious teachers ever gave a name to their teachings; they just went on teaching throughout their lives about how we should live.[34]

Buddhadasa's Buddhist way of anchoring his theological pluralism within emptiness makes an interesting contrast to those Western theological pluralists who understand diverse religions to refer ultimately to one God.

---

34. Bhikku Buddhadasa, "No Religion," in *Me and Mine: Selected Essays of Bhikkhu Buddhadasa*, ed. Donald Swearer (Albany: SUNY Press, 1989) 146–47.

12

"Without Bias"—The Dalai Lama in Dialogue

Judith Simmer-Brown

In July of 1996, an historic weeklong dialogue between twenty-five Christian and twenty-five Buddhist contemplatives took place at Gethsemani Abbey in Kentucky. Distinguished guests came from monastic communities all over the world, and the honored guest was the most famous Buddhist in the world: Tenzin Gyatso, the Fourteenth Dalai Lama of Tibet, called in the West "His Holiness."[1] Stemming from conversations that began at the World Parliament of Religions in Chicago in 1993, these dialogues were designed to explore the common features of monastic spirituality. Gethsemani was chosen because it had been the home community of Thomas Merton, who met His Holiness in India in 1968, shortly before his death. The Dalai Lama spoke of seeing "profound spirituality and love" in Merton, and in a tribute commented, "I think the important thing is that we must fulfill his wishes. I think that with our

---

1. There is no Tibetan term that is translated as "His Holiness." From the impetus of Tibetan Buddhism in exile, this term used for the Catholic pope was used for the heads of the four major schools of Tibetan Buddhism—and so from the 1960s, there have always been four "His Holinesses": His Holinesses Karmapa, Sakya Trinzin, Dudjom, and the Dalai Lama—they are all referred to in English as "His Holiness." The term in Tibetan is more often given *Kyabje*, which means "Lord of Refuge," which means the teacher has been recognized by his peers to embody all the qualities of enlightenment in his manifestation and his compassionate teaching. There is no legislative body that makes this decision. The term begins to be used over time, especially for the genuine elders of a tradition.

dialogue today we are fulfilling one of his wishes."[2] These dialogues were dedicated to the memory of Merton, about whom His Holiness said, "the impact of meeting him will remain until my last breath."[3]

In Western dialogue settings, it is commonly assumed that the Dalai Lama's inspiration for interreligious dialogue came primarily from Christian sources. Often it is said that it was Merton himself who brought His Holiness into dialogue; his meeting with Merton "opened up his perspective," causing him to develop a "new pluralism."[4] Others credit Merton's remarkable "love of Christ," who is "the source, center and object of all prayer."[5] Without an informed understanding of Tibet and its Dalai Lamas, it is easy to fall into simplistic perspectives, but this underestimates the sophistication, intelligence, and complex factors at work in the life of His Holiness.

The Fourteenth Dalai Lama has become the "leading proponent of Buddhist modernism,"[6] a reframing of traditional Tibetan Buddhism as a world religion. When he fled Tibet in 1959, he entered a world stage that rapidly broadened his horizons and placed him in the double role of chief political advocate for independence for his country as well as most visible Buddhist on the globe. These roles required him to adopt modernist stances while preserving the integrity of his own traditions. For example, under the influence of the legacy of Mahatma Gandhi, he eschewed the violence commonly practiced by his predecessors and eventually devised the ultimatum that he would resign his seat if violence were used in the Free Tibet movement, a personal policy that began in the year of his Nobel award.[7] Also unlike his predecessors, he presents Buddhism as a rational

2. Donald W. Mitchell and James Wiseman, eds., *The Gethsemani Encounter: A Dialogue on the Spiritual Life by Buddhist and Christian Monastics* (New York: Continuum, 1997) 39, 48.

3. His Holiness the Dalai Lama, "Tribute to Thomas Merton," in Mitchell and Wiseman, eds., *The Gethsemani Encounter*, 261.

4. Bettina Bauemer, "A Model for Mutual Enrichment," in *Monastic Interfaith Dialogue Journal* 78 (2007).

5. Murray Bodo, "The Dalai Lama Visits Gethsemani," in *St. Anthony Messenger*, January 1997.

6. Donald S. Lopez, Jr., *Prisoners of Shangri-la: Tibetan Buddhism and the West* (Chicago: University of Chicago Press, 1999), 185.

7. Elliot Sperling, "Orientalism and Aspects of Violence." In *Imagining Tibet: Perceptions, Projections, and Fantasies*, ed. Thierry Dodin and Heinz Rather (Somerville, MA: Wisdom, 2001), 326.

religion strongly affiliated with a scientific worldview, based on the practice of meditation that relegates ritual, deity-worship, and superstition to popular misunderstandings of its true essence. This brand of Buddhist modernism was never known in Tibet, but it has successfully supported the precarious roles the Dalai Lama has been forced to hold, gaining sympathy everywhere for the Tibetan cause and for Buddhism. [8] In addition, His Holiness serves as the chief spokesperson for an ecumenical, peaceful worldview that has rendered him the most popular religious figure in the world.

His Holiness's stance in interreligious dialogue may be part of this complex strategy, but in any case his visionary spiritual leadership in the world has been shaped by strands of his own Buddhist tradition in Tibet. In this essay, we will look especially at a little-known ecumenical movement in modern Tibet that has shaped his interreligious sensibilities. Since his exile in 1959, the Ri-me tradition has increasingly shaped the dialogue theology of His Holiness the Dalai Lama.

Ri-me (literally "without bias," pronounced Ree-May) was an ecumenical movement that began in nineteenth-century Tibet, countering strong sectarian rivalry that had dominated Tibet for centuries. Ri-me was an informal network of teachers from the mainstream lineages, who shared an inclusivist, even pluralist sensibility, wishing to preserve practices and transmissions from all lineages of Tibet. While the movement was concentrated in monastic settings, many lay yogis and yoginis of Tibet also were counted among their numbers. This movement has shaped the orientation of many lamas and incarnate teachers (*tulkus*, usually called *rinpoches*, or "precious jewels") in exile who have come to the west. This paper outlines the primary theological features of the Ri-me school of Tibet, and extrapolates its contemporary adaptation found more recently in the interreligious dialogues of His Holiness, the fourteenth Dalai Lama.[9]

8. Lopez , *Prisoners of Shangri-la*, 206–7.

9. Geoffrey Samuel describes the central role of Ri-me in shaping contemporary teachers, both in Asia and the West, in *Civilized Shamans: Buddhism in Tibetan Society* (Washington: The Smithsonian Institution Press, 1993), 307. For background on Ri-me on Chogyam Trungpa's interreligious dialogue activities, see Judith Simmer-Brown, "Heart to Heart: Interreligious Dialogue," in Fabrice Midal, ed., *Recalling Chogyam Trungpa* (Boston: Shambhala, 2005); Judith Simmer-Brown, "Preface to the Second Edition," in *Speaking of Silence: Christians and Buddhists in Dialogue* ed. Susan Szpakowski (Halifax, NS: Vajradhatu, 2005), 3–10.

Certainly Tibet has had a bitter history of sectarianism and bigotry, especially in central and western Tibet. Before the thirteenth century, rivalry between the indigenous Bon and Buddhist traditions was replaced by "modernist" polemics against the tantras of the "ancients" (Nyingma). While southern and eastern Tibet had a history of greater harmony and cooperation, by the fourteenth century sectarian issues were intensified all over Tibet by the political stakes at hand, even though the Great Fifth Dalai Lama (ruled from 1642 to 1682) pacified much bigotry and sectarianism through diplomacy. Monastic doctrinal catechisms further fueled sectarian rivalry and crushed the previous creativity of the debate traditions. By the mid-1800s, sectarian rivalry was the predominant culture in all areas of Tibet, with particular suppression of the Nyingma.[10]

The Ri-me can trace its early roots to the great Nyingma treasure-discoverer Jigme Lingpa (1730–1798), master of the yogically oriented *Dzogchen* ("great perfection") meditation lineage.[11] Dzogchen emphasizes the innate, natural state of mind, an open, expansive experience of reality unfettered by discursive thought. Ri-me developed on these yogic foundations, emphasizing the openness and purity of realization, the centrality of meditation, and the importance of scholastic study in service of practice rather than the other way around. Jigme Lingpa stated, "To become attached to intellectual models of the experience or meditational states encountered in the course of trying to achieve it is to mistake the path for the goal, whereas the real aim is to turn the goal into the path."[12]

It was the nineteenth century that nourished the full bloom of the Ri-me in Tibet. In east Tibet, a loose network of the most creative masters of meditation "concurrently exhibited an incredibly open attitude to all teachings and shared a concern for their preservation."[13] These masters included wandering yogis, prolific monastic scholars, and respected masters of meditation.[14] With the publication of the *Sheja-dzo* or *Treasury*

10. Gene Smith, "'Jam mgon Kong sprul and the Nonsectarian Movement," in *Among Tibetan Texts* (Somerville, MA: Wisdom, 2001) 237–47.

11. Samuel , *Civilized Shamans*, 534.

12. Ibid., 535.

13. Sarah Harding, trans., *Treasury of Esoteric Instructions* (Ithaca: Snow Lion, 2008), 30; Samuel, *Civilized Shamans*, 321; John Petit, trans., *Mipham's Beacon of Certainty* (Somerville, MA: Wisdom, 1999) 97–98, 488.

14. Best-known examples are Shabkar and masters of Palpung, Dzongzar, and Dzogchen—including Jamgon Kongtrul, Jamyang Khyentse Wangpo, Chokling

of Knowledge in 1864,[15] the great master Jamgon Kongtrul Lodro Thaye launched the first comprehensive demonstration of the Ri-me approach. He encyclopedically outlined the inner unity of the Buddhist teachings while preserving teachings and lineages in danger of extinction. Kongtrul wrote that Shakyamuni taught 84,000 different teachings, and since it is unknown which teaching will influence which being, "it is best to collect them all, so that no one will miss her or his unique opportunity."[16] He also collected into anthologies texts of all kinds—from philosophic to artistic to liturgical—so that they could be preserved in their original form. For practice texts, he received the *wang, lung,* and *tri*[17] and practiced each of them so that their meditative essence could be passed on unsullied by time.

Kongtrul's work laid the foundation for the effective transmission of the diverse schools of Tibetan Buddhism in a challenging environment like the twentieth-century diaspora, for as Ringu Tulku explains, it became possible to receive "the teachings of various lineages and schools from a single teacher in a single place."[18] For example, Kongtrul's *Treasury of Instructions* preserve the compendium of the most essential teachings of the eight practice lineages as a single lineage of transmission.

Features of the Ri-me Approach

Since Ri-me was not a school in the sense of the ancestral schools formulated in the fourteenth through the seventeenth centuries in Tibet, it did not constitute an organized monastic order with its own temples (*gompa*) or its own lineages. It was a collaboration of masters of several mainstream Tibetan Buddhist schools and lineages (Kagyu, Nyingma, and Sakya) who shared an orientation toward meditation, realization, and preservation of

---

Rinpoche, Dza Patrul, Zhenga, Ju Mipham Gyatso, and many others.

15. This text is also called the *Sheja Kunchab*. As Gene Smith notes: "The [*Sheja Dzö*] appears to be the earliest statement of nonsectarian thought" ("Jam mgon Kong sprul and the Nonsectarian Movement," 237).

16. Harding, *Treasury of Esoteric Instructions*, 34.

17. Literally empowerment, reading transmission, and oral instructions.

18. Ringu Tulku, *The Ri-me Philosophy of Jamgon Kongtrul the Great* (Boston: Shambhala, 2006), 12–13.

teachings and lineages of teaching. They held as central the interpretation of dharma texts without discrimination (*ris su ma chad par*); hence they were named Ri-me (*ris med*). [19]

With the promulgation of the Ri-me approach by Jamgon Kongtrul Lodro Thaye, four distinctive elements emerged that have relevance for a theological foundation for interreligious dialogue. [20]

1. *The Ri-me advocated that all traditions of meditation practice are to be appreciated, valued, and preserved, regardless of the lineages or schools from which they have come.* While many of the Ri-me proponents were from the *Nyingma* ("ancients") school, leaders of the movement derived from the various divisions of *Kagyu* ("command lineage"), *Sakya* (a hereditary royal lineage), and *Jonangpa* schools. Occasional Gelukpa teachers were also included. A contemporary Ri-me master commented in a talk in North America: "To adopt the Ri-me approach means to follow your own chosen path with dedication, while maintaining respect and tolerance for all other valid choices." [21]

For preservation, Ri-me was intent upon saving a contemplative tradition seen to be in peril of being lost or overly codified in the atmosphere of sectarianism and scholasticism of nineteenth-century Tibet. For Ri-me, it was important that all these teachings and practices be preserved so that the full resources of the dharma be available for future generations. [22] As Buddhologist Geoffrey Samuel wrote, "All methods were to be gathered together and made available. Any one might contain the liberating potential appropriate to one or another student." [23] This is why great Ri-me masters such as Jamgon Kongtrul Lodro Thaye devoted their lives to the collecting, editing, and preserving the texts of Tibet's various practice lineages, and to receiving the corresponding empowerments and oral instructions associated with those texts. [24]

19. Petit, *Mipham's Beacon of Certainty*, 98.

20. These categories are adapted especially from the work of Samuel, *Civilized Shamans*, 537–51.

21. Jamgon Kongtrul of Sechen, in a talk in Victoria, British Columbia, Canada, in the mid-1980s. Quoted in Richard Barron, trans., *The Autobiography of Jamgon Kongtrul: A Gem of Many Colors* (Ithaca NY: Snow Lion, 2003) xviii.

22. Comments of Ringu Tulku, Rinpoche, cited in Reginald Ray, *Indestructible Truth* (Boston: Shambhala, 2001) 207–8.

23. Samuel, *Civilized Shamans*, 543.

24. For a summary of Jamgon Kongtrul Lodro Thaye's treasuries, see Smith, "'Jam

2. *Ri-me's abiding interest was in meditation and contemplative practice as the ground of spiritual life.* This meant that Ri-me focused on fostering communities of practice, encouraging extensive solitary meditation retreats, preserving the texts and oral traditions of authentic practice lineages, and respecting the uniqueness of each lineage. Ri-me masters refrained from syncretism, the mixing of all kinds of spiritual paths and techniques in the name of ecumenism.[25] While it is not clear what exactly constituted "authenticity" or "validity" in a Tibetan setting, the concerns of the Ri-me masters were promulgating an unbroken lineage of oral transmission; preserving corresponding texts (both ritual and meditation) within the lineage, with accompanying oral instructions on the conduct of the practice; and supporting living teachers who could serve as the spiritual guide. Ri-me lamas are primarily *tantrikas* who experience visions, discover hidden treasure texts, and place emphasis upon intensive meditation practice in retreat. Their sainthood can sometimes take unorthodox forms, especially in settings of excessive institutionalization and scholasticism.

3. *Meditation is not to be regarded with naive passivity; rather, intelligent investigation and inquiry are crucial supports to a mature meditation practice.* In an atmosphere of sectarian rivalry, the Ri-me movement cultivated a new kind of philosophic view that refrained from obscure points of contention. Rather than drawing on recent Tibetan sectarian texts, the nonsectarian movement focused on the Indian traditions from which much of Tibetan scholasticism derived.[26] Ri-me monastic colleges (*shedras*) focused on a small number of classical scriptures from Indian Buddhism, with simple commentaries in Tibetan translation. In addition, the hermeneutical aim was to understand the meaning (*ngedon*), rather than just the literal words of the texts (*drangdon*), for it was felt that the underlying meanings of the Buddha are not in contradiction. As Jamgon Kongtrul quoted from *Net of Magical Manifestation of Manjushri*:

---

mgon Kong sprul and the Nonsectarian Movement," 262–67; for a more comprehensive list see Barron, *The Autobiography of Jamgon Kongtrul*, 515–49.

25. Barron, "Introduction," in *The Autobiography of Jamgon Kongtrul*, xvii.

26. Samuel, *Civilized Shamans*, 538; Smith, "'Jam mgon Kong sprul and the Nonsectarian Movement," 26.

> The Buddha is without beginning or end;
> The original Buddha is without bias.[27]

The emphasis of such study was comprehension that would "eliminate many controversies that arose through variant expositions of the same texts by different Tibetan exegetes."[28] As a further move away from sectarian traps, Ri-me scholars refused to accept the labels of their opponents in debate.

Still, the Ri-me movement did not have a single philosophical standpoint.[29] Many of the Ri-me masters embraced the Shentong perspective of Madhyamaka, holding that the luminous nature of mind was not merely empty, but full of the qualities of Buddhahood. This perspective is diametrically opposed to core teachings of the Gelukpa school, that hold Rangtong Madhyamaka, asserting that the highest teachings of Buddhism are the emptiness of inherent existence of all phenomena, including the nature of mind. However, key Ri-me founders like Ju Mipham departed from the Ri-me majority in also holding the Rangtong to be paramount. In any case, the Ri-me movement generated "a renewal of the academic and intellectual tradition within the non-Gelukpa schools."[30]

4. *The Ri-me movement was not merely an academic or elite spiritual movement, it also had a strongly popular side.*[31] Many of the Ri-me proponents were not from aristocratic Tibet, and they flourished outside institutional monastic Buddhism, even though many Ri-me masters were fully ordained and taught within monasteries. Pioneers like Dza Patrul Rinpoche composed works full of earthy references to nomadic and lay life, popularizing practices that could be done outside the monastery, like *chod* (severance), a practice from Machik Lapdron; *phowa* (mind transference at death); and the bodhisattva practices of *Shantideva* and *Atisa*. Ri-me also relied on folk material from the *Gesar of Ling* epic and Shambhala teachings so beloved in Tibet, as well as on the yogic traditions of *terma*, visionary and prophetic teachings, and shamanic practices. The Ri-me view was "not to reject one path (e.g., monasticism) in favor of another

27. Quoted in Harding, *Treasury of Esoteric Instructions*, 26.

28. Smith, "'Jam mgon Kong sprul and the Nonsectarian Movement," 246.

29. Samuel, *Civilized Shamans*, 543.

30. Ibid., 538; John Powers, *Introduction to Tibetan Buddhism* (Ithaca: Snow Lion, 2007) 362.

31. Samuel, *Civilized Shamans*, 539.

(such as that of the lay yogin) but to maintain all paths as possible options that might be suitable for particular students."[32] The Ri-me embraced all of these streams of practice.

As another aspect of shamanic and prophetic teachings, Ri-me teachers held the degeneration of spiritual motivation to stem from institutionalization of the teachings, lack of deep study, and the use of dharma for merely worldly gain. This is known popularly in Tibetan Buddhism as the "dark age" (*snyigs ma'i dus*), a time foretold by the Buddha as a time in which obstacles to practice and realization are monumental, requiring extraordinary means to counter it. Jamgon Kongtrul wrote:

> These days even famous lamas and geshes have a very meager vision or pure perception of the entirety (phyogs med) of the sage's doctrine other than just for that of their own traditions and a few sources. Most people, high or low, have done few studies and have little familiarity with the dharma. In particular, in these later times there are indeed many who, while they themselves do not live forthrightly and lack a religious outlook, yet with the arrogance of power proclaim which dharma traditions are good and which bad, which lineages are pure and which impure. To say nothing of other tradition, they even shun their own traditions with unfounded fears, like a blind yak that startles himself.[33]

For Jamgon Kongtrul, to exhibit such bias was "rejecting the dharma" itself, an act which he considered "grievous."[34] Ri-me developed under the prevailing Tibetan view that current times are the "dark age" in which the degeneration of truly spiritual motivation gives rise to corruption of the genuine dharma. This view provided the impetus for preservation of authentic lineages so in peril in this dangerous time.

32. Ibid., 540–41.

33. Barron, ff. 66b-67a (*Gem*, 190–91), quoted in Harding, *Treasury of Esoteric Instructions*, 34.

34. Harding, *Treasury of Esoteric Instructions*, 34, 36.

The Dalai Lama in Dialogue: A Western Ri-me?

The impact of the Ri-me on Tibetan Buddhism was powerful even in the nineteenth century,[35] but it is in diaspora that the full impact of the Ri-me has been felt. Certainly sectarianism has continued among Tibetans in the west. Some lamas have first replicated the forms familiar to them in Tibet and India, including the sectarianism; the habit of hegemony was their birthright in more traditional settings. The norm has been for these Tibetan teachers to establish meditation centers, translation committees, retreat centers, monastic study programs such as *shedras*, and curricula of systematic study and practice. As Tibetan teachers of diverse lineages have been thrown together as refugees, however, others have found that cooperation, tolerance, and mutual respect have served them more fruitfully than debate and rivalry. Many teachers have found Ri-me a helpful reference point for relating with diverse religions and cultural forces at work, especially in educational and dialogue activities. This has been especially true of the current Dalai Lama.

The remarkable fourteenth Dalai Lama was strongly influenced by Ri-me teachers in his later training in India. Though his initial tutors were exclusively Gelukpa in orientation, Kagyu lama Khunu Lama Tenzin Gyaltsen, and Nyingma masters H. H. Dilgo Khyentse Rinpoche and the third Dodrupchen, Tenpe Nyima, all served as important teachers for His Holiness. He has practiced Mahamudra and Dzogchen, and gives empowerments from many of the major lineages. Striking evidence that he has embraced a Ri-me approach is found in his denunciation of the ancestral Gelukpa protector practice of Dorje Shugden, rejected because of its aggressive brand of sectarianism toward Nyingma practitioners.[36]

35. "[T]he esteem with which [they and their collaborators] continue to be regarded are a testimonial to the tact and judgment they possessed. Although the nonsectarian movement did engender reactionary intolerance and occasionally the denigration of other traditions of Buddhist practice, even these sectarian responses were couched in the language of eclecticism and unity" (Smith, "'Jam mgon Kong sprul and the Nonsectarian Movement," 237).

36. Identifying himself more squarely with the Ri-me school has been politically dangerous for His Holiness within Tibetan Buddhism, as the orthodox branches of the Gelukpa school have continued threats toward him for betraying what they perceive to be the major protector of the Gelukpa school. This complex issue is explored impressively by George Dreyfus, "The Shuk-den Affair: Origins of a Controversy," a revised version of an article originally published in *Journal of the International Association of*

His Holiness has written a supplication for the nonsectarian approach of Tibetan Buddhism.

> In short, may all the teachings of the Buddha in the Land of Snows
>
> Flourish long into the future—the ten great pillars of the study lineage,
>
> And the chariots of the practice lineage, such as Shijé ('Pacifying') and the rest,
>
> All of them rich with their essential instructions combining sutra and mantra.
>
> May the lives of the masters who uphold these teachings be secure and harmonious!
>
> May the sangha preserve these teachings through their study, meditation and activity!
>
> May the world be filled with faithful individuals intent on following these teachings!
>
> And long may the non-sectarian teachings of the Buddha continue to flourish![37]

His Holiness's leadership in overcoming sectarianism and promoting interreligious understanding has been powerful both within Tibetan Buddhism and globally. As Ringu Tulku wrote: "At this time we Tibetans have little good fortune and little power. The only area in which we are fortunate is that the fourteenth Dalai Lama, Tendzin Gyatso, is still alive. The Dalai Lama is a proponent of nonsectarianism, and his views accord with those of Jamgon Kongtrul."[38] Early in his dialogue activities, His Holiness was tentative, even a bit stiff in his interreligious presentations. At the very first Buddhist-Christian meditation dialogue at Naropa in 1981, he spoke traditionally about Buddhist meditation, without much evidence of a Ri-me flavor of engagement with other lineages and traditions.[39] As

---

Buddhist Studies 21 (1998) 227–70, published by the Office of Tibet (http://www.tibet .com/dholgyal/shugden-origins.html). He places the current Dalai Lama's dilemma in the historical context of similar dilemmas faced by the great fifth and the thirteenth Dalai Lamas, especially with regard to practices of the Nyingma in general and Dzogchen in particular.

37. http://www.lotsawahouse.org/harmonious.html.

38. Ringu Tulku, *The Ri-me Philosophy of Jamgon Kongtrul*, 13.

39. After His Holiness launched without prelude into an extended, detailed presentation of meditation, for example, translated into technical Tibetan, the audience began to

the 1980s progressed and with the assimilation of late twentieth-century century values and ethics, His Holiness's visionary leadership, peacemaking, and dialogue activities earned him the Nobel Prize for Peace in 1989. In 1990, he met in Dharamsala with a delegation of Jewish teachers for an extensive interfaith dialogue. In his subsequent dialogues at the World Parliament of Religions in Chicago in 1993, the Monastic Interreligious Dialogue (MID) in the 1990s, and his more recent dialogues with Muslims, his stance has manifested more Ri-me sensibilities. He has since visited Israel three times and met in 2006 with the chief rabbi of Israel. He had frequent dialogues with Pope John Paul II and has met privately with Pope Benedict XVI. He has also met the late Archbishop of Canterbury and the late President of the Church of Jesus Christ of Latter-day Saints (Mormons), as well as senior Eastern Orthodox Church, Muslim, Hindu, and Sikh spiritual leaders and officials. There is probably no more prolific and accomplished dialogue partner on the interreligious scene today.

Dialogue and Discernment: A Ri-me View

Working from the foundation of the Ri-me movement in Tibet and extrapolating what appears to be the application of Ri-me in a Western environment, let us delineate a theological structure for the Dalai Lama's engagement in interreligious dialogue. The word theology has been assumed consciously in the context of current thinking on the subject, in which theology refers *rhetorically* to formal discourse concerning meaning within Buddhism with relation to other religions, and *functionally* to engagement with other religious traditions about fundamental questions that pertain to all of them.[40] This investigation will pursue four fundamental questions.

1. *For contemporary Tibetan Buddhists in diaspora, why would one dialogue?* This is probably best addressed by the fourth characteristic of Ri-me described above, the extraordinary skillful means necessary in a

---

inexplicably laugh. His Holiness responded in English: "What happened? I don't know. (Laughs.) Anyway, laughing is good. Laughing is much better than remain like this" (unpublished transcripts, Naropa University Archives, 1981).

40. Jose Cabezon, "Buddhist Theology in the Academy," in Roger Jackson and John Makransky, eds., *Buddhist Theology: Critical Reflections by Contemporary Buddhist Scholars* (Surrey, UK: Curzon, 2000) 25–26.

period characterized by the "dark age." From a Ri-me perspective, we live in a time in which spiritual vocation is under threat from the forces of materialism that have placed the needs of the few above the needs of the many. As Tibetans have lost control of their own homeland, the matter has become more pressing. As the social, political, and spiritual leader of the Tibetan people, His Holiness now speaks of the urgency for dialogue and interreligious understanding, drawing on the creative potential of the world's religions to bring peace and harmony everywhere. He is not confident that such leadership can come from social and political forces. Because we all share our lives on the planet, it is very important to live in harmony and peace—in fact, it is a necessity. At the 1996 Gethsemani dialogues, His Holiness lamented how unfortunate it is that there are so many divisions, even conflict and bloodshed in the name of religion. But different religious traditions "have a great potential to help humanity by promoting human happiness and satisfaction."[41]

Still, His Holiness asks the world's religions to challenge each other a bit in "constructive competition" in order to deepen the authenticity of personal practice. Truly applying one's spiritual teachings to daily life could have a transformative effect on the world, overcoming apathy and hypocrisy. As he challenges his colleagues, "the Buddhists should implement what we believe in daily life; and our Christian brothers and sisters should also implement their teachings in daily life. . . . Since each side would like to be better practitioners, there is no harm in such competition—it is really constructive."[42] The point of such competition is a truly Ri-me one: deepening authentic spirituality of the living contemplative traditions of the world, especially in the daily life of the practitioner. "We need to experience more deeply the meanings and spiritual values of our own religious tradition—we need to know these teachings not only on an intellectual level but also through our own deeper experience. We must practice our own religion sincerely; it must become part of our lives."[43]

41. His Holiness the Dalai Lama, "Harmony, Dialogue and Meditation," in Mitchell and Wiseman, eds., *The Gethsemani Encounter*, 47.

42. Mitchell and Wiseman, eds., *The Gethsemani Encounter*, 49.

43. Quote from Murray Bodo, "The Dalai Lama Visits Gethsemani," *St. Anthony Messenger*, January 1997.

2. What theological stance is taken with regard to other religious tradi-tions? The Ri-me approach is always inclusive, assuming that the multi-plicity of teachings in Tibet are an expression of the skillful means of the Buddha in providing different paths and practices for students of differ-ent temperaments and propensities. On a more global stage, Ri-me says that there is no place in dialogue for advancing the superiority of one's own tradition. His Holiness commented, just as the Buddha Shakyamuni deliberately taught different philosophies for people of different abilities, there is no point in "determining that one interpretation of reality is true, and that since another is false you therefore should follow this first inter-pretation. You cannot say that. Even Buddha could not say that."[44] When asked questions about God in Buddhist-Christian dialogue, His Holiness has demurred, saying that that the creator is beyond our concepts anyway and that there is not much benefit in such debates. He goes on to say that it is more important to talk about meditation practice and cultivation of the mind and heart.

Yet, His Holiness has at times acknowledged the philosophical dif-ferences that his tradition has with, for example, Christianity. He speaks of his own belief that there can be no "first cause and hence no creator; nor can there be such a thing as a permanent, primordially pure being."[45] Still, asserting this is in no way a denigration of a Christian's belief that God is the creator and that "his will is beneficial and soothing, and so for that person such a doctrine is worthwhile."[46] It is important that the Buddhist not denigrate the creator when in dialogue with Christians. When Brother Wayne Teasdale presses the point, saying that Buddhists need to see that "God *does* exist, that God is not merely a concept, or the result of a reasoning process, but is essentially experiential," His Holiness responds with respect. "Although I do not personally accept the notion of a creator, because we Buddhists follow the view of dependent arising, or the interdependence of all beings, I do feel that the experience of God is valid and true. There is definitely something to this theistic mysticism,

---

44. Mitchell and Wiseman, eds., *The Gethsemani Encounter*, 48.

45. Dalai Lama, "'Religious Harmony'; and Extracts from the Bodhgaya Interviews," in Paul J. Griffiths, ed. *Christianity through Non-Christian Eyes* (Maryknoll, NY: Orbis, 1990). Excerpted in Dan Cohn-Sherbok, ed., *Interfaith Theology: A Reader* (Oxford: One World, 2001) 72–73.

46. Cohn-Sherbok, 73.

and I strongly respect it."[47] There is no conflict between respect for other traditions and the commitment to one tradition as best for oneself. His Holiness remarks, "However on an individual basis we can say that a particular religion is good for us. For example the Buddhist way is best *for me*. There is no doubt! But this does not mean that Buddhism is best for everyone."[48]

The reason why holding an exclusivist view does not fit the Ri-me approach is that the spiritual founders of the world's great traditions skillfully understood the diversity of needs of the many peoples of the world. Just as there are many types of peoples in the world with different sensibilities and propensities, just so there are practices and teachings that are suitable for those different types of people. A traditional analogy is that of medicine: just as there are many illnesses and sicknesses that afflict various beings, so the variety of the world's religions provides many ways to "cure the pains and unhappiness of the human mind. Here too, it is not a question of which religion is superior as such. The question is, which will better cure a particular person."[49] Another analogy used by His Holiness is that of food: "one religion, like a single type of food, cannot hope to satisfy all. Depending on their different mental dispositions, some people benefit from one teaching, others from another."[50]

From this perspective, it is not desirable to create one universal religion in the name of harmony, as some dialogue leaders advocate. The specificity and richness of the world's diverse traditions are precious, and must be preserved. For that matter, harmony is not achieved through oneness but through respect of difference. His Holiness says, "If we try to unify the faiths of the world into one religion, we will also lose many of the qualities and richnesses of each particular tradition. Therefore, I feel it is better, in spite of the many quarrels in the name of religion, to

47. "Pope John Paul II and Christian-Buddhist Dialogue: His Holiness, the XIVth Dalai Lama, An Interview by Wayne Teasdale," in Byron L. Sherwin and Harold Kasimow, eds., *Pope John Paul II and Christian-Buddhist Dialogue* (Maryknoll, NY: Orbis, 1999) 90–91.

48. Mitchell and Wiseman, eds., *The Gethsemani Encounter*, 48.

49. Ibid., 47; Dalai Lama, *Ethics for the New Millennium*, 225–29, quoted in Kristin Beise Kiblinger, *Buddhist Inclusivism: Attitudes toward Religious Others* (Hants, UK: Ashgate, 2005) 61.

50. Mitchell and Wiseman, eds., *The Gethsemani Encounter*, ix.

maintain a variety of religious traditions."[51] This is why Ri-me has always emphasized education about the specific traditions we are striving to preserve. It is not enough to meditate; it is important also to understand the view of each tradition, as well as the lineages, practices, and ethics of each tradition.

Rejecting, denigrating, or despising spiritual teachings from genuine religious traditions has serious consequences for the Buddhist. The Vajrayana Buddhist vows entail acknowledging deluded attitudes that can damage the integrity of the very vows themselves. One of the root downfalls to be eschewed is the transgression of the Buddha's teachings, even ones from different schools or levels of vow, saying that they do not matter or that they are not true. Jamgon Kongtrul Lodro Thaye wrote: "to disrespect or reject the teachings [of the Buddha], even when due to lack of understanding of them, qualifies as a downfall."[52] This means that the Vajrayana practitioner is not to reject the teachings of what is known as the Hinayana or the teachings of the "hearers" or "solitary realizers," for these teachings form the foundation of the Buddhist path. She or he is also cautioned to respect the teachings of the noble Mahayana, which "forms the very heart of the definitive meaning" of the Vajrayana tradition.[53]

Jamgon Kongtrul goes on to say that denigration of other spiritual traditions "means to disparage [one's own or] other religions out of desire for personal gain."[54] What other motivation would there be for denigrating another tradition? Bias in religious matters goes against the core of Vajrayana vows to maintain sacred outlook (*daknang*) in all matters, assuming the intrinsic goodness of all traditions one may encounter. To depart from this view in order to aggrandize one's own tradition and practice can come only from ego clinging. However, in its parochialism, Kongtrul's commentary rates the denigration of non-Buddhist religions as a minimal offense, and adds that showing disrespect toward non-Buddhist traditions "with the intention of spiritually inspiring their adherents

---

51. Dalai Lama, *The Good Heart: A Buddhist Perspective on the Teachings of Jesus* (Somerville, MA: Wisdom, 1996) 42.

52. Jamgon Kongtrul Lodro Taye, *Treasury of Knowledge, Book Five: Buddhist Ethics* (Ithaca, NY: Snow Lion, 1998) 258, quoted in Harding, *Treasury of Esoteric Instructions*, 37.

53. Taye, *Treasury of Knowledge*, 260.

54. Ibid.

[to follow the Buddhist path], one not only does not incur this downfall, but actually acquires merit[!]"[55] In diaspora, there are probably Tibetan lamas and disciples who actually hold this view as true, but for the contemporary Ri-me practitioner, a view like this would not be compatible with an unbiased approach. His Holiness the Dalai Lama emphasizes the appreciation of "all the religions in the world, particularly the major world traditions."[56]

3. *What is the particular theological framework for discerning what is valuable and true in another religion?* First, the Ri-me holds that preservation of meditation and spiritual practices, teachings, and lineages is of the highest priority of the movement, especially for authentic practice traditions. However, Ri-me was fashioned in an environment of some insularity, in which the diversity of religions was limited, and which assumed homogeneity of peoples and spiritual aspirations. In Tibet, an abiding concern with "authenticity of lineages" was based on an assumption of cultural cohesion, and in a diverse and dispersed western environment outside of this cohesion, it may be difficult to define "authenticity."

Rather than concern for the authenticity of spiritual lineages, the Dalai Lama focuses on the results of contemplative practice. For him, the litmus test is the quality of heart. The measure of a faith is its ability "to produce fine warmhearted human beings,"[57] he writes. His Holiness has spoken frequently of meeting a Christian hermit at a Benedictine monastery in Montserrat, Spain. When asked about his practice, the monk responded, "love, love, love." His Holiness commented, "And he was not meditating on just the word. When I looked into his eyes, I saw evidence of profound spirituality and love—as I had during my meetings with Thomas Merton."[58] Later, His Holiness spoke of this hermit as a modern Milarepa, and credited meetings like this with his growing respect for Christianity.[59]

In the Bodhgaya Interviews, he states that religious traditions share values of "human improvement, love, respect for others, sharing other

55. Ibid.

56. Mitchell and Wiseman, eds., *The Gethsemani Encounter*, 48.

57. Ibid., ix.

58. Dalai Lama, *The Good Heart*, 39.

59. Dalai Lama, *Freedom in Exile: The Autobiography of the Dalai Lama* (New York: Harper Perennial, 1991) 189.

people's suffering."[60] All the major world religions also emphasize that their followers "must be honest and gentle, in other words, that a truly religious person must always strive to be a better human being."[61] This emphasis on human caring, concern, and decency is what deems a religious tradition "authentic" and "valuable" from the point of view of His Holiness.

4. *What are the most important dialogue subjects?* Contemporary Ri-me continues its interest in meditation and contemplative practice as the ground of spiritual life, fostering communities of practice, preserving and respecting the uniqueness of authentic practice lineages. For the Ri-me practitioner, the most beneficial content to dialogue is the sharing of wisdom of the actual practice traditions. When His Holiness was a presenter at that very first Naropa University dialogue conference, he spoke in detail about calm abiding (*shamatha, shi-ne*) and clear-seeing (*vipashyana, lhakthong*) meditation,[62] as he has done at countless dialogues since. At the Gethsemani encounter, His Holiness taught meditation "as a way to enrich one another,"[63] providing suggestions for how Christians could adapt the practice for their own theological concerns. He especially emphasized analytic meditation (comparable to what is called "meditation" in Christian circles), taking a word or idea as the object upon which to focus the mind. In each of these settings, His Holiness took great pains to teach the practice precisely, with a wealth of information about how to refine both analytic and formless meditations. These are clear Ri-me sensibilities about preserving the full authenticity of the practice traditions.

The reason that meditation is so prized by the Ri-me dialogue partner is the conviction that the undeveloped mind is the source of all suffering and the trained mind is the source of all happiness. Our mental outlook is the "key factor for the future—the future of humanity, the future of the world, and the future of the environment. Many things depend on our mental attitude, both in the personal and public spheres. Whether we are happy in our individual or family life is, in a large part, up to us. Of course, material conditions are an important factor for happiness and

---

60. Cohn-Sherbok, *Interfaith Theology: A Reader*, 72.

61. Ibid., 73.

62. From unpublished transcripts, Naropa University archives.

63. Mitchell and Wiseman, eds., *The Gethsemani Encounter*, 50.

a good life, but one's mental attitude is of equal or greater importance."[64] The purpose of the world's religions is not so much to construct huge worldly temples but "to create temples of goodness and compassion inside, in our hearts" through mental cultivation.[65] From this perspective, sharing mind-cultivation is viewed in the Ri-me as the most compassionate possible gift for the benefit of the many.

For the Ri-me, meditation and contemplation practice have the potential to heal many of the world's ills, especially prejudice and disharmony. These practices calm and clarify the mind, providing spiritual nourishment and cultivating the heart of compassion that is so pivotal in interreligious tolerance and understanding. His Holiness has often taught meditation to practitioners of other religions, saying that spiritual depth will bring us to the point where we might "feel totally convinced of the preciousness of and need for compassion and tolerance" and "a sense of being touched, a sense of being transformed from within."[66] His Holiness says there is no need to be a Buddhist to engage in these practices. Once we have a transformative experience, it must be cultivated and stabilized. For Tibetan Buddhism, this is done through contemplation practice that clearly sees the benefits of compassion and tolerance and consciously deepens them through practice.

The Ri-me dialogue partner hesitates to engage in philosophical debate or polemics. Philosophical perspectives are less important than religions' desires "to help and benefit others," and so it is important in dialogue to view philosophy as a support to this more important purpose: "If we go into the differences in philosophy and argue with and criticize each other, it is useless. There will be endless argument; the result will mainly be that we irritate each other—accomplishing nothing. Better to look at the purpose of the philosophies and to see what is shared—an emphasis on love, compassion and respect for a higher force."[67] Placing philosophy in service of compassion, rather than the reverse, is a classic Ri-me stance in which scholarship serves meditative practice.

5. *What are the best ways to extend and deepen interreligious understanding?* In 1996, I asked His Holiness in a private interview how to

64. Dalai Lama, *The Good Heart*, 38.

65. Ibid., 39.

66. Ibid., 46.

67. Cohn-Sherbok, *Interfaith Theology*, 72.

counter the sectarianism and misunderstanding between religious traditions, and he gave an answer similar to ones he has given elsewhere: we must have plenty of contact with practitioners of other traditions.[68] From this perspective of Ri-me, interreligious dialogue becomes an ongoing extension of one's contemplative practice. His Holiness suggests five ways to initiate such contact. First, organize conversations between scholars "to clarify the differences and similarities between their traditions."[69] He also suggests four additional types of contact between religions, gatherings of practitioners to discuss their practice, interreligious pilgrimage, social-engagement projects sponsored by different religious traditions, and community forums in which religious leaders appear publicly for simple conversation.[70] (For the latter, His Holiness feels that it is beneficial for people just to see leaders together, no matter what was actually said between them.)[71]

Throughout his travels and dialogues, His Holiness has fostered the strength of practice communities he has encountered all over the world. At a Benedictine seminar in London, His Holiness recommended the very best way to overcome conflicts in the name of religion is "close contact and an exchange among those of various beliefs, not only on an intellectual level, but in deeper spiritual experiences. This is a powerful method to develop mutual understanding and respect."[72] Ultimately, however, appreciation for other contemplative traditions comes from the depth and integrity of one's own meditation practice. His Holiness says, "I believe the best way to counter that force [of sectarianism] is to experience the value of one's own path through a meditative life, which will enable one to see the value and preciousness of other traditions."[73] This Ri-me theme has prevailed for more than a century.

---

68. Judith Simmer-Brown, "Commitment and Openness," in *Heart of Learning: Spirituality in Education* (New York: Tarcher/Putnam, 1999) 103–4; Mitchell and Wiseman, eds., *The Gethsemani Encounter*, 48–49.

69. Mitchell and Wiseman, eds., *The Gethsemani Encounter*, 49.

70. Ibid., 49–50; Dalai Lama, *The Good Heart*, 39–40.

71. Simmer-Brown, "Commitment and Openness," 104.

72. Dalai Lama, *The Good Heart*, 38.

73. Ibid., 41.

Dialogue Tensions with Pope John Paul II

It has not always been easy for His Holiness in dialogue, as can be seen in the public criticisms that came from His Holiness John Paul II in his book, *Crossing the Threshold of Hope*. In his scathing chapter on Buddhism, John Paul refers to the Dalai Lama's tradition of "negative soteriology," in which the central conviction is that "the world is bad, that it is the source of evil and of suffering for man."[74] The heart of the pope's criticism is that Buddhism is "indifferent to the world," which is diametrically opposed to Catholic theology.[75] In addition, he takes issue with the Dalai Lama's bringing Buddhism "to people of the Christian West, stirring up interest both in Buddhist spirituality and in its methods of praying." The implication is that the Dalai Lama is proselytizing, in spite of his frequent statements that it is important for peoples of the West to practice the traditions of their own heritage, with few exceptions.[76]

Buddhists throughout the world were deeply offended by Pope John Paul's criticism of their tradition. When he visited Sri Lanka in 1995, protests broke out, eliciting from Catholic bishops a public apology, insisting that the pope had not meant to hurt the feelings of Buddhists.[77] In Thailand and Taiwan, His Holiness John Paul was denounced for his misinformed attacks on Buddhist traditions. The normally mild Vietnamese teacher Thich Nhat Hanh wrote that the book displayed an attitude that "excludes dialogue and fosters religious intolerance and discrimination. It does not help."[78] The Tibetan Nyingma teacher Ven. Thinley Norbu, Rinpoche, wrote a biting refutation of *Crossing the Threshold*, point by painstaking point, most definitely not a Ri-me tome.[79]

Other observers note the historic shift in rhetoric from Pope John Paul during the early 1990s. Previously, in resonance with the famous

---

74. Pope John Paul II, *Crossing the Threshold of Hope* (New York: Knopf, 1994) 85.

75. Ibid., 86–88.

76. Dalai Lama, *The Good Heart*, 45.

77. Tad Szulc, *Pope John Paul II: The Biography* (New York: Scribner, 1995) 467.

78. Thich Nhat Hanh, *Living Buddha, Living Christ* (New York: Riverhead, 1995) 193.

79. Norbu, *Welcoming Flowers: Across the Cleansed Threshold of Hope* (New York: Jewel, 1997).

encyclical *Nostra Aetate*,[80] John Paul depicted Buddhism in generally positive, though cautious, light. The shift to a more oppositional stance was most likely a response to the eagerness with which many Western people, including many Catholic monastics, have embraced Buddhist meditation practice. As Buddhist theologian Jose Ignacio Cabezón, notes, "The distorted picture of Buddhism in John Paul's more recent writings arises from what is an increasing fear of Buddhism as a competitor in the spiritual, especially the contemplative, sphere . . . [T]he Pope is declaring Buddhism itself to be the threat, and now a threat not to Asia but to the Christian West."[81] In a pluralistic age like the present, however, we can no longer speak of the Christian West.

Ri-me dialogue partners have certainly been criticized before, given the long history of sectarian rivalry in Tibetan Buddhism, and current tensions are no exception. His Holiness the Dalai Lama downplays the controversy, saying that he and Pope John Paul had a "very good" personal relationship. Both of them had experienced the tyranny of Communist regimes and shared concern for the value of spirituality in the contemporary world.[82] When asked in an interview why Pope John Paul would be so negative toward him and Buddhism, the Dalai Lama observed that Pope John Paul did not have a very deep understanding of Buddhism, and that his remarks were both "sad and amusing. They are sad because his approach moves in the direction of polemics, and amusing because so superficial."[83] This is one reason why, in the Ri-me approach, it is so important to be educated in the traditions with which one is in dialogue, and to show them respect even when beliefs and practices are not one's own.

On another occasion the Dalai Lama remarked that the criticism was, in part, because of Buddhist monks' lack of social action. "Buddhists are inclined to withdraw from the world . . . We have to learn from our Christian brothers and sisters. We should have more socially engaged

80. Francesco Gioia, ed., *Interreligious Dialogue: The Official Teaching of the Catholic Church (1963–1995)* (Boston: Pauline, 1997).

81. Jose Ignacio Cabezón, "A Buddhist Response to John Paul II," in Sherwin and Kasimow, eds., *John Paul II and Interreligious Dialogue* (Maryknoll, NY: Orbis, 1999) 120.

82. Teasdale, "John Paul II and Christian-Buddhist Dialogue," 86–87.

83. Ibid., 87.

activities."[84] These perspectives mirror his view that while Buddhists have powerful practices for cultivating compassion, Tibetan Buddhists in general and monastics in particular are not socially engaged enough.

Conclusion: Ri-me as Pluralism

The Ri-me perspective was forged in Tibet late in its history, after centuries of sectarian rivalry added to a toxic mixture of religion and politics. It represented in nineteenth century Tibet a kind of "fresh start" that returned to the roots of Buddhist teachings in India and looked for the commonalities rather than the differences. It sought preservation of lineages of spirituality and meditation practice, without prejudice concerning doctrinal differences. Still, Ri-me did not seek syncretism or a mere relativism. It honored the differences of lineages, practices, and textual heritages of each of the traditions it encountered.

In diaspora, Ri-me has grown in some quarters, expanding its scope and its appetite for dialogue with non-Buddhists. His Holiness the Dalai Lama is the leading proponent for contemporary Ri-me, as can be seen in his dialogue activities throughout the world. In its new form, the primary features of the nineteenth-century Tibetan manifestation of Ri-me remain: its respect and appreciation for diverse traditions from the world's religions, and desire to preserve their heritages; its abiding interest in contemplative practice as the foundation of spiritual life; its emphasis on study of texts, philosophies, and traditions as a way to foster and support those contemplative practices, rather than the reverse; and an appreciation of the popular dimensions of spirituality, rather than merely scholastic ones.

In addition, contemporary Ri-me in the dialogue activities of His Holiness the Dalai Lama can be seen to have added additional elements that enrich its view and application. His Holiness seems to have altered the criteria for "authentic" spiritual traditions based on their capacity to promote harmony and peace for both individuals and the world, and to produce warm-hearted human beings. He has developed skill in dialoging with theistic, Abrahamic traditions that have so historically advocated their own traditions as the ultimate, and has done so with appreciation

84. Bodo, "The Dalai Lama Visits Gethsemani."

and respect and, in many cases, a strong sense of friendship. He has done so without promoting that religions are essentially the same, a view that has often clouded contemporary dialogue endeavors. He has brought to the forefront a more human, less polemical approach to dialogue that has enriched contacts between religious traditions.

When I read Diana Eck's seminal description of pluralism, I see many elements of the contemporary Ri-me approach. She says that pluralism is the recognition that truth is not exclusively (or inclusively) the property of any one religious tradition, and that the myriad understandings of truth or the ultimate in religious traditions provide an opportunity for celebration and dialogue rather than providing obstacles to be overcome.[85] She also speaks of the compatibility between interreligious dialogue and personal religious commitment that is also central to Ri-me's basic approach. The give-and-take of dialogue does not produce philosophic agreement: "We do not enter into dialogue to produce an agreement, but to produce real relationship, even friendship, which is premised upon mutual understanding, not upon agreement."[86] Ri-me's appreciation of the diversity of religions and commitment to preservation of the practices, texts, and communities of many spiritual traditions in the face of modernity may provide a ground for a truly pluralistic understanding.

85. Diana Eck, *Encountering God: A Spiritual Journey from Bozeman to Benares* (Boston: Beacon, 1993) 192; Judith Simmer-Brown, "A Buddhist Approach to Pluralism: The Dialogue Relationship," in *Buddhist Theology: Critical Reflections by Contemporary Buddhist Scholars*, Roger Jackson and John Makransky, eds. (Surrey, UK: Curzon, 2000).

86. Eck, *Encountering God*, 197.

13

Comparative Theology with a Difference: A Shin Buddhist View in Pedagogical Perspective

Mark Unno

The notion of "dialogue and discernment" in the context of comparative theology offers a unique opportunity to explore dialogue and comparison, two closely related but distinct endeavors in the study of religion. Here I show how, building on past experience in dialogue, one can begin to form an effective approach to comparative theology within a pedagogical context. Specifically, one can use theological differences in a complementary manner, opening up possibilities for religious insights that might not occur within the narrower scope of a single religious or theological perspective.

It is like the fact that one can gain unique insights into the way language works when one learns more than one language. However, just as one cannot learn about languages in general without learning a specific language, this view of comparative theology and pedagogical complementarity begins with a specific religious tradition. The author takes his own experience as an illustration; his views have evolved through his own engagement with Buddhist tradition, specificially that of Shin Buddhism, one of the largest developments of Pure Land Buddhism in east Asia.

The paper begins by describing key features of Shin Buddhism that have influenced the author's engagement with religious dialogue and comparative theology. It goes on to describe how these features have helped to shape a pedagogy of theological complementarity. And it illustrates this view with a number of case studies.

Shin Buddhism

Twofold truth. Shin Buddhism, a school of Pure Land Buddhism that originates with the work of the Buddhist priest and thinker Gutoku Shinran (1173–1262), is one of the largest developments of east Asian Buddhism. As a school within Mahayana Buddhism, it subscribes to the twofold truth of form and emptiness, of conventional truth and highest truth. In this view, form is understood as the world of appearances, multiplicity, as defined by language and conceptual difference; the truth of emptiness is realized when one sees into and through the illusory nature of the distinctions defined by language. When the Buddhist practitioner realizes the emptiness of form—concept, conventional truth—she is freed from the strictures of finite definitions and attains the freedom of the emptiness or oneness beyond or before words, the highest truth. This realization of emptiness or oneness, however, does not mean that one permanently discards the world of words or of form. Rather, one comes to see that the very nature of form is emptiness, that words themselves can be vehicles for the wordless truth of oneness.

Mountain not a mountain. There is the well-known Zen saying, "Before enlightenment, a mountain is a mountain. During enlightenment, a mountain is not a mountain. After enlightenment, a mountain is a mountain." Before enlightenment, one approaches the mountain with a preconceived notion of what to expect and thus one does not see the mountain. Rather, one's vision is obscured by a conceptual filter that predetermines the image that will be admitted into the mind. During enlightenment, the mountain is not a "mountain," because one has let go, or emptied the mind, of any preconceived notion of "mountain." The conceptual filter separating knower and known is dropped. In that moment, in a sense, one does not see the mountain, because the mountain is not objectified. Yet, in another sense, one sees the mountain most vividly, as person and mountain unfold intimately together. Finally the mountain is again a "mountain," but to the knower, it is not the same mountain as before, for now, when she speaks of it, she does so intimately, as if speaking of a close friend, of a lover, of a reality that is now a part of her. The realization of oneness does not obliterate difference; rather, it paradoxically heightens the subtle and vibrant awareness of difference. Whether it is the face of a lover or a wildflower growing by the wayside, the less I am preoccupied with my own thoughts, the more I become intimately aware of the being to whom I am relating in all her nuances and particularity.

Blind passion. Yet if the knower is not able to let go of his preconception of the mountain, remains attached to his dogmatic insistence that he knows what a mountain is, then he is deluded or, in the language of Shin Buddhism, he is bound by blind passion, blinded by his desire to possess the mountain on his terms. Such a one is called *bombu* ("foolish being"), for he is foolish in his blindness. Yet at the very moment in which he is made to realize his blindness, he is illuminated by the larger truth of emptiness or oneness, and in that moment, he is freed from his blindness and released into the light of oneness. Without the illumination of oneness, one remains imprisoned, alone, in the darkness of blind passion, a foolish being. The recognition of blindness is made possible by illumination; blindness and insight coincide in the moment of awakening.

Saying the Name. In Zen Buddhism, one of the central practices for cultivating the awareness of one's delusional attachments or blind passions is *zazen,* seated meditation. In Shin Buddhism, the central practice for cultivating this awareness is the recitation of the Name of Amida Buddha, "Namu Amida Butsu." *Namu* derives from the Sanskrit, *Namas,* "to entrust," and "Amida Buddha" derives from *Amitâbha Buddha,* "the buddha of infinite light." Thus the Name means, "I entrust myself to the buddha of infinite light." Yet because Amida Buddha is not a static entity but the dynamic unfolding of emptiness/oneness from moment to moment, it is more accurate to say that Amida Buddha signifies the awakening of infinite light, so that the saying of the Name, Namu Amida Butsu, really means, "I, a foolish being, entrust myself to the awakening of infinite light." Just as seated meditation is said to embody awakening in Zen Buddhism, the saying of the Name is said to embody awakening in Shin Buddhism. Thus, Shinran states that there is no Amida apart from the Name, and no Name apart from Amida Buddha.[1]

---

1. Shinran, *Mattôshô,* in *Shinran chosaku zenshû (SCZ),* ed. Daiei Kaneko (Kyoto: Hôzôkan, 1964) 593. In this passage Shinran states that there is no Vow apart from the Name, and no Name apart from the Vow, but for all intents and purposes this is the same

Formless body of truth. Emptiness in itself is neither light nor dark, neither good nor bad; it is a oneness beyond words: colorless, odorless, and formless. In Shin Buddhism, this is called the formless *dharmakaya* *(hôben hosshin),* or the body of truth (dharma) in its aspect beyond form. Yet the experience of having one's blind passion illuminated by the truth of emptiness is like emerging from a dark tunnel into the light of day; it is a palpable experience of being illuminated, embraced, and dissolved into infinite light. Shinran calls this the entrance into the "ocean of light."[2] This is also called the *dharmakaya*-as-compassion, or the body of truth in its aspect as compassionate light.

True entrusting. The act of entrusting oneself to the Name is called *shinjin,* or "true entrusting." While the Shin Buddhist practitioner ever remains a foolish being filled with blind passion in this world, she is simultaneously awakened to the depths of her own reality, which is none other than emptiness, oneness, the limitless awakening of light. When one looks closely, one sees that the saying or chanting of the Name does not occur from the side of the ego self, or through what Shin Buddhists call "self power" *(jiriki),* but through the unfolding of the depths of reality that continually exposes and dislodges the static grid of illusory preconceptions by which the foolish being had previously sought to pigeonhole reality. Thus the voiceless voice of truth, of the *dharmakaya,* of the awakening of infinite light, arises from the most intimate reality that is "other power" *(tariki),* so called because it is other than ego.

Thus, Shinran states, "True entrusting is none other than the expression of buddha-nature,"[3] just as the Zen meditator realizes that to truly engage in seated meditation is to completely give oneself over to one's buddha-nature. As the Zen Master Dôgen states, "When one completely lets go of body and mind and forgets them, and one throws oneself into the realm of the buddha, all unfolds from the side of the buddha; . . . then, without any force or artificial striving, one leaves behind life-and-death

---

as saying there is no Amida apart from the Name.

2. Ocean of light: *kômyô no kôkai.* Shinran, *Kyôgyôshinshô,* SCZ, 68. "Thus, when one has boarded the ship of the Vow of great compassion and sailed out on the vast ocean of light, the winds of perfect virtue blow softly and the waves of evil are transformed." Translation taken from, Shinran, *Kyôgyôshinshô,* Shin Buddhism Translation Series, *The Collected Works of Shinran, Vol. 1: The Writings* (Kyoto: Jôdo Shinshû Honganji-ha, 1997) 56.

3. Shinran, *Yui shinshô mon'i,* SCZ, 550.

and attains buddhahood."[4] True entrusting, *shinjin,* is itself the unfolding of other power, the awakening of infinite light as one's deepest truest reality.

Twofold Truth

form	emptiness
conventional Truth	highest Truth
words	beyond words
multiplicity	oneness
blind passion	boundless compassion
foolish being	Amida Buddha
self power	other power
body of form	body of truth
samsara	nirvana
defiled world	Pure Land
Namu	Amida Butsu

Stages of Awakening

There are several ways to describe the process of religious awakening in Shin Buddhism, but for present purposes, three stages are described in which one moves from the deluded ego of self power into the embrace of the ocean-light of other power. In order to relate this to the following section on pedagogy and theological complementarity, we borrow some illustrative passages from the Daoist classic *Zhuangzi* as well as Buddhist sources that resonate with Shin Buddhist understanding. The three stages are perspectival awareness, dissolution of boundaries, and realization of oneness.

Perspectival Awareness. The deluded ego self is led to seek a deeper truth when it is made to confront the inescapable suffering caused by attachment to the rigid boundaries of its dogmatically defined world. The recognition of a wider horizon of possibility begins to open up when the ego learns to relativize its own perspective through taking into account

---

4. Dôgen, "Shôji," *Shôbôgenzô,* vol. 4, *ao 319-3,* annotated by Yaeko Mizuno (Tokyo: Iwanami Shoten, 1993).

the differing perspectives of others. As Zhuangzi suggests, no one person, in fact no single living species, can define the standard of truth, goodness, or beauty:

> If a man sleeps in a damp place, his back aches and he ends up half paralyzed, but is this true of a loach? If he lives in a tree, he is terrified and shakes with fright, but is this true of a monkey? Of these three creatures, then, which one knows the proper place to live? . . . Men claim that Maoqiang and Lady Li were beautiful, but if fish saw them they would dive to the bottom of the ocean, if birds saw them they would fly away, and if deer saw them they would break into a run. Of these four, which knows how to fix the standard of beauty for the world?[5]

One who clings to dogmatic views and fails to recognize the relative nature of his own perspective becomes entrapped by his own knowledge. As the Vietnamese Master Thich Nhat Hanh states,

> In Buddhism, [dogmatic] knowledge is regarded as an obstacle to understanding, like a block of ice that obstructs water from flowing. It is said that if we take one thing to be the truth and cling to it, even if truth itself comes in person and knocks at our door, we won't open it. For things to reveal themselves to us [and for us to become aware of our true humanity], we need to be ready to abandon our views about them.[6]

In Shin Buddhism, if one clings to the notion that one is a "good" Buddhist, for example, then that knowledge prevents one from seeing beyond the artificially defined boundary between good and bad Buddhist, or even "Buddhist" and "non-Buddhist":

> Even a good person attains birth in the Pure Land [realm free of distinctions], how much more so the evil person . . . the person of self-power, being conscious of good, lacks the thought of entrusting himself completely to other power, [and] he is not the focus of the Primal Vow of Amida [the unfolding of boundless compassion]. But when he turns over self-power and entrusts himself to other power, he attains birth in the land of True Fulfillment [realm

---

5. Burton Watson, trans, *Zhuangzi: Basic Writings* (New York: Columbia University Press, 2003) 41. Osamu Kanaya, trans. and annotated, *Sôji, ao 206-1* (Tokyo: Iwanami Shoten, 1971) 74.

6. Thich Nhat Hanh, *Being Peace* (Berkeley, CA: Parallax, 1987) 42.

of boundless compassion]. Thus, even a good person attains birth in the Pure Land, how much more so the evil person.[7]

The implications for interreligious dialogue and comparative theology are readily apparent. On the one hand, if one is to truly realize emptiness, oneness, the ocean of infinite light, then all of one's foolish attachments must be illuminated and dissolved in the ocean of infinite light, including one's attachments to religion, even to Shin Buddhism itself as a discursive entity. On the other hand, only with this awakening can one begin to see, hear, and appreciate the perspective of those who embrace other religious paths and perspectives.

Dissolution of Boundaries. For the Shin Buddhist's own ultimate religious realization, it is not enough to relativize one's own perspective vis-à-vis others' in a purely discursive sense, but one must allow conceptually defined boundaries to fall away. Returning once again to the *Zhuangzi*, the well-known episode of the butterfly dream helps us to appreciate this:

> Once [Zhuangzi] dreamt he was a butterfly, a butterfly flitting and fluttering around, happy with himself and doing as he pleased. He didn't know he was [Zhuangzi]. Suddenly he woke up and there he was, solid and unmistakable [Zhuangzi]. But he didn't know if he was [Zhuangzi] who had dreamt he was a butterfly, or a butterfly dreaming he was [Zhuangzi]. Between [Zhuangzi] and a butterfly there must be *some* distinction! This is called the Transformation of Things.[8]

The butterfly episode calls into question any discursively defined self-identity. At first, it appears self-evident to Zhuangzi that he has just awakened from a dream in which he was a butterfly. Upon further reflection, however, it is not clear whether the butterfly was a dreamlike apparition or whether his own life as a human being with arms and legs is a product of some other being's imagination. The fact that Zhuangzi is able to feel and embody the existence of the other, in this case the butterfly, raises doubts as to what his true body is, where his true subjectivity resides.

It is one thing to listen to another person's opinion, understand it intellectually, yet remain at a distance personally. It is another thing altogether to listen deeply to another, to allow the truth of another person's

7. Taitetsu Unno, trans., *Tannisho: A Shin Buddhist Classic* (Honolulu: Buddhist Study Center Press, 1996) 6. *Tannishô, SCZ,* 676.

8. Watson, *Zhuangzi,* 45. Kanaya, *Sôji,* 89.

life to enter into one's heart and mind. That is certainly a tall order, and yet one can argue that unless one is able to walk a mile in another person's moccasins, one cannot truly appreciate the perspective that she brings before one.

Shinran expresses a similar attitude when he states that, in the realization of the oneness of the Name, one comes to know all beings intimately, as if they were close family members: "All beings have been fathers and mothers, brothers and sisters in the timeless process of birth and death."[9]

To truly engage in interreligious dialogue, then, and to come to a deeper comparative understanding theologically, it is not enough to read about others' theologies or to hear a few public lectures. One must in some way be willing to walk together with them in deeper humanity, to listen to and to hear the voices of experience as well as the sounds of ideas. I see myself still at the beginning stages of this journey, but I have been fortunate to be welcomed into many religious quarters and to share experiences and ideas with people of diverse backgrounds and commitments; It is not just other people but also other creatures that my heart must open to—cats and dogs, the deer and the wild turkey that walk through my own neighborhood, even perhaps, the cries of planet earth itself, the voiceless voice of the sun, stars, and moon.

All beings are one with me; I am led to become one with all beings. At the deepest level of awakening, all boundaries dissolve into the ocean of oneness. Yet just as one cannot sleep forever, one cannot remain endlessly immersed in oneness. Refreshed by the warm waters of the ocean, one emerges into the world of words and appearances with a renewed appreciation for the sustaining life and light of all beings. Paradoxically, the realization that, at bottom, we are all already one leads to a powerful sense of responsibility for realizing the oneness in relation to all sentient beings in this world of form. This is called the working of the Primal Vow of Amida to bring all beings to the realization of oneness.

> When one contemplates the great ocean of true entrusting, it chooses not between the rich and the poor, has nothing to do with being male or female, old or young, makes nothing of karmic evil great or little, does not weigh the length of practice, is not to be found in [the distinctions of] relative practices or goods, . . . medi-

9. Unno, *Tannisho*, 8. *Tannishô, SCZ,* 677.

tative or non-meditative, orthodox or heterodox . . . but [is found]
just in this *shinjin* inconceivable, inexplicable, ineffable.[10]

Such a realization of ineffable oneness, if in fact it is possible, cannot be
forced, but unfolds only when all contrivance falls by the wayside.

A Pedagogy of Theological Complementarity

My primary teaching responsibilities consist in offering survey, intermediate, and seminar courses in Asian religions, especially Japanese Buddhism.
Beyond those, I regularly offer two courses in comparative religion, REL
407 (Women's Religious Narratives East and West), and REL 353 (Dark
Self East and West), the latter a course on comparative conceptions of
selfhood that focuses on the dark or problematic dimension, as defined in
terms of sin, delusion, alienation, karmic evil, and so forth. As part of the
curriculum of a religious studies department in a public university, it is
crucial to maintain the separation of church and state, and so we are very
clear that we teach about religion, not religion itself.

Nevertheless there are legitimate and significant ways in which we
provide *tools* for students to explore theological questions. In fact, I would
argue, there can be certain advantages to the religious-studies setting for
students who wish to explore religious issues of personal significance, especially when theologies and philosophies are presented in comparative
perspective.

First, the indirect approach of religious studies allows students leeway to reflect inwardly on theological concerns and religious issues without feeling forced to confront them explicitly; it also frees the instructor
from student expectations that we are responsible for the personal religious questing of students. Of course, instructor and student will have
fulfilled their requirements in the course by the former helping the latter
to develop critical reading, writing, and discussion skills, and there is no
need to pursue theological questions directly. Yet, indirectly, instructors
raise questions of religious significance that bear on students' own self-
understanding, and students can explore their religious self-understanding according to their own inner disposition and level of engagement.

10. Shinran, *Kyôgyôshinshô, SCZ*, 119–20.

Second, in courses on comparative religion, instructors may be able to represent the sympathetic understanding of each theological perspective more forcefully than in single-tradition courses, as well as raise critical questions about them; when done skillfully and in a balanced manner, the comparative context frees the instructor from potential accusations of "selling" any one religion. Through lecture as well as discussion, students may be more readily able to engage texts and ideas at multiple levels of cognition involving intellectual, intuitive, as well as affective modes of knowing.[11] This allows students to "try on" different religious perspectives, to question their own assumptions, and to question diverse religious perspectives without feeling that they are being forced into a mold.

Third, the examination of diverse religious perspectives taken as a whole can have a synergistic effect, spurring reflection on themes that span multiple religious perspectives.

The case studies that follow illustrate these points. Where necessary, the names and circumstances have been changed to protect the identities of the individuals involved. In all essential details, however, they reflect actual experiences taken from my classroom experiences.

Jake, Indirect Communication, and the Existential Self

I have taught some version of my course on comparative conceptions of selfhood in East and West at the three colleges and universities where I have held appointments, including my present appointment at the University of Oregon, where I teach "Dark Self East and West" as an intermediate-level lecture/discussion course. In an earlier incarnation, when it was taught as a large lecture course, a student, Jake, came to me in my office hours during a portion of the course in which we were covering a segment on Japanese Buddhism. I had had Jake in a previous class and had known him to be an intelligent but somewhat lackadaisical student, a fact that was reflected in his coursework. He had a bit of an unhappy expression of his face, and I asked him, "What can I do for you?"

He replied, "I want to be Japanese." Now, he was most assuredly about as far away from being Japanese as one might imagine, but in any

11. See, Mark Unno, "Four Modes of Knowledge and the Representation of Text," in *Counterpoints: Issues in Teaching Religious Studies,* eds. Mark Unno and Mark Hadley (Providence, RI: Department of Religious Studies, Brown University, 1995) 75–82.

case, I gave a quick reply that I believe was jovial but neutral, and by now entirely forgotten. This brief exchange, however, would become significant later on.

A few weeks later, he came back again during office hours, and he asked for a consultation. He said that he was thinking of quitting school to pursue his dream of becoming a musician. His parents were supporting him through school, and they threatened to cut off his funds if he dropped out, but he felt that they should support his musical efforts. He wanted me to affirm his brilliant career move, including looking at some of his songs and evaluating their value. First of all, I know very little about music, but one glance at the small jottings he had made, and it was fairly evident that we did not yet have a musical prodigy on our hands. Again I said something jovial and neutral, as well as suggesting that perhaps his parents were somewhat within their rights to deny him support should he embark on his musical endeavors.

As the weeks went by, however, I kept this conversation in mind in light of his naïve and romanticized view of Japanese Buddhism as well as of his musical career. When we reached the section on Kierkegaard, I felt I had an opening to say something that might be meaningful. I did not change what I had planned for my regular lecture, but I subtly emphasized certain key points. We were reading excerpts from two works by Kierkegaard: *Fear and Trembling* and *The Sickness Unto Death*,[12] and as we were discussing the latter, I explained that Kierkegaard, through the pseudonym of Anti-Climacus, conceived the self as a synthesis of polar factors: finite and infinite, necessity and freedom, temporal and eternal. This is an ongoing synthesis, such that the self reconstitutes itself in each moment, as a new synthesis; the self decides what it becomes in each moment. Failure to recognize the reality of the self and to properly constitute itself leads to self-deception, despair, and sin.

In order to illustrate the workings of this model of the self, I gave a few analogies, including the following:

> When Kierkegaard says that the self is a synthesis of finite and
> infinite, necessity and freedom, it is like saying that one needs to
> be grounded in reality but also leave room for the imagination. For
> example, expressing creativity and pursuing one's dreams is part of

12. Søren Kierkegaard, *"Fear and Trembling"* and *"The Sickness unto Death,"* trans. Walter Lowrie (Princeton: Princeton University Press, 1941).

the infinite freedom of imagination, but this needs to be balanced against the practical necessities of life, such as paying bills and eating right. For Kierkegaard, the existence of the self is brought into relief in each moment of decision as it attempts to effect this balance between the self and its aspect of freedom and imagination on the one hand, and the practical limitations of everyday life, on the other. He describes the self in existential tension from moment to moment.

As instructors, we often do not learn of the effects of our teaching on our students until much later, sometimes years afterwards. In fact, we may in many instances never receive feedback even when students have had an impactful experience. In Jake's case, however, I did receive feedback a few weeks later, as he came to me again during office hours. It was totally unexpected given my previous experiences with him:

> Professor Unno, I've been doing some thinking, especially after listening to some of your lectures recently. I think maybe I need to rethink some of my goals. Maybe I can think about my music in the future, but I've decided to focus on my studies in school for now. I'm going to finish my major in chemistry, but I need to ask you for something. I'm applying for some PhD programs in chemical research and green technology, and I'm wondering if you could write a recommendation letter for me.

I was very happy to learn that he had reconsidered his career move, but now I was posed with a different problem. He was at best an average student who until that moment had failed to show real motivation or a competent sense about making practical commitments. It would not help him for me to write a letter that showed any negative traits, but I could not write a letter that was unrealistically positive. Writing effective letters is one of the most important aspects of our jobs as instructors, and I felt I wanted to highlight positives appropriately so that it maximized the possibility that his advisors, were he admitted into a PhD program, would be able to bring out the best in him. I felt like I was playing twister as I wrote the letter, but I did the best I could. To make a long story short, not only was Jake accepted into a first-rate doctoral program, but I received a nice message from his advisor that he was the star of his cohort group.

Kierkegaard was himself the master of indirect communication.[13] Thus, not only did I benefit from his work in the pedagogical context of "Dark Self East and West," but I am indebted to him even in the manner in which I was able to convey his insights indirectly.

Theologically, Kierkegaard's emphasis on intensifying the existential self-consciousness of self before God in many ways stands in stark contrast with the Shin Buddhist emphasis on dissolving the ego self in the ocean of Amida's infinite light. Yet, for this very reason, and for other contextual considerations, it seemed best to make my point indirectly through Kierkegaard. Here, having previously had the horizon of my own religious and philosophical self-understanding expanded through dialogue with Christian thinkers and having learned from my study of Kierkegaard, theological difference with my own tradition functioned in a complementary manner that benefited both student and instructor. When students come to me with an interest in the personal dimension of religious questioning, I generally refer them to religious specialists, to various schools of Buddhist practice, such as Zen, Vipassana, or Tibetan centers as appropriate, or to Christian churches, synagogues, or to schools of psychological thought, such as Object-Relations, Jungian, or Transpersonal psychology, and so on. In most of these cases, I have colleagues and acquaintances who have taught me about the particular strengths of each through interreligious or interphilosphical dialogue.

From within my own religious path, Shin Buddhism provides ways in which to enter into this pedagogical circle of theological complementarity. First, in the realm of form, of multiplicity and religious diversity, I am ever the foolish being blinded by my attachments. Thus, in order to awaken beyond the limited horizon of my own religious perspective, I need to allow other perspectives to enter into and enrich my being. Second, from within the ocean of oneness, which is, as Shinran states, "beyond orthodox and heterodox," there is a point from which all theological perspectives are embraced. Emptiness is not emptiness unless all is embraced; the ocean of light loses its brilliance if it is divided. This can be seen in the exchange between Manjusri and Vimalakirti in *The Holy Teaching of Vimalakirti*:

13. See Søren Kierkegaard, "On My Work as an Author," in *The Point of View for My Works as an Author*, trans. Howard V. Hong and Edna Hong (Princeton: Princeton University Press, 1998) 7.

Mañjushri: Householder, where should emptiness [oneness] be sought?

Vimalakirti: Mañjushri, emptiness should be sought among the sixty-two "heterdox" [non-Buddhist] convictions.

Mañjushri: Where should the sixty-two "heterodox" convictions be sought?

Vimalakirti: They should be sought in the liberation of the Tathagatas [buddhas].

Mañjushri: Where should the liberation [realization of oneness] of the Tathagatas be sought?

Vimalakirti: It should be sought in the prime mental activity of all living beings.[14]

Ashley, Authenticity, and Theological Complementarity

One day, when my teaching assistant Ashley came into talk with me, she had an ashen look on her face. "What's the matter, Ashley?" I said.

"Mark, I'm not sure what to do. One of the students in my discussion section just came to talk to me, and she confided that she has been going to Seattle on the weekends where she has become involved with some highly problematic activities."

"Ashley, before you go any further, I need you to stop. I cannot be privy to confidential information. You may not know, but when a student takes you into confidence, you cannot tell others, even her parents, due to laws of strict confidentiality."

I proceeded to explain this further and to tell her that there were people and offices within the college that she could refer the student to. However, once she allowed the student to confide in her, there were some things that she could perhaps convey to the student as advice. I was quite concerned from that point onwards, as Ashley was quite clearly shaken, and we were still in the middle of the course.

Toward the end of the course, however, Ashley began to look much better, and she came to my office to tell me what happened.

---

14. Robert Thurman, trans., *The Holy Teaching of Vimalakīrti* (University Park: Pennsylvania State University Press, 1976) 44.

"Mark, the situation has been cleared up, and I feel so much better. The student came into talk to me, and she has completely extricated herself from the situation she got caught up in and the people she was involved with. She's no longer taking off for Seattle on the weekends, and she is much more focused on her schoolwork.

"She told me that each week we read about a new thinker or a new religious or philosophical perspective, she wanted to see how what she was doing on the weekends might or might not fit into the particular worldview that was being discussed. Regardless of the philosophy or religion, though, she couldn't find a model of the self in which she could continue to do what she was doing and call it authentic. Even though each text and perspective presented a different view of the self and its dark side, there was no view of the self presented to her by which she could continue her Seattle activities and see her present self as authentic." Ashley seemed happy and relieved.

"Ashley, I'm really glad things worked out well. They don't always work out, but in this case, it did, and as her teacher, you played a crucial role." I myself was also quite relieved and pleased for Ashley and her student. Had someone sermonized the student directly, or presented a particular religion as *the answer*, the student might not have engaged in the rigorous, wide-ranging examination of her options and her life in the way she did. The diverse theologies and philosophies we studied in the course often did not agree with one another. Although I did point out points of resonance and overlap between specific texts and perspectives, it was the student herself who embarked on the search for selfhood and found authenticity as the thread that ran through all of the sources she studied. In fact, had I made an explicit claim about universal selfhood in the lecture, she may not have accepted it or been spurred on the path to self-discovery.

Here we see that the emphasis on theological and philosophical variety and difference that is the basis of the course constitutes a circle of complementarity by which the students organically discover their mutual intimacy on the theme of authenticity. One might argue that this is similar to the way that interreligious dialogue works, not just in the formal setting of scholarly exchange, but among ordinary people coming from diverse theological backgrounds. Individuals, once they are comfortable with one another, might begin to exchange their views about religion.

When things go well, they discover common threads organically, based on themes of mutual interest informed by personal experience.

The Monk, the Vow of Silence, and the Bow of Oneness

In intermediate level lecture/discussion courses and in seminars, I often begin the first class meeting with student self-introductions, by having them give their name, brief background, and interest in the course. One year, as we were doing this in "Dark Self East and West," I noticed an older student who looked to be in his seventies, whom I had had before in an earlier survey course. He was a taller gentleman with a gentle, gapped-tooth smile. He had an unusual appearance, as he always wore a black robe with a hand-stitched insignia, and he had a matching, pointed hat.

We sat in a circle as we went through self-introductions, going in order counterclockwise. When it came time for this older man to introduce himself, instead of speaking he handed the student sitting next to him a small piece of paper. The student looked at it and began to read, "You can call me 'monk.' I have decided to take to take a vow of silence for three years, and so I will not be speaking for the duration of the course. I would, however, like to audit this class, and just listen, if that is all right."

"That would be fine, Mr. Monk," I replied.

As the weeks went by, the Monk was always there, attentively listening to the goings on. After awhile, I began to notice his presence more and more even though he remained utterly silent. It was the quality of his attention. He smiled at every bad joke I made, he was attuned to every insight offered by the students, he pondered every complex question.

On the last day of class, as we all sat in a circle, I had students go around once again, this time to share their impressions of the class. The Monk was there, and when it came his turn, he seemed to be holding something in his hand. I thought it was a piece of paper, and as he stood up, I thought he was bringing it to me. But as he came closer, I realized that it was not a piece of paper. It was a flower, a single white Camellia blossom. He slowly came up to my desk chair, placed the blossom on my desk, and took one step back. He grinned widely, revealing his gapped tooth smile, placed his palms together, and bowed, deeply.

Spontaneously, I was moved to put my palms together, and I bowed in return. I was at a loss for words.

Theologically he was not just from another world, he was from another planet, and to this day, I have no idea which planet. He was from another era, a completely different cultural background. Yet, in that moment, when he laid that flower on my desk, and he bowed, I felt that the tips of his fingers pierced my heart through and through, and there was nothing left to do but to return his bow.

According to Shinran, the founding figure of Shin Buddhism, the path of Pure Land Buddhism, of saying the Name, only applies to one person, himself: "When I ponder the compassionate vow of Amida [the embrace of emptiness/oneness] . . . I realize it was for myself, Shinran, alone."[15] In this way, the Shin Buddhist generally does not feel that the path applies to anyone else but himself. In fact, the Shin path of the foolish being and the awakening of infinite light opens the way for the follower of the Name to let go of all constructs and to seek the point of encounter with what was until then defined as different, as other. But as Zhuangzi states, if one delves deeply enough into that point of mutual contact, between the butterfly and Zhuangzi, teacher and student, Monk and Professor, self and other, then one begins to realize that what were previously seen as polar opposites can interpenetrate each other and may ultimately be one: "There is nothing bigger than the tip of a strand of hair in autumn. The great mythic Mount Tai is tiny. No one has lived longer than a dead child, and the great mythic Peng bird died young. Heaven and Earth were born at the same time I was, and the myriad creatures are one with me."[16] It is significant here that the passage ends with Zhuangzi stating, "Heaven and Earth were born at the same time I was, and the myriad creatures are one *with me*." These last two words, "with me," indicate the fact that, for the author of the *Zhuangzi*, the oneness of the Dao is not a metaphysical speculation but only takes on meaning as lived realization, and it echoes Shinran's sentiment when he states, "I realize it was for myself, Shinran, alone."[17]

15. Translation adapted from Unno, *Tannisho*, 33. *Tannishô, SCZ,* 694.

16. Translation adapted from Watson, *Zhuangzi*, 38. Kanaya, *Sôji,* 67.

17. Translation adapted from Unno, *Tannisho* 33. *Tannishô, SCZ,* 694.

In the Face of Uniqueness

The foregoing approach of theological complementarity requires a religious perspective that is inclusive of theological difference or of religious diversity. What happens, however, when one considers a religious perspective that insists upon its own unique, and in various ways, exclusive truth?

In the context of comparative theology, there are several facets to this question that require further elaboration: What do the terms *unique* and *proposition* mean, and what is the nature of *dialogue*? Beginning with this last term, one must consider the relation between the people involved in dialogue and the doctrines or propositions they are considering. It doesn't make sense that someone should engage in dialogue with a system. Rather, adherents of diverse faiths engage in dialogue with one another, and in that dialogue various commitments, propositions, and practices may be involved.

In terms of the question of what is signified by the term *unique*, the adherent of a faith who makes claims regarding the unique truth of his faith and its propositions can take a range of positions. For our purposes we can identify three points along this spectrum that may be called isolative uniqueness, totalitarian uniqueness, and relative uniqueness. Isolative uniqueness represents the perspective of an adherent who insists that one cannot understand the doctrines or propositions of his unique faith unless one is a member of his religious community. In that case, no dialogue with adherents of other faiths is possible. Totalitarian uniqueness represents the perspective of one who insists that her faith has exclusive claims over religious truth and insists that others adopt the same truth. Due to the insistence on absolute difference (uniqueness) and absolute universality (truth), there is no chance for dialogue. For such a person, the universe of truth exists exclusively within the domain of her own discourse (propositions), and so everything else is inferior or nonsense. In the case of both isolative and totalitarian uniqueness, one is reminded of the Simon and Garfunkel song, "I Am a Rock," which suggests the experience of profound isolation and impenetrability. In the case of isolative uniqueness, there is no dialogue because you can only enter as a permanent resident of the island, or an adherent of the faith. In the totalitarian uniqueness, there is no dialogue because one is forced to become a resident or an adherent.

In relative uniqueness one asserts the uniqueness of one's own religious truth but allows that others may also make such claims. How can two unique truths inhabit the same dialogical space? In the same way that two unique people can enter into dialogue with one another. No two people are exactly the same, and in this sense each person is unique. Yet two unique individuals enter into dialogue with one another because they share some common ground. Furthermore, claims of relative uniqueness are accompanied by recognition of the potential limits of that claim, and that is what makes dialogue meaningful. For one person to claim possession of the unique truth, he must have as thorough a knowledge of all other religions or faiths as his own, and have evaluated the claims of all others as thoroughly as his own. Yet, in practice, most people can provide a much thicker account of their own religion than they can of others'. One of the reasons people enter into religious dialogue is to gain a fuller understanding of others' religions so that they can more fully understand and evaluate their own. The variety and range of religious truth is vast and arguably inexhaustible. Even within one religion or one sect, there is a wide range of interpretations, and religious traditions continually renew themselves through adaptation and innovation. In this sense, the work of attempting to gain self-knowledge concerning one's own religion through interaction and dialogue with others is a never-ending process.

One can also consider the issue of relative uniqueness in the context of history and of belief. That is, a claim to unique truth is a matter of religious *belief*, not of *knowledge*, and therefore not a proven fact but logically a kind of hypothesis still in need of verification. Historically, religions have come and gone, and none have proven to be absolutely and uniquely in possession of the truth, since the truths of religion continue to be debated. Thus, although adherents of some religions may *believe* that their religion is uniquely true, such a claim is contested by other religions' claims to truth and even to unique truth. Genuine dialogue can only occur if the two parties in question agree to the relative status of their claims to uniqueness. Otherwise it is not an equal or symmetrical dialogue, but that which begins by favoring one side over the other. One cannot enter into a true dialogue with a consideration of one side's claim to uniqueness as the main focus of that dialogue. If the discussion revolves around a particular adherent's claim to the unique truth of his or her faith, then it is a debate about one religion, not dialogue.

One who acknowledges the relative character of unique religious expressions also sees that the exegetical and dialogical horizon of religious truth is limitless, and that the hermeneutical circle is never closed. This is the case as long as the followers of the world's religions have not all come to an agreement that there is one superior theology, and that all have agreed it expresses the unique truth. The possibilities for truth, both historically and speculatively, are endless and the permutations virtually infinite. It can even occur that adherents of one religion may find closer affinity with the views presented by some adherents of other religions than with certain of those of one's own faith. Such a moment occurred when Catholic theologian and Father David Burrell stated, "I'm such a negative theologian that I think I may be Buddhist!" Of course, he was not saying that he had a negative view of theology or that he was really Buddhist. Rather, by using the term "negative theology," he was making reference to the *via negativa,* well established in such Catholic thinkers as St. John of the Cross and Meister Eckhart, and a form of theology that has sometimes been identified as resonating with the Buddhist logic of such thinkers as Nagarjuna and Candrakirti. Now, whether such resonances prove theologically worthy under rigorous scrutiny is itself a topic for serious interreligious dialogue. Nevertheless, Burrell may in fact find friendlier company among some Buddhists than among certain other Catholics. Of course, some Buddhists may find greater affinity with certain followers of other religions than with some of their own.

Historically, a large percentage of adherents of the world's religions inherit their faiths from their parents and ancestors. One of the interesting things that come to light through dialogue and through comparative theology is that many of these followers believe that their religion is at least superior to other religions if not in exclusive possession of the truth. It seems remarkable that such a large number of people happen to be so fortunate as to be born into the religion with superior truth claims. Serious dialogue helps one to recognize that the uniqueness of the truth claims of one's own religion cannot be the focus of dialogue; rather, one must begin with the relativity of truth claims among religions.

The consideration of the unique truth of religious propositions requires further logical and epistemological underpinning. For example, how is the term *proposition* understood? *Proposition*, considered under Aristotelian logic and the law of the excluded middle, on the one hand, carries different formal properties from the *catus-koti* or tetralemma of Nâgârjuna and other Mahayana Buddhist thinkers, whose logic contravenes the law of the excluded middle, on the other. In mathematics, there are both Euclidean and non-Euclidean geometries, each with distinct applications, so that what *parallel* means in one differs from what it means in another. In Euclidean geometry, two parallel lines are defined as never meeting. In some forms of non-Euclidean geometry, parallel lines may intersect under certain circumstances. The reason that we have both Euclidean and non-Euclidean geometries is because they have diverse applications. In considering the curvature of gravitational fields, for example, certain non-Euclidean geometries with potentially intersecting parallel lines are more effective in describing actual conditions.

Similarly, the meaning of *proposition* may differ considerably depending upon the requirements of the given logic. In some forms of Buddhism, the insistence on identifying essential beliefs in the form of discursive propositions is itself considered a hindrance to understanding religious truth. For Nâgârjuna, the exclusive use of discursive reasoning and the conceptual proliferation it begets are called *prapanca,* "discursive chatter." In its place, he appeals to the nondiscursive logic of the tetralemma, which is expressed as follows:

A exists.

A does not exist.

A both exists and does not exist.

A neither exists nor does not exist.

In terms of the twofold truth introduced earlier, the first line corresponds to the truth of "form," based on the existence of distinct realities as defined by the conventions of language and concept formation. The second line corresponds to the truth of "emptiness," that is, the lack of any fixed essence that be said to exist in any discursive or conceptually reified sense. Thus the third and fourth lines signify "both form and emptiness" and "neither form nor emptiness." One can see that both the third and fourth lines contravene the law of the excluded middle. However, the fourth line appears logically to simply be the double negative of the third line. For Nâgârjuna and in general for Mahayana Buddhist thinkers, the fourth line is necessary because it indicates that the significance of the twofold truth cannot be realized in discursive, conceptual terms. That is, the truth of the formulation, "form is emptiness," cannot be grasped merely in discursive terms.

"Emptiness" defies discursive definition, yet it includes discursive logic. The distinctive character of the twofold truth issues from the fact that it weds the discursive truth of form with the nondiscursive truth of emptiness as inseparable from each other. For Nâgârjuna, of course, there was never any need to wed the two together since for him, they logically inhere in each other. This logic, however, does not conform to the law of the excluded middle.

If one understands the third line purely discursively, then this is a distortion or delusion. The fourth line reinforces the nondiscursive aspect of the third line. Logically speaking, the tetralemma expresses the discursive negation of discursive logic and points to the positive realization of the nondiscursive. For this reason, Nâgârjuna also states that one must realize the "emptiness of emptiness," *sunyata-sunyata*. To realize emptiness, one must empty the mind of the concept of emptiness.

A fuller consideration of the definition of *proposition* and its function in diverse forms of religious logic lies beyond the scope of the present essay. However, from this brief discussion it should be evident that comparative theology and interreligious dialogue may help us to expand our examination of the character and meaning of religious truth as well as its content, and to place them in the larger context of history, logic, and epistemology. In considering the various meanings of *proposition* as found in Aristotelian, Nâgârjunian, or other forms of logic, a key point is that, just as in the case of diverse geometries and their application in physics, these logics were designed to articulate diverse applications in the practice of different religions. For this reason, it is not enough simply to stay on the plane of abstract reasoning; it is through the living encounter with followers of diverse faiths that we begin to see diverse logics embodied and why interreligious dialogue involving personal encounter is indispensable to deeper mutual understanding. Let us then return to the question, what, if in dialogue with another religion, you encounter a belief system that insists on the unique truth of its own propositions? As a response, I would offer precisely the foregoing consideration of this question as a way to examine, contextualize, and to begin to understand what "the unique truth of its own propositions" could possibly mean.

Conclusion

We often hear about the celebration of religious diversity, the need for dialogue, and the significance of comparative religion. It is often difficult to carry them out in practice. For every enjoyable tale of theological encounter I can dig up, there are a thousand broken ones. Nevertheless, each time, I feel that I am being led into the secret treasure trove of someone's heart, of the divine spark, the mysterious Dao, of existential meaning, the ocean of light. So I conclude by saying this is yet another beginning, another opening into that unknown world where theological difference is precisely the portal to renewed self-understanding, a world of complementarity through which I am led to discover more of the world, and just as importantly, more of myself.

List of Contributors

Mustafa Abu Sway is Professor of Philosophy and Islamic Studies at Al-Quds University, Palestine. He graduated from Bethlehem University, Palestine, and Boston College, USA. Dr. Abu Sway taught at the International Islamic University—Malaysia, and was Visiting Professor at Florida Atlantic University and at Bard College. He is author of *Islamic Epistemology: The Case of Al-Ghazzali* (1995), and *Fatawa Al-Ghazzali* (1996). He is also editor and co-author of *Al-Thaqafah Al-Islamiyyah* (Islamic Culture) (2007).

Asma Afsaruddin is Professor of Islamic Studies in the Department of Near Eastern Languages & Cultures at Indiana University, Bloomington. Her research focuses on the religious and political thought of Islam, Qur'an and hadith, Islamic intellectual history, and gender. She is the author and/or editor of four books, including *The First Muslims: History and Memory* (2008), and *Excellence and Precedence: Medieval Islamic Discourse on Legitimate Leadership* (2002). Afsaruddin is currently completing a book manuscript about competing perspectives on *jihad* and martyrdom in premodern and modern Islamic thought. Her research has won funding from the Harry Frank Guggenheim Foundation and the Carnegie Corporation of New York.

Reinhold Bernhardt is the Professor for Systematic Theology / Dogmatics at the University of Basel (Switzerland). He earned his Dr.theol. (1989) and Habilitation (1998) at the Faculty of Theology, University of Heidelberg. His work focuses on theology of religions. He has books published in German, Spanish, and English. Among them are *Der Absolutheits-*

anspruch des Christentums: Von der Aufklärung bis zur Pluralistischen Religionstheologie (1990, 1993); *Für ein Christentum ohne Absolutheitsanspruch* (1994); English ed.: *Christianity without Absolutes* (1994); *Ende des Dialogs? Die Begegnung der Religionen und ihre theologische Reflexion* (2006); *Wahrheit in Offenheit: Der christliche Glaube und die Religionen* (2007). He is editor of the series Beiträge zu einer Theologie der Religionen, and of the periodical *Theologische Zeitschrift*, and co-editor of the series Scientia & Religio, and Studien zur systematischen Theologie und Ethik.

David Burrell, C.S.C., Theodore Hesburgh Professor emeritus in Philosophy and Theology at the University of Notre Dame, where he taught from 1964 to 2007, is currently serving the Congregation of Holy Cross in the District of East Africa, assisting at Uganda Martyrs University. He has been working since 1982 in comparative issues in philosophical theology in Judaism, Christianity, and Islam, as evidenced in *Knowing the Unknowable God: Ibn-Sina, Maimonides, Aquinas* (1986), *Freedom and Creation in Three Traditions* (1993), *Friendship and Ways to Truth* (2000), and two translations of al-Ghazali: *Al-Ghazali on the Ninety-Nine Beautiful Names of God* (1993), and *Al-Ghazali on Faith in Divine Unity and Trust in Divine Providence* (2001). With Elena Malits he co-authored *Original Peace* (1998). Blackwell published a collected set of his essays: *Faith and Freedom* (2005).

Catherine Cornille is Associate Professor of Comparative Theology at Boston College. Her teaching and research focus mainly on methodological questions in the study of religions, inculturation, and interreligious dialogue. Her books include *The Guru in Indian Catholicism: Ambiguity or Opportunity of Inculturation* (1991); editor, *Many Mansions: Multiple Religious Belonging and Christian Identity* (2002); editor, *Song Divine: Christian Commentaries on the Bhagavadgita* (2007); and most recently *The Im-Possibility of Interreligious Dialogue* (2008). She is managing editor of the series Christian Commentaries on non-Christian Sacred Texts.

Gavin D'Costa is Professor of Catholic Theology, Department of Theology and Religious Studies, University of Bristol. Some of his publications include: *Theology and Religious Pluralism* (1986), *John Hick's Theology of*

Religions (1987), *The Trinity and the Meeting of Religions* (2000), *Sexing the Trinity* (2000), *Theology in the Public Square* (2005), and *Disputed Questions in the Theology of Religions* (2009). His research interests are in Catholic theology, theology of religions, and gender and psychoanalysis. Gavin D'Costa is a consultant to the Church of England, the Catholic Bishop's Conference, and the Vatican on issues regarding other religions.

David Elcott holds a PhD from Columbia University in Political Psychology and Middle East Studies, and has academic expertise in Islamic and Jewish studies. He is the author of *A Sacred Journey: The Jewish Quest for a Perfect World* (1995). As a Visiting Scholar and Senior Research Fellow at the Wagner Graduate School of Public Service, Dr. Elcott advises organizations, government officials, media, and political leaders on issues of global concern. He has served as Executive Director of the Israel Policy Forum and as U.S. Director of Interreligious Affairs at the American Jewish Committee. He was Vice President of CLAL: The National Jewish Center for Learning and Leadership for sixteen years.

Joseph E. B. Lumbard is Assistant Professor of Classical Islam at Brandeis University and former adviser on interfaith affairs to King Abdullah II of Jordan. His research focuses upon Quranic exegesis and Islamic intellectual traditions, with an emphasis on Sufism and Islamic philosophy. He is the editor of *Islam, Fundamentalism, and the Betrayal of Tradition* (2004), a collection of essays that examines the religious, political and historical factors that have led to the rise of Islamic fundamentalism. His forthcoming *Towards a Judeo-Christian-Islamic Tradition* (2010), examines the thematic continuity between the Old Testament, the New Testament, and the Quran. He is currently working as an Associate Editor for the *HarperCollins Study Quran* (Forthcoming, 2011).

Jonathan Magonet was born in London in 1942, received rabbinic ordination from Leo Baeck College and his PhD from the University of Heidelberg. From 1974 he was Head of the Department of Bible Studies at Leo Baeck College, then Principal (1985–2005), and is currently Emeritus Professor of Bible. He is editor of *Forms of Prayer for Jewish Worship*, vol 1, *Daily, Sabbath and Occasional Prayers*, 8th ed. (2008) and of the journal *European Judaism*. For four decades he has co-organized an annual

Jewish-Christian Bible Week and an annual Jewish-Christian-Muslim Student Conference in Germany.

John Makransky is Associate Professor of Buddhism and Comparative Theology at Boston College and senior advisor to Kathmandu University's Centre for Buddhist Studies in Nepal. Within the American Academy of Religion (AAR), he is co-chair of the Buddhist Critical-Constructive Reflection Group. He is the author of *Buddhahood Embodied: Sources of Controversy in India and Tibet* (1997) and of *Awakening through Love: Unveiling your Deepest Goodness* (2007), co-editor of *Buddhist Theology: Critical Reflections by Contemporary Buddhist Scholars* (1999), and the author of many articles and essays. He is also the co-founder and guiding meditation teacher of the Foundation for Active Compassion, which brings contemplative training to people who work in areas of social service and social justice (www.johnmakransky.org).

Anantanand Rambachan is Professor of Religion, Philosophy, and Asian Studies at St. Olaf College. Rambachan's monographs include *Accomplishing the Accomplished: The Vedas as a Source of Valid Knowledge in Sankara* (1991), *The Limits of Scripture: Vivekananda's Reinterpretation of the Authority of the Vedas* (1994), and most recently, *The Advaita Worldview: God, World, and Humanity* (2006).

Deepak Sarma is Associate Professor Religious Studies at Case Western Reserve University. He received his MA and PhD at the Divinity School of the University of Chicago. His areas of teaching and research specialization include Indian philosophy, Vedanta, Hindu theology, method and theory in the study of Hinduism, and the comparative philosophy of religions. Sarma is the author of *An Introduction to Madhva Vedanta* (2003), *Epistemologies and the Limitations of Philosophical Inquiry: Doctrine in Madhva Vedanta* (2004), and *Hinduism: A Reader* (2007). He is currently completing *Indian Philosophy: A Reader* for Columbia University Press.

Judith Simmer-Brown is Professor of Religious Studies at Naropa University in Boulder, Colorado. She is an officer in the Society of Buddhist-Christian Studies, and served on the Cobb-Abe Dialogue from 1984–2004. Currently she is on the steering committee of the American

Academy of Religion's Buddhist Critical-Constructive Reflection Group. She lectures and writes on Tibetan Buddhism, American Buddhism, women and Buddhism, and interreligious dialogue. She is author of *Dakini's Warm Breath: The Feminine Principle in Tibetan Buddhism* (2002).

Mark Unno is Associate Professor of East Asian Religions in the Department of Religious Studies at the University of Oregon. Professor Unno's primary research is in Classical Japanese Buddhism, and he also has strong research interests in modern Japanese religious thought, comparative religion, and Buddhism and psychotherapy. He is the author of *Shingon Refractions: Myoe and the Mantra of Light* (2004), a study and translation of the medieval Japanese Buddhist practice of the Mantra of Light. He has also edited volumes on Buddhism and psychotherapy, including *Buddhism and Psychotherapy across Cultures: Theories and Practices* (2006); and he is the translator of *Hayao Kawai, The Buddhist Priest Myoe—A Life of Dreams* (1992).